Matter as an Image of the Good

VERITAS
Series Introduction

"... the truth will set you free" (John 8:32)

In much contemporary discourse, Pilate's question has been taken to mark the absolute boundary of human thought. Beyond this boundary, it is often suggested, is an intellectual hinterland into which we must not venture. This terrain is an agnosticism of thought: because truth cannot be possessed, it must not be spoken. Thus, it is argued that the defenders of "truth" in our day are often traffickers in ideology, merchants of counterfeits, or anti-liberal. They are, because it is somewhat taken for granted that Nietzsche's word is final: truth is the domain of tyranny.

Is this indeed the case, or might another vision of truth offer itself? The ancient Greeks named the love of wisdom as *philia*, or friendship. The one who would become wise, they argued, would be a "friend of truth." For both philosophy and theology might be conceived as schools in the friendship of truth, as a kind of relation. For like friendship, truth is as much discovered as it is made. If truth is then so elusive, if its domain is *terra incognita*, perhaps this is because it arrives to us—unannounced—as gift, as a person, and not some thing.

The aim of the Veritas book series is to publish incisive and original current scholarly work that inhabits "the between" and "the beyond" of theology and philosophy. These volumes will all share a common aspiration to transcend the institutional divorce in which these two disciplines often find themselves, and to engage questions of pressing concern to both philosophers and theologians in such a way as to reinvigorate both disciplines with a kind of interdisciplinary desire, often so absent in contemporary academe. In a word, these volumes represent collective efforts in the befriending of truth, doing so beyond the simulacra of pretend tolerance, the violent, yet insipid reasoning of liberalism that asks with Pilate, "What is truth?"—expecting a consensus of non-commitment; one that encourages the commodification of the mind, now sedated by the civil service of career, ministered by the frightened patrons of position.

The series will therefore consist of two wings: (1) original monographs; and (2) essay collections on a range of topics in theology and philosophy. The latter will principally be the products of the annual conferences of the Centre of Theology and Philosophy (www.theologyphilosophycentre.co.uk).

Conor Cunningham and Joseph Terry, *Veritas Series Editors*

Available from Cascade Books

Anthony D. Baker	*Diagonal Advance: Perfection in Christian Theology*
D. C. Schindler	*The Perfection of Freedom: Schiller, Schelling, and Hegel between the Ancients and the Moderns*
Rustin Brian	*Covering Up Luther: How Barth's Christology Challenged the* Deus Absconditus *that Haunts Modernity*
Timothy Stanley	*Protestant Metaphysics After Karl Barth and Martin Heidegger*
Christopher Ben Simpson	*The Truth Is the Way: Kierkegaard's* Theologia Viatorum
Richard H. Bell	*Wagner's Parsifal: An Appreciation in the Light of His Theological Journey*
Antonio Lopez	*Gift and the Unity of Being*
Toyohiko Kagawa	*Cosmic Purpose*, translated and introduced by Thomas John Hastings
Nigel Zimmerman	*Facing the Other: John Paul II, Levinas, and the Body*
Conor Sweeney	*Sacramental Presence after Heidegger: Onto-theology, Sacraments, and the Mother's Smile*
John Behr et al. (eds.)	*The Role of Death in Life: A Multidisciplinary Examination of the Relation between Life and Death*
Eric Austin Lee et al. (eds.)	*The Resounding Soul: Reflection on the Metaphysics and Vivacity of the Human Person*
Orion Edgar	*Things Seen and Unseen: The Logic of Incarnation in Merleau-Ponty's Metaphysics of Flesh*
Duncan B. Reyburn	*Seeing Things as They Are: G. K. Chesterton and the Drama of Meaning*
Lyndon Shakespeare	*Being the Body of Christ in the Age of Management*
Michael V. Di Fuccia	*Owen Barfield: Philosophy, Poetry, and Theology*
John McNerney	*Wealth of Persons: Economics with a Human Face*
Norm Klassen	*The Fellowship of the Beatific Vision: Chaucer on Overcoming Tyranny and Becoming Ourselves*
Donald Wallenfang	*Human and Divine Being: A Study of the Theological Anthropology of Edith Stein*
Sotiris Mitralexis	*Ever-Moving Repose: A Contemporary Reading of Maximus the Confessor's Theory of Time*
Sotiris Mitralexis et al. (eds.)	*Maximus the Confessor as a European Philosopher*
Kevin Corrigan	*Love, Friendship, Beauty, and the Good: Plato, Aristotle, and the Later Tradition*
Andrew Brower Latz	*The Social Philosophy of Gillian Rose*

1. Note: Nathan Kerr, *Christ, History, and Apocalyptic*, although volume 3 of the original SCM Veritas series, is available from Cascade as part of the Theopolitical Visions series.

D. C. Schindler	*Love and the Postmodern Predicament: Rediscovering the Real in Beauty, Goodness, and Truth*
Stephen Kampowski	*Embracing Our Finitude: Exercises in a Christian Anthropology between Dependence and Gratitude*
William Desmond	*The Gift of Beauty and the Passion of Being: On the Threshold between the Aesthetic and the Religious*
Charles Péguy	*Notes on Bergson and Descartes*
David Alcalde	*Cosmology without God: The Problematic Theology Inherent in Modern Cosmology*
Benson P. Fraser	*Hide and Seek: The Sacred Art of Indirect Communication*
Philip John Paul Gonzales	*Exorcising Philosophical Modernity: Cyril O'Regan and Christian Discourse after Modernity*
Caitlin Smith Gilson	*Subordinated Ethics: Natural Law and Moral Miscellany in Aquinas and Dostoyevsky*
Michael Dominic Taylor	*The Foundations of Nature: Metaphysics of Gift for an Integral Ecological Ethic*
David W. Opderbeck	*The End of the Law? Law, Theology, and Neuroscience*
Caitlin Smith Gilson	*As It Is in Heaven: Some Christian Questions on the Nature of Paradise*
Andrew T. J. Kaethler	*The Eschatological Person: Alexander Schemann and Joseph Ratzinger in Dialogue*
Emmanuel Falque	*By Way of Obstacles: A Pathway through a Work*
Paul Tyson (ed.)	*Astonishment in Science: Engagements with William Desmond*
Darren Dyk	*Will & Love: Shakespeare and the Motion of the Soul*
Matthew Vest	*Ethics Lost in Modernity: Reflections on Wittgenstein and Bioethics*
Hanna Lucas	*Sensing the Sacred: Recovering a Mystagogical Vision of Knowledge and Salvation*
Philip Gonzales et al. (eds.)	*Finitude's Wounded Praise: Responses to Jean-Louis Crétien*
Martin Koci et al. (eds.)	*God and Phenomenology: Thinking with Jean-Yves Lacoste*
Steven E. Knepper (ed.)	*A Heart of Flesh: William Desmond and the Bible*
James Madden	*Thinking About Thinking: Mind and Meaning in the Era of Techno-Nihilism*
Tyler Dalton McNabb	*An Analytic Theology of Evangelism: A Classical Theist's Approach*
John Milbank et al. (eds.)	*New Trinitarian Ontologies, Volume 1*
Duncan Reyburn	*The Roots of the World: The Remarkable Prescience of G. K. Chesterton*
Pablo Irizar et al. (eds.)	*To Die of Not Writing: Doing Philosophy of Religion with Emmanuel Falque*

Matter as an Image of the Good

Ferdinand Ulrich's Metaphysics of Creation

RACHEL M. COLEMAN

Foreword by Adrian J. Walker

CASCADE *Books* · Eugene, Oregon

MATTER AS AN IMAGE OF THE GOOD
Ferdinand Ulrich's Metaphysics of Creation

Veritas

Copyright © 2025 Rachel M. Coleman. All rights reserved. Except for brief quotations in critical publications or reviews, no part of this book may be reproduced in any manner without prior written permission from the publisher. Write: Permissions, Wipf and Stock Publishers, 199 W. 8th Ave., Suite 3, Eugene, OR 97401.

Cascade Books
An Imprint of Wipf and Stock Publishers
199 W. 8th Ave., Suite 3
Eugene, OR 97401

www.wipfandstock.com

PAPERBACK ISBN: 979-8-3852-3021-1
HARDCOVER ISBN: 979-8-3852-3022-8
EBOOK ISBN: 979-8-3852-3023-5

Cataloguing-in-Publication data:

Names: Coleman, Rachel M. [author]. | Walker, Adrian J. [foreword writer]

Title: Matter as an image of the Good : Ferdinand Ulrich's metaphysics of creation / by Rachel M. Coleman.

Description: Eugene, OR: Cascade Books, 2025 | Series: Veritas | Includes bibliographical references and index.

Identifiers: ISBN 979-8-3852-3021-1 (paperback) | ISBN 979-8-3852-3022-8 (hardcover) | ISBN 979-8-3852-3023-5 (ebook)

Subjects: LCSH: Metaphysics. | Ulrich, Ferdinand. | Ontology. | Christian philosophy. | Creation. | Thomas, Aquinas, Saint, 1225?-1274.

Classification: BD313.U473 C65 2025 (paperback) | BD313.U473 (ebook)

06/30/25

This book is dedicated to the John Paul II Institute MTS class of 2010, in whose fellowship I first began to see.

Contents

Foreword by Adrian J. Walker xi
Acknowledgments xix
Abbreviations xxi

Introduction 1
    1. Matter in Thomas Aquinas's Metaphysics of Creation 14
    2. The Basic Structure of Ferdinand Ulrich's Metaphysics of Creation 45
    3. Ferdinand Ulrich's Understanding of Matter 88
Conclusion 133

Bibliography 145
Author Index 149
Subject Index 151

Foreword

Rachel M. Coleman's *Matter as an Image of the Good: Ferdinand Ulrich's Metaphysics of Creation* is an original work of scholarship and speculation richly deserving of recognition by her fellow philosophers and theologians.

Doctor Coleman's thematic focus—the role that Ferdinand Ulrich sees matter playing in the manifestation of divine goodness *ad extra*—provides her with a lens through which to exhibit the architecture of Ulrich's entire metaphysics without sacrificing precision, economy, or grace. In so doing, she has produced one of the first, as well as one of the finest, accounts of Ulrich's metaphysical vision in any language.

Doctor Coleman does more, however, than offer an outstanding synthetic reconstruction of a still underappreciated monument of twentieth-century Catholic thought. She also beautifully expounds and defends an exciting speculative thesis that is both wholly Ulrichian and wholly her own.

Inspiring this thesis is Doctor Coleman's Ulrichian vision of God's creative causality as a loving self-donation: God gives himself away to the creature without losing himself in the process. Now, since God is *ipsum esse subsistens*,[1] the first, all-encompassing fruit of his creative self-giving likewise deserves the name "*ipsum esse*." "To create," as Aquinas says, "is to give *esse*."[2] Of course, the *esse* the Creator thus gives is itself creaturely; it is not God himself, but a

---

1. This is not a definition of the divine essence. If anything, it is an account of why the divine essence exceeds definition. *Esse*, after all, is not a being among beings. It is "the actuality of all things, including the very forms" (*ST*, I, q. 4, a. 1, ad 3), and, as such, it is present in everything without being exhausted by anything. For the same reason, its nature doesn't consist in being posited over against something that it's not. Rather, it comprehends all differentiation, and so all differential non-being, in itself. (This applies even to the *nihil* "out of which" God draws the creature; this nothingness is not a void that the Creator fills up, or a potential that he actualizes, but the creature's utter lack of being, its pure "zerohood," apart from the gratuitous gift of being bestowed on it by the subsistent *esse* that, in its infinity, is a one without a second.) In this sense, *esse* is as much an enabling ground, a letting be, as it is a plenitude of actuality.

2. *In Librum Sententiarum*, I, 37, 1, 1.

"similitude of the divine goodness."[3] Nevertheless, *esse*-as-similitude is not an object that could be compared with God and found similar to him. Rather, it is the principle of the creature's dynamic assimilation to God, which is to say: the energy whereby it participates in the Divine without being divine. The *esse* of creatures is the Godward act by which they exist in themselves, and to call this act "created" is to name the most formal root of its primary Godwardness: its status as God's "proper effect"[4]—and so as the immediate fruit, and transparent mediation, of the Creator's causal self-donation *ad extra*.

Following Ulrich, Doctor Coleman displays the inner structure of *essecreatum* as similitude in light of Aquinas' dictum that created *esse* "signifies something complete and simple, but non-subsistent."[5] Insofar as God holds nothing back in creating, but imparts himself unreservedly to the creature, the primary fruit (and medium) of his self-bestowal, namely: *esse creatum*, can only be "complete and simple"; insofar, however, as the aim of God's creative self-giving is to let creatures exist, and so to give them to themselves as subjects of their own being and action, the *esse* they receive from him must also be "non-subsistent," lest it merge pantheistically with his.

This last point is decisive: unless *esse creatum* is non-subsistent, it cannot be cleanly distinct from *ipsum esse subsistens*; unless *esse creatum* is cleanly distinct from *ipsum esse subsistens*, however, it cannot be truly given over to the creature; and, unless *esse creatum* is truly given over to the creature, it cannot be the fruit and medium of the self-donation in which God's creative act consists.

For Doctor Coleman, then, the non-subsistence in question here is God's inspired device for cleanly distinguishing created *esse* from his own *ipsum esse subsistens* without thereby undermining or diminishing the former's character as *esse*, as the act-fullness he lovingly knows it to be in himself. Created *esse*'s non-subsistence, in other words, enables it to be the gift that, in its perfect distinction from the Giver, contains the entire Giver himself—not as a dead object, but as a living, self-communicating origin. By the same token, the non-subsistence of *esse creatum* allows the Creator to be more interior to his creature than the creature is to itself—and thus to pervade the creature, not as an intrusive competitor, but as the generous, liberating source of the latter's own inmost sourcehood. Corollary: the ongoingly received, abidingly receptive character of the creature's exercise of *esse creatum* does not diminish its proper originality, but establishes, shapes, and orients this originality as a living image of God's (and, indeed, God the Father's) own fontal plenitude.

3. *DV*, XXII, 2, ad 2.
4. *ST* I, 8, 1.
5. *DP*, I, 1, ad 1.

In showing all of this, Doctor Coleman helps us appreciate the meaning of Ulrich's description of *esse creatum* as "pure mediation."[6] The point of this description, we realize, is precisely *not* that created *esse* is a thing-like entity interposed between God and his creature. Put positively, Ulrich's point is that *ipsum esse creatum*, being at once the proper effect of God and the fundamental act of the creature (and the latter *because* it is the former), is nothing but a communion between God and his creature. The nature of created *esse*, in other words, isn't to subsist as a thing in its own right, but to be the "tent of meeting" in which creature and Creator enact their *admirabile commercium* without confusion or separation. The energy of creaturely be-ing is at once a "Neoplatonic" participation and a "biblical" covenant, the two coinhering in an *admirabile commercium* of their own.

The foregoing highlights another aspect of created *esse* that Doctor Coleman uncovers for us: the selfless transparency that inwardly completes its ecstatic communicativity. It as if created *esse* had always already "foregone" any subsistence of its own in order to let created substances subsist by exercising *it*. Of course, it is not *esse creatum* that makes this kenotic choice. Rather, it is the Creator who makes the choice for it. In so doing, however, he "builds into" *esse creatum* an expressive image of his own creative self-giving. This image centrally includes the above-mentioned selfless transparency, which efficaciously manifests, sacrament-like, God's power to be non-invasively discreet in his very omnipresence.

In one sense, of course, *esse creatum* pre-contains all creatures and posits them in existence, together with their actions and accidents.[7] Since, however, created *esse* is not a subsistent agent, but the fruit and vehicle of the Creator, it must pre-contain and posit creatures in a corresponding manner. It must pre-contain and posit them, in other words, by being immemorially given over to them as the subjects that exercise it, created *esse*, in their own name (and so to say adapt it to the dimensions of their respective essences). In this sense, *ipsum esse* presupposes the very creature that it pre-contains and posits; it is as much a kenotic *letting be* as an energetic *making be*.[8] It's by this gesture of letting be, we can add, that created *esse* faithfully images God's archetypal letting

---

6. "*Reine Vermittlung.*" Ulrich, *Homo Abyssus*, 15.

7. On *esse*'s precontaining everything else, see *ST*, I-II, 2, 5, ad 2: "*Esse* pre-contains in itself all subsequent goods."

8. The kenosis in question here, of course, is not a self-cancellation, because *esse creatum* never has a self to cancel in the first place. We are dealing, rather, with a selflessness, an outpouredness, that is coincident with the simple fullness of *esse creatum* itself—and that therefore represents a distant analogue of the subsistent relationality constitutive of the persons of the Trinity.

be—and, therefore, the above-mentioned discretion of the One who displays his omnipotence by liberating his creatures into their own sourcehood (which sourcehood is original *because* it is participatory communion with him, the Source of sources).

In laying out this metaphysical vision, Doctor Coleman makes it clear that non-subsistence is not a deficiency that would threaten created *esse*'s simple fullness, but that it belongs co-essentially to, and inwardly characterizes, this fullness as the act-plenitude it is. Indeed, on her Ulrichian account, created *esse*'s kenotic-ecstatic outpouredness essentially co-constitutes it as a sacrament-like similitude, or efficacious icon, of the divine goodness. Precisely by being the fullness of act in the state of being given away; precisely by presupposing what it posits; precisely by letting be in making be—precisely in all these ways, created *esse* not only mediates God's creative act, but also images it forth as what it is: the self-expression of the omnicausal Good whose nature is to be a subsistent identity of being and self-giving, of being and love.

The foregoing sketch of the first main part of Doctor Coleman's central thesis leads us up to the threshhold of the second: Just as the non-subsistence of created *esse* enters constitutively into its imaging of the divine goodness, this imaging is reflected in, and extended by, the *informitas* of matter in turn. Matter—precisely as potency and *prope nihil*—iconizes the kenotic-ecstatic "renunciation" of subsistence by which created *esse* itself iconizes God's subsistent identity of being and loving.

To be sure, matter, like the form with which it is concreated, owes its existence to *esse creatum*. Nevertheless, to the extent that matter, thus concreated, functions as a non-subsistent letting be of corporeal substances, it indeed constitutes an icon, a sacrament-like medium, of created *esse* in *its* non-subsistent letting be of the very same substances. And, in imaging and vehicling *that*, matter uniquely contributes to manifesting *activa creatio* as what it is: a divine self-impartation that itself efficaciously expresses God as the subsistent identity of being and loving we call "the Good."

As the foregoing suggests, Doctor Coleman offers Thomists attractive reasons for engaging with Ulrich's reading of the Angelic Doctor. In particular, she highlights, and makes accessible, Ulrich's contribution to the mid-twentieth-century rediscovery of Thomistic metaphysics as the crowning synthesis of Aristotelianism and Neoplatonic thought. Not the least merit of *Matter as an Image of the Good* is that it helps re-introduce *this* Thomas—creatively and faithfully Aristotelian *because* creatively and faithfully Dionysian, and *vice versa*—at a moment when his voice is sorely needed.

For Ulrich—and for Doctor Coleman following him—the Dionysian contribution to Thomas' metaphysics is not limited to the Areopagitic vision of the creative act as a bestowal of participation in God, or even to the consideration of *ipsum esse* as the iconic mediator of this participatory gift. On Doctor Coleman's telling, the Dionysian contribution also extends to the intuition that even the lowest entity in the hierarchy of created reality—namely, matter—enjoys an immediacy to, and plays a unique part in revealing, the perfection of the creative cause that transcendently comprehends the hierarchy as a whole. We see Thomas' awareness and approbation of this insight reflected in his programmatic remark that "as Dionysius teaches in Chapter II of the *Celestial Hierarchy*, it is more fitting that divine things be transmitted in Scripture under the figures of vile bodies than under those of noble ones."[9]

The just-mentioned intuition is bound up, in its turn, with the further Dionysian insight that the secret motor of divine causality is a beautiful *eros*, a fruitful yearning that moves God to go "outside" himself,[10] even to the point of pouring himself out into what, at first, looks least like himself—in this case, matter.[11] To be sure, the divine *eros* is a purely spontaneous, purely gratuitous self-motion; it is entirely a freely self-given implication of God's own self-donation.[12] Nevertheless, the spontaneity and gratuity in play here serve to underscore the extent to which God reveals his transcendent freedom from need like the master in Christ's parable of the talents: by delighting to receive back his gift with interest—the interest that is the creature's own being and acting in communion with him, the discreetly omnipresent Creator. As Hans Urs von Balthasar puts it, God's greatest gift is to be himself in the all he is not.[13]

The Areopagite's contemplation of God's creative goodness is wholly Neoplatonic in being wholly biblical, and *vice versa*. For him, Christ's kenosis unto death on the cross crowns the revelation of divine *eros* begun in creation.[14]

---

9. Thomas Aquinas, *ST*, I, 1, 9, ad 3.

10. Dionysius, *De Divinis Nominibus*, IV, 13.

11. Matter, lying below the threshold of the distinction between inside and outside, images God's capacity to go outside of himself without departing from himself, which is to say: his power to give himself away without self-cancellation or self-diminishment.

12. The Areopagite describes the divine *eros* as a self-moving reality, indeed, as the transcendent archetype of self-motion itself: "*autokinêton*." *De Divinis Nominibus*, IV, 14; PG 1: 712C.

13. "God is God so much that he can be in the All that he is not." Balthasar, "The Fathers, the Scholastics, and Ourselves," 391.

14. Dionysius himself makes this plain in passages such as these: "But the divine *eros* is ek-static, not allowing the lovers to belong to themselves, but to the beloved. . . . Wherefore even the great Paul, entirely possessed by divine *eros*, and partaking of its ek-static power, says with divinely inspired mouth 'I live no longer, but Christ lives in me.'" Dionysius, *De Divinis Nominibus*, IV, 13; *PG* 1: 712A.

Ulrich, too, conjoins the erotic and the kenotic in his own consideration, at once Christian and philosophical, of the non-subsistence of *esse* as the effective icon of God's creative letting be. The Creator's omnipotent "*fiat*," Ulrich shows, provides itself with an answering echo in matter, which lets be—better: is a pure letting be of—material substance's reception of the *actus essendi*.[15] In the fullness of time, this answering "*fiat*" attains its crowning recapitulation in the "Yes" by which the Theotokos lets be the incarnation of God the Word. The Mother of God is the personification of matter, indeed of all creaturely receptivity, which she raises to the level of an efficient causality whose dignity lies in its very handmaidenly hospitality.

As Doctor Coleman ably shows, Ulrich draws from his meditation on matter as an image of the Good a beautiful but often overlooked metaphysical truth: the truth that making room, letting be, receiving—in short, the gestures we typically associate with matter and we see personified in the *Virgo Mater*—are perfections, and that these perfections find a primary analogate, not only in the non-subsistent fullness of *esse*, but also in the self-outpouring *eros* that coincides with Pure Act.[16]

To be sure, Ulrich takes quite seriously the phenomenon that often generates anti-corporeal resentment in us: the exposure, rooted in our bodily individuality, to deformity, humiliation, pain, sickness, and death. Yet Ulrich's resolute confrontation with this negativity does not prevent him from insisting that it manifests, rather than contradicting, the essential, abiding goodness of our corporeal existence. God's providence, he shows, turns the vanity overshadowing our post-lapsarian existence into an indirect reminder of, and occasion to recapitulate, the gratuitous outpouredness inscribed in the non-subsistence of *esse creatum*. The light of being continues to shine in the very midst of the darkness that cannot overcome it. What insight could be more timely—or more timelessly important—than this vision of God's irrevocable fidelity to the vulnerable flesh in which being's non-subsistence shines forth as ecstatic-kenotic love?

---

15. To be sure, it is "by means of *form* that the substance becomes the proper receiver of *esse*" (*SCG*, II, 55, 2; emphasis added). Nevertheless, in the case of *corporeal* substance, form constitutes this "proper receiver" only in hylomorphic union with matter, thus actualizing matter's potential to become (and to be the material for) a bodily substance that, as such, is the subject of its own being and action.

16. Neither Ulrich nor Doctor Coleman intends to eliminate, or even to weaken, the division between act and potency. Their intention is rather to explain better the analogy between the two co-principles—and, in so doing, to deepen our understanding of how potency originates entirely in, while remaining distinct from, act. It does so, they show, in virtue of the non-subsistence of *esse* as an inner completion, rather than a diminution, of its act-fullness.

FOREWORD

In laying out with elegant rigor this Ulrichian valorization of matter as an image of the Good, Doctor Coleman has made it her own; she has let Ulrich's thought bear fruit in hers. Placing herself where Ulrich himself has stood and creatively recapitulating his own philosophical gesture, she invites us to marvel at the God who, acting through the medium of *esse creatum*, lays himself in the womb of matter (a womb he creates and distinguishes from himself in this very act); the God who shows his humble majesty in the fragility of the lowly body with its subjection to change, contingency, and chance; the God who manifests the omnipotence of his love in the passivity of a freely assumed suffering and death. Doctor Coleman, like Ulrich, deserves our gratitude for offering this full-throated, and most timely, re-affirmation of the goodness of individual embodiment. In so doing, she reminds us of a perennial task of the philosopher, which is also a perennial task of the believer: the mission of bearing witness to, and stewarding, the Creator's unreserved "fidelity to the earth."

ADRIAN J. WALKER

Acknowledgments

Though it can sometimes feel utterly isolating, I have learned over the years that writing is never actually a solitary endeavor. From those who actively participate in the editing and review process to those whose quiet but steady presence allow the author the rest she needs in order to move forward, it almost goes without saying that this work is a work of communion.

Still, there are those I need to thank in particular. First, all those at the John Paul II Institute who fostered and deepened my thinking while I was there. In that vein, I must also thank Stephen Loughlin, Larry Chapp, and Rodney Howsare, in whose classes and under whose tutelage I first caught sight of the Good.

There are a few I must thank especially with regard to my work on Ulrich. In particular, Martin Bieler, who was the first to suggest the (what I at the time deemed laughable) idea that I write on Ulrich. As it turns out, he saw something that I was perhaps still too afraid to look at myself. I also thank Katrina and Jonathan Bieler, whose support guided me through the earliest stages of this process. I owe a debt of gratitude to the members of the Johannesgemeinschaft, who have all been with me in this work in one way or another. And to Adrian Walker, whose friendship has made this book and all of my thought much deeper, more expansive, and simultaneously more simple.

Lastly, I thank my family, especially Barbara and Rebekah, without whom I would not be sane.

Abbreviations

BSP	Etienne Gilson, *Being and Some Philosophers*
Disp.	Francisco Suárez, *Disputationes metaphysicae*
DP	Thomas Aquinas, *De potentia*
DPN	Thomas Aquinas, *De principiis naturae*
DV	Thomas Aquinas, *De veritate*
ES	Ferdinand Ulrich, *Erzählter Sinn*
FG	Martin Bieler, *Freiheit als Gabe*
GA	Marine de la Tour, *Gabe im Anfang*
GV	Ferdinand Ulrich, *Gabe und Vergebung*
HA	Ferdinand Ulrich, *Homo Abyssus* (trans. D. C. Schindler)
"Inwiefern"	Ferdinand Ulrich, "Sein und Materie. Inwiefern ist die Konstruktion der Substanzkonstitution maßgebend für die Konstruktion der Materiebegriffes bei Suárez, Duns Scotus und Thomas?"
Meta.	Aristotle, *Metaphysics*
MMS	Stefan Oster, *Mit-Mensch-Sein*
MTTA	John F. Wippel, *The Metaphysical Thought of St. Thomas Aquinas*
Op. Ox.	John Duns Scotus, *Opus Oxoniense*
SCG	Thomas Aquinas, *Summa contra gentiles*
ST	Thomas Aquinas, *Summa theologiae*
TMC	Susan Canty Selner, "The Metaphysics of Creation in Thomas Aquinas' *De Potentia Dei*"

Introduction

WHY SHOULD THERE BE material being? Given that man is microcosmos, that is, the little world who both encapsulates and incarnates the unity of matter and spirit, the reason for material being would seem to be a question that is most natural for him to ask. And yet, it is rarely considered in the history of thought. At first it seems very close to what Heidegger names as "the first of all questions": "Why are there beings at all rather than nothing?,"[1] but this question is somewhat different; the question of *material* being asks why there should be beings *in this way*. That is to say, the question of material being asks why it is given to matter, which is nothing in itself[2]—a kind of nonbeing—to reveal something about the nature of being itself.

If we look at the works of Dionysius the Areopagite, we receive some initial reflection on and insight into our question. He writes in the *Divine Names* that

> the Beautiful is therefore the same as the Good, for everything looks to the Beautiful and the Good as the cause of being, and there is nothing in the world without a share of the Beautiful and the Good. And I would even be so bold as to claim that nonbeing also shares in the Beautiful and the Good, *because nonbeing, when applied transcendently to God in the sense of a denial of all things, is itself beautiful and good*. This—the One, the Good, the

---

1. Heidegger, *Introduction to Metaphysics*, 1.
2. *ST* I.44.2: Sed contra est quod dicit Augustinus, *XII Confess.*, duo fecisti, domine, unum prope te, scilicet Angelum, aliud prope nihil, scilicet materiam primam.

Beautiful—is in its uniqueness the Cause of the multitudes of the good and the beautiful. From it derives the existence of everything as beings, what they have in common and what differentiates them ... the return upward by those of lower status, the protecting and unchanged remaining and foundations of all things amid themselves. Hence, the interrelationship of all things in accordance with capacity. Hence, the harmony and the love which are formed between them but which do not obliterate identity.[3]

Earlier in the *Divine Names* Dionysius writes that unity is the result of "the supra-essential being of God—transcendent Goodness transcendently there," and also that God is "unity above being."[4] To be sure, there are several types of nonbeing for Dionysius, but he understands that the nonbeing below being (i.e., matter) in some way images the nonbeing above being (i.e., God, the Good), and does so in such a way that nothing else can, *precisely because of its "status" as nonbeing*. Dionysius writes,

> Given that the Good transcends everything, as indeed it does, its nature, unconfined by form, is the creator of all form. In it is nonbeing really an excess of being. It is not a life, but is, rather, superabundant Life. It is not a mind, but is superabundant Wisdom. Whatever partakes of the Good partakes of what preeminently gives form to the formless. *And one might even say that nonbeing itself longs for the Good which is above all being.* Repelling being, it struggles to find rest in the Good which transcends all being, in the sense of a denial of all things.[5]

This theme of nonexistence desiring and imaging the higher is also found in *Celestial Hierarchy* wherein Dionysius explains the use and purpose of dissimilar symbols: "So, then, forms, even those drawn from the lowliest matter, can be used, not unfittingly, with regard to heavenly being. Matter, after all, owes its subsistence to absolute beauty and keeps, throughout its earthly ranks, some echo of intelligent beauty. Using matter, one may be lifted up to the immaterial archetypes."[6]

Also in *Celestial Hierarchy* we find Dionysius's explanation for the whence of material creation:

> One truth must be affirmed above all else. It is that the transcendent Deity has out of goodness established the existence of

3. 704B–C, emphasis added.
4. 593C and 641C, respectively.
5. 697A, emphasis added.
6. 144B–C.

everything and brought it into being. It is characteristic of the universal Cause, of this goodness beyond all, to summon everything to communion with him to the extent that it is possible. Hence everything in some way partakes of the providence flowing out of this transcendent Deity which is the originator of all that is.[7]

And again in the *Divine Names* we find an "explanation" for creation, as well as all causality, which is love:

> To those listening properly to the divine things the name "love" is used by the sacred writers in divine revelation with the exact same meaning as the term "yearning." What is signified is a capacity to effect a unity, an alliance, and a particular commingling in the Beautiful and the Good. It is a capacity which preexists through the Beautiful and the Good. It is dealt out from the Beautiful and the Good through the Beautiful and the Good. It binds the things of the same order in mutually regarding union. *It moves the superior to provide for the subordinate*, and it stirs the subordinate in return toward the superior.[8]

Reflecting on these selections from Dionysius, we can see that he in some sense connects non-being to that which is above being—that is, God. The lowest in the hierarchy of being can, according to Dionysius, reveal the highest, and importantly, can only do so because it is the lowest. Because of its nature, matter, which is below being, so to speak, is uniquely suited to reveal that which is above being, God. Thus we might initially say that the reason for matter (and therefore material being) is to reveal aspects of God accessible to nothing else in creation.

The second theme we might see emerging in these brief excerpts is that the reason for matter and material being is *love*. Not only does nonbeing "long for" (=love) the Good above being, but the Good has brought everything in creation into being—including matter—out of love, and in some way unites itself to creation while not becoming one with it. Love binds without subsuming, according to Dionysius. And so we see, if we pay attention to matter, that the Good loves matter and the rest of creation into being.

Love then, according to Dionysius, should be our entrance into thinking about matter and material being. And indeed in this book we will take his suggestion and follow this path.

---

7. 177C.
8. 709D, emphasis added.

I must admit immediately that this is not a book about Dionysius the Areopagite. I start, however, with some of his most provocative and insightful statements about matter and nonbeing (which are not always exactly coincident, but as we shall soon see, also not completely different) for two main reasons: First, Dionysius asks us not only to think about a component of our reality that we often take for granted—that is, matter—but also to think about it as radically as possible: that is, as a unique image of God himself. This alone would be enough to at least include Dionysius's reflection on matter in any serious study of the subject.

There is however a second reason to begin this book in particular with Dionysius, even though he will not be our main subject. This work seeks to answer our question—why should there be material being?—in and through the work of the German philosopher Ferdinand Ulrich. As I will explain in much more detail in what follows, the foundation of Ulrich's thought is the work of Thomas Aquinas, and Thomas in turn is deeply influenced by Dionysius—indeed, Dionysius is one of the most quoted authors across all of Thomas's corpus. Ulrich himself does not highlight Dionysius's influence on the Common Doctor—in fact, it is unclear how much Ulrich is aware of the Areopagite's influence on Thomas. And yet, Ulrich, in his creative dialogue with Thomas, and perhaps without knowing it himself, retrieves and highlights the deep Neoplatonic influence on and structure of the Angelic Doctor's work. And this is perhaps nowhere more clear than in Ulrich's treatment of matter.

This book seeks to answer the question of why there should be material being, and to do so in and through the work of Ferdinand Ulrich. Ulrich's metaphysics is also and necessarily a meta-anthropology, because, as Ulrich writes, "being and man belong together in a primordial way."[9] Man himself is material being; he therefore cannot escape the question of matter, which is in some sense the question of why he exists as he does. Though the question "why is there anything at all?" has in some form or another guided philosophy from the beginning, the question of why this being should be *material* is not one to which the philosophical tradition has systematically given its attention. Among his many other contributions, Ulrich not only brings this question to the fore, but also makes it one of the foci around which his metaphysics revolves.

Ulrich is still a somewhat unknown philosopher, and though there have already been several excellent studies on his thought, none of them draws attention to the central role matter plays in his metaphysics. Since I will be concentrating on matter in Ulrich's thought, the reader should know about

---

9. Ulrich, *Homo Abyssus* [hereafter=*HA*], 1. Unless otherwise noted, all English translations of *HA* are from D. C. Schindler's translation.

the other major treatments of Ulrich's work even if—or perhaps especially because—they are few in number. In German, we encounter systematic commentary on Ulrich's work the first time in book-form in Martin Bieler's *Freiheit als Gabe* (1991). Here, Bieler asks what it means that finite freedom's *Urgestalt* is the freedom of the Trinity, engaging primarily with Thomas Aquinas, and also with Augustine and Richard of St. Victor. When Bieler begins to address finite freedom specifically, he moves from those interlocutors to Gustav Siewerth and Ferdinand Ulrich, who help frame the discussion of a so-called more traditional understanding of freedom, while also taking the modern emphasis of human freedom into account. Here Bieler begins to trace the influence of Thomas on Ulrich, but *Freiheit als Gabe* is not entirely dedicated to Ulrich's work, and therefore this reflection is not sustained. It should also be noted that while Bieler's work is very clear and gets to the heart of Ulrich's thought, it is strictly theological and does not thematize the philosophical character of Ulrich's work. Bieler has also written the introduction to several of Ulrich's books, including *Homo Abyssus* (1998), *Leben in der Einheit von Leben und Tod* (2000), and *Erzählter Sinn* (2002).

The most prominent text on Ulrich is probably Stefan Oster's *Mit-Mensch-Sein* (2004),[10] which addresses Ulrich's phenomenology and anthropology of gift; Oster's particular concern is opening up Ulrich's ontology through human experience. Oster's main interlocutors are Habermas, Hegel, and Derrida. One chapter addresses Ulrich's metaphysics of creation, but Ulrich's understanding of matter is not thematic in the discussion.

Marine de la Tour's *Gabe im Amfang: Grundzüge des metaphysischen Denkens von Ferdinand Ulrich* (2016)[11] is another excellent introduction to Ulrich. In it, de la Tour concentrates on what Ulrich calls the "self-realization of reason." According to de la Tour, this is the core of Ulrich's thought: the self-realization of reason as reflexive act, in which man must constantly refer to the "beginning" of being, which is, for Ulrich, being's very giftedness. This, de la Tour says, is the original gesture of thinking: to "be" constantly—that is, to draw the source of one's self—from the beginning, and to understand this beginning as gift. De la Tour then traces this philosophical approach in Ulrich's engagement with other thinkers such as Scotus and Suárez, but especially Hegel, Schelling, and Heidegger.

Resources in English are somewhat scant, though there is a growing awareness of Ulrich's work in English-language philosophy and theology, and thus a growing number of articles on his work. There is an excellent short introduction, again by Stefan Oster, entitled "Thinking Love at the Heart of

10. Oster, *Mit-Mensch-Sein* [hereafter=*MMS*].
11. de la Tour, *Gabe im Amfang* [hereafter=*GA*].

Things: The Metaphysics of Being as Love in the Work of Ferdinand Ulrich" (2010), in which Oster very clearly identifies the main principles of Ulrich's metaphysics: (1) an understanding of being as love, (2) the importance of Thomas's insight of *esse non subsistens* to Ulrich, and (3) the central place the *Subsistenzbewegung*, or the movement into subsistence, takes in Ulrich's metaphysics. Martin Bieler has also published an article in English entitled "*Analogia Entis* as an Expression of Love according to Ferdinand Ulrich" (2011). In it, Bieler writes, "Like the *bonum* and its causality, which aims at that which is not yet, the *materia prima* is in a certain sense wider than being,"[12] and he begins to situate Ulrich's thought in regard to Thomistic metaphysics. Bieler even touches upon the fact that matter plays a central role for Ulrich, but he does not develop the latter point. The article is more introductory and focuses on what the *analogia entis* is in Ulrich's work. Ricardo Aldana reflects on the meaning of time for Ulrich in "The Experience of the Unity of Time and Christian Faith in the Thought of Ferdinand Ulrich" (2016). Finally, we should mention D. C. Schindler's *A Companion to Ferdinand Ulrich's* Homo Abyssus (2019), which, as the title suggests, guides the reader through *Homo Abyssus* and includes two helpful analytical appendices.

Ulrich's work is as profound as it is lengthy, and so it is not as a corrective to all these works that I propose to interpret matter as central to his metaphysics, but rather as a different, though important, path into and through the density of his metaphysics. As will be shown in what follows, Ulrich's thought penetrates reality to its utmost depths, and so in order to follow his metaphysics of creation as radically as possible, as it were, we will follow it all the way down to the lowest of all created effects: matter itself.

Before moving directly into our explication of Ulrich's metaphysics of creation and his understanding of matter, a short introduction to his life and work is necessary given his relative obscurity. Though he was born in Odry, Czechoslovakia, Ulrich spent most of his life in Bavaria, where he was educated and eventually taught. He studied philosophy, theology, and psychology, and eventually received his doctorate in philosophy from the Ludwig Maximilian University of Munich, with a dissertation entitled "Sein und Materie: Inwiefern ist die Konstruktion der Substanzkonstitution maßgebend für die Konstruktion der Materiebegriffes bei Suárez, Duns Scotus und Thomas?" (1955).[13] Ulrich's habilitation, written in Salzburg, would eventually be published as his first book, *Homo Abyssus: Das Wagnis der Seinsfrage* (1998). *Homo Abyssus*, subtitled "the drama of the question of being," lays out Ulrich's basic metaphysical framework, starting with the question of being in itself and

---

12. Bieler, "*Analogia Entis* as an Expression of Love," 329.
13. Hereafter="Inwiefern."

moving on to the question of man and being: what does it mean that man is both the shepherd of being and its highest incarnation? Ulrich's work is deeply metaphysical, but this does not mean he forecloses other questions that are not strictly philosophical. Indeed, the opposite is true: Ulrich's approach to the study of being is radical and comprehensive; he knows that how we understand the shape, so to speak, of being itself will in turn affect every aspect of our thinking, our living, our existence. It is because of the depth of his vision that Ulrich can comment on other areas from the question of evolution[14] to fairy tales,[15] from the question of death[16] to the meaning of language.[17] Our understanding of being will necessarily affect everything, and therefore nothing is off limits for Ulrich.

As stated above, Ulrich sees a deep and intimate connection between metaphysics and anthropology, as evidenced by the two main sections of *Homo Abyssus*,[18] and this profound joining also informs the rest of his work. He takes a special interest in psychology in his work *Leben in der Einheit von Leben und Tod* (2000), in which Ulrich ponders how man can live with the specter of death. The question is not superficially psychological—that is to say, Ulrich is not here asking questions of strategy or coping mechanisms— but rather, given the fact that death is, both factually and ontologically, *Leben* then explores the implications for man as a finite creature, and a creature who knows he is finite.

This interest in anthropology and psychology naturally unfolds into a concern with and explanation of freedom, which could be said to be man's defining trait. As with all the themes that we will here mention, the theme of man's freedom runs throughout Ulrich's work, but he explicitly and systematically addresses it in his *Gegenwart der Freiheit* (1974), in which he takes up Nietzsche's challenge to mankind: What is freedom? Are we really free? How can we really be free?

---

14. See Ulrich, "Evolution—Geschichte—Transzendenz."

15. Ulrich, *Erzählter Sinn: Ontologie der Selbstwerdung in der Bilderwelt des Märchens* [hereafter=ES].

16. Ulrich, *Leben in der Einheit von Leben und Tod*.

17. Ulrich, *Logo-Tokos*.

18. They are as follows: Part A: "To Be and the Being of Beings" and Part B "Man as *Totum Potestativum*: Unfolding the Human Essence from the Perspective of Being's Movement of Finitization." Additionally, Ulrich wrote two works before "Inwiefern"; their titles also indicate Ulrich's understanding of the intimate connection between metaphysics and anthropology: *Sein und Wesen: Spekulative Entfaltung einer anthropologischen Ontologie* (1954), and *Anthropologischen Urgrundlehre: Eine Auseinandersetzung mit der anthropologischen Theologie A. Günthers* (1955).

The concern with man as both incarnation and primary asker of the question of being, and how he takes up this task in freedom leads to the theme of childhood, since in material and historical creatures, the beginning will always shape and affect everything else. Childhood is yet another theme that is carried through all of Ulrich's work, though perhaps nowhere so explicitly as in *Der Mensch als Anfang: zur philosophischen Anthropologie der Kindheit* (1970). There Ulrich addresses what childhood means, and ultimately concludes that the child is, in a sense, the form of human being. This theme is also explicitly addressed in *Atheismus und Menschwerdung* (1966).

If the child is the form of human being, then the next step, as it were, is to explore how the child develops and grows into his understanding of who he is, what the world is, and what being is, and so Ulrich also addresses language. In *Logo-Tokos* (2003), he reflects on language as task and gift—that is, to be given the capacity to say what is true as refracted and incarnated in one's own being—but also as temptation for man: the temptation to make idols, that is, knowingly to say and worship what is false.

Language is a great gift: it is with language that man can tell himself his own story—whether it be history or myth—and it is also with language that man can worship. In *Erzählter Sinn* (2002), Ulrich explores the former, meditating on the meaning of fairy tales anthropologically, psychologically, and ontologically; in *Gebet als geschöpflicher Grundakt* (1973), Ulrich explores the metaphysical and ontological meaning of prayer. If childhood is in a certain sense the form of human being, then prayer is simply the form of creaturely being, because prayer is the ultimate and perfect creaturely expression of gratitude, which is the meaning of being itself.

Here we reach both Ulrich's most recent work[19] and perhaps the intimate heart of the entirety of his metaphysics: that being is gift, and that we can know being as gift most profoundly in and through a biblical ontology. It would be difficult to overstate the importance of the theme of gift in Ulrich's work—indeed, calling it a theme is not really sufficient. That being is gift is the *Gestalt* of Ulrich's work: it gives everything else shape, and it is that out of which everything else flows. We will explore Ulrich's metaphysics of being as gift more deeply in what follows, but its import is such that we should comment on it even here in our introduction. To say that being is gift already implies both a giver and a receiver, and indeed Ulrich does not foreclose on revelation as part of the philosophical equation, so to speak, or out of some

---

19. There are currently five volumes of Ulrich's work published by the Johannes Verlag, all mentioned above (note: *Der Mensch als Anfang, Atheismus und Menschwerdung,* and *Gebet als geschöpflicher Grundakt* are not considered part of this series); there will be a sixth on the subject of fruitfulness.

narrow sense of needing to think "purely" philosophically.[20] Rather, like Thomas Aquinas—who provides the inspiration and groundwork for all of Ulrich's thought—Ulrich takes revelation into account in his probing of the deepest metaphysical questions. Not to do so would be to impose blinders on oneself in the name of some superficial understanding of the division of the sciences. Ulrich is interested in reality as it is, and this includes the fact that it is created.

To describe being as gift, as just stated, implies a giver and receiver, but also—and crucially—it also implies that this gift has *already been given*, or the flipside, that being has *already been received*. Being is not meted out to creation in a stepwise fashion, but rather given entirely to the world in the act of creation. This means that being is not a mediator standing between God and the world, but pure mediation: God creates subsistent being, and being is the pure mediation through and in which God creates. Stefan Oster puts it this way:

> Being is a gift by which the absolute Giver, God, creates. Being is the non-subsistent similitude of the love of God. Thus, it is not the Giver, not some free-standing center alongside God out of which creation could proceed. By the same token, neither the "reception" of being nor the receiver itself stands in any kind of opposition to the gift. Rather, it is itself a really distinct presupposition of the gift, even as it is the gift itself that (again: by virtue of the Giver present in, but distinct from, the gift) establishes the receiver as its prior condition.[21]

That being is gift is thus the foundation of Ulrich's metaphysics and the intuition out of which all of his work flows. Indeed, we might say that Ulrich's insights with regard to every other aspect of reality are all an unfolding of this most fundamental intuition.

With perhaps the exception of *Homo Abyssus*, Ulrich's book *Gabe und Vergebung: Ein Beitrag zur biblischen Ontologie* (2006)[22] delves into the theme of being as gift most explicitly and most systematically. Ulrich does not unfold

---

20. Balthasar writes this about *Homo Abyssus*: "[It] has one great advantage over all the other ontologies with which I am familiar: It stands in intimate contact with the mysteries of revelation, offers an access to them, and yet never abandons the strictly philosophical domain. In this sense, it overcomes the baneful dualism between philosophy and theology, and it does so perhaps more successfully than ever before." This passage is from a letter Balthasar wrote to Ulrich on May 28, 1962, and is quoted in Oster, "Thinking Love at the Heart of Things," 660–61.

21. Oster, "Thinking Love at the Heart of Things," 677.

22. Ulrich, *Gabe und Vergebung* [hereafter=GV].

the theme here strictly metaphysically, as is the case in *Homo Abyssus*, but explores it more phenomenologically, though of course, as is the case in all of Ulrich's work, this phenomenological exploration has both deep metaphysical roots and profound metaphysical implications. In *Gabe und Vergebung*, Ulrich uses the parable of the prodigal son as a path into unfolding the implications of being's being gift, as well as the implications of this fact in a fallen world; the temptations to grasp the gift, to receive it poorly, or not at all, are all explored here, as well as what it means to receive the gift in a proper creaturely fashion.

Perhaps the most important insight explicated in *Gabe und Vergebung* is the presupposition of the other. Quoting Søren Kierkegaard, Ulrich explains that "Love presupposes what it does."[23] Ulrich takes this to mean that in any act, the cause presupposes the effect: if this were not the case, the effect would be slave to the cause and/or only an extension of the cause—that is to say, not a true other. This is one of the reasons the most appropriate title for being is gift, according to Ulrich, for in the act of giving, the receiver in some sense must already be there—whether in reality or psychologically, for lack of a better word—in order for a gift to be given, and therefore, in order for the giver truly to be giver. The giver presupposes the receiver (as truly other) in the act of giving. We can perhaps see this basic principle most clearly in creation, which is *ex nihilo*: there is no "before" this act, no receiver to receive creation before the giving. However, in creation, in order for the creature really to be free, the giver must presuppose that the creature really exists, and is already himself, as it were, in the act of giving. The logic of presupposition is then one that runs through all of creation.[24]

---

23. "Der Liebe setzt voraus, was sie tut" (*GV*, 206). Kierkegaard writes, "Love edifies by presupposing that love is fundamentally present, therefore love also edifies there, where, humanly speaking, love seems to be lacking, and where, humanly understood, it seems first and foremost necessary to tear down, not indeed for the sake of pleasure but for the sake of salvation. . . . But when the lover edifies, then it is exactly the opposite of tearing down, because the lover does something through himself: he presupposes that love is present in the other man—which is certainly exactly the opposite of doing something through the other man" (*Works of Love*, 177).

24. The logic of presupposition is perhaps most easily seen in light of *creatio ex nihilo*, but reaches its creaturely apex in redemption. Ulrich writes: "In its eternal self-communication (in the unity of being), generating (*gignere est dare*) love presupposes *in itself*, what it does. The Son, who proceeds from the Father, has never not been the Son. . . . This Trinitarian mystery reveals itself not only in creation (created being as gift *presupposes* beings, which in their procession from the gift (from ipsum esse) in the *real difference*, receive it: *substantia* est proprium susceptivum eius quod esse [*substance is the proper recipient of being*]), but even more wonderfully in the redemption, in what the eternal love itself does for the fallen world, for sinners (liberation from guilt and sin, deliverance from death) in the person of the pure creation, in the libertas immaculata, in the

INTRODUCTION

We intend to demonstrate this by looking at creation through the lens of matter, to which Ulrich dedicated his dissertation, "Inwiefern." As the lowest of all created effects, matter gives us a peculiar insight into the logic of presupposition: matter cannot exist by itself, and thus in a sense must be understood as presupposed by what causes it. Matter does not first subsist by itself and then creatures are built on or out of it, but rather only exists in an-other, which itself has been presupposed (and presupposed as *material*). It is precisely matter's relative nothingness that forces us to look more radically at the meaning and implications of creation and causality. Ultimately, we will see that in the logic of Ulrich's metaphysics, matter provides us with a unique insight into what it means that love presupposes what it does, which in turn means that answering the questions of whence and why material being helps us to understand more fully and deeply why a metaphysics of being as gift grounds a truly Christian philosophy.

Matter is often a marginalized theme in metaphysics, but it is central to Ulrich's understanding of creation, and as such, explaining his interpretation of matter is an effective way of communicating the heart of this thought. Ulrich often refers to the "little way" in his metaphysics: the seemingly insignificant, that which is poor, is given special privilege to image and therefore shed light on the meaning of being. Because matter is itself nothing, it has often been depicted as the opposite of the perfection and fullness that is being itself. For Ulrich, however, it is precisely this poverty of matter that opens up a decisive insight about the meaning of being itself: that being is gift, and therefore its task is to give itself, and to give itself wholly and entirely.

I will explain this in three chapters, the first of which is dedicated to an explication of Thomas Aquinas's metaphysics of creation. Ulrich refers to

---

Immaculata conceptio, the eternal love *presupposes* creation has never fallen, that is, is without sin" ("In ewiger Selbstmitteilung [in der Einheit des Wesens] setzt die zeugende [gignere et dare] Liebe *an ihr selbst* voraus, was sie tut. Der Sohn, der aus dem Vater hervorgeht, ist niemals nicht Sohn gewesen.... Dieses trinitarische Geheimnis enthüllt sich *nicht nur* in der Schöpfung [das geschaffene Sein als Gabe *setzt* das aus der Gabe [dem ipsum esse] hervorgehende, sie empfangende Seiende *sich* in *realer Differenz voraus: substantia* est proprium susceptivum eius quod est esse], sondern noch wunderbarer in die Erlösung, in der die Ewige Liebe eben das, was sie der gefallenen Welt, den Sündern tut [die Befreiung von Schuld und Sünde, die Rettung aus dem Tod] sich in der Person der reinen Schöpfung, der libertas immaculata, der Immaculata conceptio, der Virgo-Mater *voraussetzt*, die nie gefallen, d.h. sündenlos ist" GV, 206n81). That the logic of presupposition is intrinsic to both creation and redemption shows that from the point of view of God, these are not two separate actions, but rather simply the earthly unfolding of the inner-Trinitarian logic, which is love.

Thomas more than any other philosopher in his work and both "Inwiefern" and *Homo Abyssus* explicitly state Thomas's insight about *esse* as their central tenet: *esse est completum et simplex sed non subsistens* (being is complete and simple yet nonsubsistent).[25] The first chapter will therefore provide some necessary Thomistic background in order to understand Ulrich's metaphysics of creation more deeply. Here I will also point out what seems to be a significant lacuna in scholarship on Thomistic metaphysics: a discussion of the meaning of matter in itself, and what it reveals about creation. Though there is agreement that matter (potency) in one way or another limits being (act), there is not much discussion about how or why this should be the case, which would seem especially important in a Christian metaphysics, given the significance of the flesh. Ulrich's metaphysics, which has the meaning of matter at its core, helps us to begin to fill this lacuna.

Chapter 2 is an introduction to and explanation of Ulrich's metaphysics of creation and also demonstrates its continuity with Thomistic metaphysics. This chapter concentrates on the first half of *Homo Abyssus*, "To Be and the Being of Beings," and explains the meaning of some of Ulrich's idiosyncratic and neologistic vocabulary, including the "necessary sense of being," the *Subsistenzbewegung* or "movement into subsistence," and the three "ontological moments of reality, ideality, and bonicity." Not only is this vocabulary necessary to understand Ulrich's metaphysics, but it is also indispensable for understanding the importance of matter for a metaphysics of being as gift.

The third and final chapter specifically addresses Ulrich's understanding of matter. It does so primarily by engaging the arguments made in Ulrich's dissertation, "Inwiefern," in which Ulrich addresses how our understanding of being affects our conception of matter, and vice versa. He does so by comparing and contrasting Thomas's understanding of *esse* as *completum et simplex sed non subsistens* and its implication for matter with the Suarezian and Scotist understandings of being, respectively. During this comparison, Ulrich also explicates the ontological moments of reality and ideality, and demonstrates that when not thought together—and with the third moment, bonicity—neither is sufficient to the metaphysical whole. Our metaphysical reality is never a static structure in which one part or constituent can be isolated from another, but always a living, breathing whole, so to speak, and as such, must always be approached and studied as a whole which gives space and life to communion. The nature of the Good is to unite without collapsing, a truth to which Dionysius has already pointed us.

Finally, the book will conclude with a brief account dedicated almost entirely to Ulrich's explanation of his understanding of matter in *Erzähler*

25. *DP* 1.1.c.

INTRODUCTION

Sinn. There, in a section devoted to the fairy tale *Die Drei Sprachen*, by the Brothers Grimm, Ulrich lays out his understanding of matter, though he does it by using the language and insights of the fairy tale, which puts a different accent on his explanation than one finds in his more strictly metaphysical accounts in "Inwiefern" and *Homo Abyssus*. The metaphysical foundation does not change, but the light in which we look at matter alters slightly, and it is here that Ulrich most clearly states his understanding of material being, and why it is fitting, we might say, that creation should be material—that is to say, why there should be material being at all.

1

Matter in Thomas Aquinas's Metaphysics of Creation

THE CENTRAL QUESTION OF this book is why there is material being at all; this is a departure from—and perhaps refinement of—what Heidegger considered to be the question of metaphysics: Why is there something rather than nothing? *That* matter should be, *why* it should be, and why it should be *good* is not at all self-evident, as the history of philosophy demonstrates.[1] One of the key questions that arises when it comes to matter is how that which seemingly does not exist in itself—i.e., a kind of nonbeing—can limit

---

1. This of course goes back all the way to Plato. He writes the following about *chôra* in the *Timaeus*: "[it] always is, admitting not of destruction and providing a seat for all that has birth, itself graspable by some bastard reasoning with the aid of insensibility, hardly to be trusted, the very thing we look to when we dream and affirm that it's necessary somehow for everything that is to be in some region and occupy some space, and that what is neither on earth nor somewhere in heaven is nothing" (52A–52B). Peter Kalkavage writes in his glossary for the *Timaeus* that "This ordinary Greek word defies translation once Timaeus breathes new meaning into it. A common enough word, *chôra* refers to a place, space, or field. It is the room or expanse in which something is or belongs . . . as Timaeus' third kind (52B), the *chôra* (or receptacle) is neither mere place (since it is constantly in motion) nor empty space (because it is full of 'powers' and 'traces' of the four elements). . . . The word 'Space' conveys the appropriate indeterminateness of the *chôra* to construct the four elementary bodies. Nevertheless, it is abundantly clear from what Timaeus says about the *chôra* that no name seems capable of doing justice to this deeply mysterious nonbeing" (141), in *Plato's* Timaeus. Though Plato does not use ὕλη here, the parallel between what he describes with *chôra* and what will come to be understood as matter are clear.

and define being itself. That is to say, the question of matter is in some sense the question of limitation: how and why matter limits being, and whether this limitation is good, is at the core of answering our question. Let us then immediately state the central Ulrichian insight out of which this book grows and which this book intends to prove: the limitation of being by matter is something positive and revelatory. This is because matter, precisely in its nothingness, is an image of the Good.

In order to demonstrate Ulrich's point in all it sharpness and profundity, we need first to understand his basic metaphysical framework, which is entirely Thomistic. As Martin Bieler puts it, "Whoever really wishes to understand Ulrich must inevitably delve into Thomas Aquinas, the thinker to whom Ulrich owes the most."[2] Thomas's work of course has a much more extensive commentary tradition than that of Ulrich, and so I must narrow my explanation in some way since this is after all not a book primarily on Thomas but rather Ulrich. However, we need to understand some basics about Thomas's metaphysics in order to understand Ulrich, and in this task I will be guided by the work of John F. Wippel, specifically in his virtuosic treatment of the subject, *The Metaphysical Thought of Thomas Aquinas*.[3] This work will help to provide the background necessary for understanding Ulrich's metaphysical framework, and thus will also aid in demonstrating that an Ulrichian metaphysics of creation is not a departure from a Thomistic metaphysics, but rather a sharpening and radicalization thereof.

Thomas's Metaphysics of Creation

Thomas's metaphysics can be approached from many starting points, but if we are to concentrate on his and his followers' understanding of matter, there is probably no better starting point than his understanding of the doctrine of *creatio ex nihilo*. Thomas's is truly a Christian metaphysics, and as such, the fact of creation touches every part of his understanding of reality. As G. K. Chesterton puts it in his book about the Angelic Doctor, "the man we study may specially be called St. Thomas of the Creator."[4]

Thomas's knowledge of creation will make his understanding of God and his relationship to the world different from either the Aristotelian or

---

2. "Wer Ulrich wirklich verstehen will, wird nicht darum herumkommen, sich eingehend mit Thomas von Aquin zu befassen, den Denker, dem Ulrich am meisten verdankt" (Bieler, "Einleitung," xv, in Ulrich, *Homo Abyssus: Das Wagnis der Seinsfrage*).

3. Wippel, *The Metaphysical Thought of Thomas Aquinas* [hereafter=*MTTA*].

4. Chesterton, *Saint Thomas Aquinas*, 119.

Neoplatonic traditions. The world comes about as an act of neither indifference nor necessity and indicates God's complete and total transcendence. In no way is God a part of the world, but at the same time, he is also completely immanent. There is here neither the co-eternity of God and the world from the Aristotelian tradition nor an uninterested overflow of the Good from the Neoplatonic. Rather, the world has a beginning, which means that creation is in the fullest sense an act.

Explaining the contours of this act is where Thomas's genius shines. For Thomas, knowing as he does that creation is an act of God, the why of creation is asked radically. In question 47 of the *Summa*, Thomas addresses the question of the why of multiplicity.[5] Earlier in the same treatise, Thomas asks just what exactly creation is; the first article in question 45 asks, "whether to create is to make something from nothing?" Thomas answers with a resounding yes, being careful to distinguish creation from the emanation of one already existing thing to another; he states that creation is "the emanation of all being from the universal cause."[6] There is no-thing before this emanation, and therefore creation cannot have come from anything preceding. "If the emanation of the whole universal being from the first principle be considered, it is impossible that any being should be presupposed before this emanation. For nothing is the same as nonbeing."[7]

An interesting objection to this article states that action, motion, and change are judged by their terms—that is, what causes the action and what is caused by the action. "The nobility of action and of motion is considered from their terms. Action is therefore nobler from good to good, and from being to being, than from nothing to something. But creation appears to be the most noble action, and first among all actions. Therefore it is not from nothing to something, but rather from being to being."[8] Does this mean that

---

5. *ST* I.47 addresses "The Distinction of Things in General." The first article asks "whether the multitude and distinction of things comes from God?" Thomas ultimately answers, "Hence we must say that the distinction and multitude of things come from the intention of the first agent, who is God. For He brought things into being in order that His goodness might be communicated to creatures, and be represented by them; and because His goodness could not be adequately represented by one creature alone, He produced many and diverse creatures, that what was wanting to one in the representation of the divine goodness might be supplied by another. For goodness, which in God is simple and uniform, in creatures is manifold and divided and hence the whole universe together participates the divine goodness more perfectly, and represents it better than any single creature whatever" (corpus).

6. *ST* I.45.1.c.

7. *ST* I.45.1.c.

8. *ST* I.45.1.ob.2.

creation, coming from nothing, is less than nothing? First, Thomas reminds us in the reply to this objection that change receives its dignity "not from the term 'wherefrom,' but from the term, 'whereto.'"[9] We must remember that nonbeing is not the cause of creation, but simply the "wherefrom." The fact that the "whereto"—that is, creation itself—is so much more dignified than the "wherefrom" in this case does make creation the noblest of acts. It is also the case that creation is not simply an act of change or alteration: we never encounter motion akin to it *within* the world. The closest is generation, which, rather than alter a substance, produces a new substantial form, though of course not *ex nihilo*. Thus, "creation is more perfect and excellent than generation and alteration, because the term 'whereto' is the whole substance of the thing; whereas what is understood as the term 'wherefrom' is simply nonbeing."[10]

We include this objection because it is important to understand that nonbeing is not the cause of creation, as if God has some sort of co-eternal, co-cause beside him, out of which creation arises. Thomas addresses this in the second article of question 44, in which he asks whether "primary matter is created by God, or if it is an independent coordinate with him." In it, Thomas shortly traces the history of philosophers' understanding of matter, starting with the fact that the only thing man immediately perceives is sensible bodies. But, "an advance was made when they understood that there was a distinction between the substantial form and matter, which later they imagined to be uncreated." Thomas continues: "But we must take into consideration that matter is contracted by its form to a determinate species."[11] All of this, even matter, says Thomas, is considered "being," and as such, must be created by God,[12] for "whatever is the cause of things considered as beings, must be the cause of things, not only according as they are 'such' by accidental forms, nor according to as they are 'these' by substantial forms, but also according to all

---

9. *ST* I.45.1.ad.2.
10. *ST* I.45.1.ad.2.
11. *ST* I.44.2.c. The full sentence is "But we must take into consideration that matter is contracted by its form to a determinate species, as a substance, belonging to a certain species, is contracted by a supervening accident to a determinate mode of being; for instance, man by whiteness." This is fairly quickly passed over by Thomas, but it is interesting to note here that he is saying that in some sense it is form that limits prime matter, which in itself is unlimited, and also, again in some sense, that substance is given subsistence ("a determinate mode of being") by its accidents; the subsistence of creatures is not a simple equation of potency limiting act but rather always a question of the whole—that is, the subsisting creature—and how its metaphysical constituents interact.
12. "It is necessary to say that all things were created by God" (*ST* I.45.2.c).

that belongs to their being at all in any way. And thus it is necessary to say also that primary matter is created by the universal cause of all things."[13]

One objection to this article we should keep in mind states that if prime matter is simply potency, then "it is against the nature of prime matter to be a thing made." True enough, responds Thomas, but this "does not show that matter is not created, but that it is not created without form; for though everything created is actual, still it is not pure act. Hence it is necessary that even what is potential in it should be created, if all that belongs to its being is created."[14] Everything is created by the first universal cause, which is God.

Act and potency

Before moving on to what Ulrich understands to be the central tenet of Thomas's metaphysics, we need to address Thomas's reception of the Aristotelian categories of act and potency. Susan Canty Selner argues that Thomas's metaphysics of creation and participation come largely from Plato, but is "radically informed by the metaphysics of act and potency"[15] from Aristotle. Selner points to the *Summa contra gentiles*, in which Thomas writes, "everything participating in something is compared to that which is participated as potency to act: for the participated thing is made actual by that which is participated."[16]

Thomas reiterates the now-familiar Aristotelian principle in question 6 of the *De potentia*: "act is prior to potency, both in nature and in time, simply speaking."[17] Aristotle thinks of act and potency mostly in terms of a concrete substance's form; indeed, for Aristotle, the main term in metaphysics is always substance. A substance's form is its principle of act, and all substances, save the unmoved mover and the celestials, are composed of act and potency. Potency is that which has yet to be moved into act.

One of Aristotle's greatest metaphysical questions is how act and potency are composed in substances—that is, how the composition of this particular being occurred. Aristotle admits that this question is a bit strange to ask, because it is also the case that in some sense, every substance is responsible for its own being: "there is no other thing responsible for the being-one of any of

---

13. *ST* I.44.2.c.

14. *ST* I.44.2.ob. and ad.3.

15. Selner, "The Metaphysics of Creation in Thomas Aquinas' *De Potentia Dei*" [hereafter=TMC], 51.

16. *SCG* II.53.c.

17. *DP* 6.2.

these."¹⁸ Still, in order to understand reality we must push a little deeper into the unities that we encounter.

This leads Aristotle to develop his understanding of fourfold causality. A substance's form is "the look [of a thing] that is disclosed in speech,"¹⁹ that is, how we identify it and what gives the substance identification. A substance, however, is not unchanging, and thus form cannot be all there is to a substance. Aristotle identifies change as a movement from potency to act, and reasons that this motion must be toward something—things move according to a certain rationality—and this "something" is a substance's final cause. A substance's final cause is in some way simply the perfection of its form, and so final and formal causes are, we could say, two different ways of looking at the "how" of a substance. Aristotle also endeavors to understand how the composition of any substance occurs, and this leads him to the efficient cause. "At the very end of *Metaphysics* VIII," writes Selner, "Aristotle takes up the question of the unity of composite being," but because each thing's unifying principle is in fact itself, "it is in itself, in a way, its own principle of composition."²⁰ However, Aristotle does not deny that there is composition—that is, principles of actuality and potency, even though in the thing itself those principles are one—and so it must be the case that there is another cause by which the principle of potency moves into actuality. This is the efficient cause.²¹ The efficient cause is the means by which act and potency come together in a substance, which is first in the substance itself, but is also supplied, as it were, from without, as we

18. *Meta.* VIII.6, 1045b.
19. *Physics*, 193a31.
20. TMC, 58.
21. I use the word efficient for *kinoun* because this is what Selner uses and is also most often used to describe this cause. Joe Sachs and others have pointed out that this term is anachronistic for Aristotle and one that incorrectly overlays a modern scientific worldview onto the Stagirite; Sachs prefers to translate it the "moving" cause. Sachs writes, "we tend to speak of causes as events that lead to other events, since that is the only kind of causality that remains possible in a mathematically-reduced world, but Aristotle understands everything that is the case as resulting from causes, and every origin of responsibility as a cause. Something called the 'efficient' cause has been grafted onto Aristotle's account; it means the proximate cause of motion, like the bumping of billiard balls. Efficient cause is something even used as a translation of one of Aristotle's four kinds of cause, but not correctly.... All of Aristotle's causes stem from beings, and they are found not by looking backward in time, but upward in a chain of responsibility" (*Aristotle's* Physics, 24). Aristotle introduces this "third" cause in Book II.3 of the *Physics*. Sachs translates this as "In yet another way [cause is meant by] that from which the first beginning of a change or of rest is as the legislator is a cause, or the father of a child, or generally the maker of what is made, or whatever makes a changing thing change" (194b30).

will see shortly. Another way of putting this: that whatever moves a thing from potency to act is the efficient cause.

Lastly for Aristotle, there must be some ultimate end for all four causes. Thus, both form and ultimate final cause secure two things: (1) that there is no infinite regress or progress, which is against the nature of the good, and (2) the ultimate priority of act over potency. This ultimate cause is the unmoved mover, and its existence vis-a-vis the world helps to explain all motion and change; all substances move toward this highest good in an effort to be like that which is most perfect. The unmoved mover is efficient cause of the world insofar as all things are drawn to it in its perfect actuality. All forms tend toward its perfection as their ultimate final end. Indeed, any other efficient and final causality can only be enacted because of the unmoved mover, which is perfect actuality in itself. "In order to be ultimate in actuality, having no potency, and yet also have the ability to cause change or motion in another, this efficient cause must exercise its efficiency within its finality."[22] The unmoved mover is efficient cause of the world precisely by being ultimate final cause.

Selner points out that in this explanation, two causes are neglected—the formal and the material—and that Thomas endeavors to present a more complete picture.[23] In the eighth book of the *Metaphysics*, Aristotle writes that a substance has no other cause than itself "except something which as it were moves from potency to act,"[24] but in Thomas's commentary on that text, "he removes the qualifying *ut quasi* and simply says, 'Therefore there is no other cause which unifies those things which are composed of matter and form, except that which moves [them] from potency to act.'"[25] It seems that Thomas comprehends something different and more expansive than Aristotle when

---

22. TMC, 213.

23. Selner's understanding here is that "Aristotle does not understand the power of the prime mover to extend to the realm of formal causality" (TMC, 213). To put it perhaps over-simply, for Aristotle, form explains itself, because form as the principle of actuality needs no further explanation. Though I must side-step this discussion for this project, I am not sure this is entirely true to Aristotle, since form does need, in a sense, the "explanation" of the unmoved mover. However, I think Selner makes a strong case for Thomas understanding Aristotle in this way and then making certain moves in his metaphysics to "correct" the problems. Fortunately, since in his metaphysics Thomas simply tries to give reality its proper due—as does Aristotle—these "corrections" seem to me truer to Aristotle than perhaps Thomas even knew, though of course Thomas's insights, we might say, penetrate reality more deeply than Aristotle's could because revelation casts a new light on the meaning of creation.

24. *Commentary on the Meta.* 1767a.

25. TMC, 59.

it comes to efficient causality. This will in turn affect his understanding of the other three causes.

Creation is responsible for this difference. For Thomas, neither matter nor form—neither potency nor act—is simply self-explanatory. In the classic father-son example of causality, "Thomas is not satisfied to understand the father as setting a pre-existing potency 'forward' into actuality, Thomas wants to know, whence this potency?"[26] The answer for Thomas lies in efficient causality, but one that is necessarily thought differently than for Aristotle.

We cannot—or rather, for Thomas, it is not sufficient to—explain material being by pointing to an active formal principle and a passive material principle, which are directed by their efficient and final causes. We need to ask, Selner says, how a thing (or anything) comes to be in the first place. "In order to do that we must move beyond the thing itself and ask about the origin of its existence."[27]

Thomas points out that for the ancients *ex nihilo, nihil fit*,[28] and he maintains that this is true in particular agents. But when speaking of the existence of the world, this is not the case. As Thomas understands it, the ancients knew of no actuality that could cross the abyss between nothing and something, and thus posited an eternal prime matter.[29] Thomas, rather than rejecting prime matter, simply transforms our understanding of it, acknowledging its existence (however partial or incomplete) as created, and as completely consistent with the rest of reality. For Thomas, creation does not make the world

---

26. TMC, 59–60.

27. TMC, 60.

28. See especially *ST* I.a.45.2.0b. and ad. 1.

29. Again, I must prescind from the question of whether this "substantial" version of prime matter is entirely true to Aristotle, or Plato for that matter. It seems to me that if one reads Aristotle's *Metaphysics* closely, one can see that Aristotle does not propose a co-eternal force of prime matter over against the unmoved mover, but rather, because of the eternality of the world, proposes that matter—that is, potency—is always there as a result of the final/efficient causality that is the unmoved mover. Of course, the act of creation still makes a difference in our metaphysics because it reveals that the world is not eternal but in fact has a beginning; I would argue that this, we might say, radicalizes Aristotle's insights rather than negates them or makes them substantially different. Again, Selner makes a strong case for Thomas's understanding Aristotelian prime matter as substantial—and it is clear, as we will see in chapter 3, that Ulrich also understands Aristotle this way, and understands Thomas to take Aristotle in this way as well—but I wonder if the revelation of the doctrine of creation does not in this case bring something to light that was already there in Aristotle, albeit ambiguously. My thanks to Adrian J. Walker for many conversations on Aristotle's understanding of matter that helped bring this point to light.

metaphysically inconsistent, it actually makes the world more consistent, metaphysically speaking.

In view of the doctrine of *creatio ex nihilo*, Thomas can combine Aristotle's notion of act and potency with a Neoplatonic understanding of participation, thereby transforming each of these from the inside without violating their inner principles. Selner writes that if we "were to remain in the realm of particular agents, [we could not break] an endless chain of act-potency-act-potency. All causes are on the same dependent level as their effects."[30] But Thomas is able to break this chain using his understanding of participation. "Once the metaphysical tool of participation is brought to bear, suddenly it is possible to conceive of a cause which is not on the same level as its effect."[31] We will address the metaphysical notion of participation shortly, but for now it is important to note that because of it, Thomas can understand the possibility of a cause being formally both prior to and higher than its effect. Aristotle's understanding of act and potency is consistently applied to all four causes. "Participation allows an efficient cause to exercise its causality in terms of formality and not just finality,"[32] writes Selner. Form is no longer the ultimate principle of actuality. In a metaphysics of participation, we know that a universal efficient cause can exercise its causality in an intrinsic manner, that is, in terms of formality. This is essentially to say that a metaphysics of participation combined with a metaphysics of act and potency allows us to understand what it means to cause something to be at all. Participation allows us to understand unequal cause and effects, while the metaphysics of act and potency "maintains a radical otherness between God and creature as between pure actuality and limited actuality."[33] Understanding both these metaphysical structures as coincident with and mutually reinforcing each other, creation can be understood radically: that is, as brought out of nothing.

Esse subsistens and *esse creatum*

Perhaps Thomas's most distinctive contribution to metaphysics is his situating all of creation in the framework of being itself, or *esse creatum*. We will see in the next two chapters that central to Ulrich's understanding of Thomas's metaphysics is Thomas's insight that *esse* is "complete and simple yet

---

30. TMC, 216.
31. TMC, 216.
32. TMC, 217.
33. TMC, 219.

non-subsistent."[34] Ulrich will make this the centerpiece of his own metaphysics, but again, in order to see the radicality of Ulrich's arguments, we must give an overview of what this means and how it unfolds in Thomas's metaphysics of creation. Later in *De potentia*, Thomas defines *esse* as "the actuality of all acts and thus the perfection all perfections."[35] As with most of his arguments, and certainly all of his arguments about created things, Thomas proceeds from effect to cause. He reasons that because everything that exists has precisely this in common—that is, existence—it then must be the case that there is some fullness of existence itself. It is also the case that every concrete finite being we encounter is composed, and therefore each has varying degrees of existence, or *esse*. And again, therefore, there must be some single perfect source of the fullness of being. "Because being," writes Thomas, "is common to all things, it must be the effect of a single cause"[36] and three articles later, he states that because we meet being in everything, we may "infer that there must pre-exist an incorporeal substance wherein there is the perfection of being, not in a particular manner, but within a universal fullness."[37]

God is the act of all acts, or the fullness of actuality, but this by itself does not explain creation. Here we come to one of the perennial philosophical questions: the question of the One and the Many. It is around this question that Wippel situates Thomas's metaphysics of creation.

Given Thomas's understanding of God as the fullness of actuality, Wippel says it only makes sense to look at creation through the lens of participation. He refers to Thomas's *Expositio in Librum Boethii De Hebdomadibus*, quoting, "when something receives in particular fashion that which belongs to another in universal (or total) fashion, the former is said to participate in the latter."[38] This could be one way to understand creation: all of creation has *esse* to a lesser degree than that which has *esse* in perfect, infinite,

---

34. *DP* 1.1.c: Verbi gratia esse significat aliquid completum et simplex sed non subsistens.

35. *DP* 7.2.ad.9.

36. *DP* 6.6. This is also a different articulation of Thomas's "4th way" in *ST* I.2.

37. *DP* 6.9. That this universal fullness is infinite is not perfectly self-evident, as it was not for Aristotle. However, again, the revelation of creation is key here: Aristotle's unmoved mover does not bring something out of nothing, nor does the Demiurge (at least with such radicality) in the *Timaeus*, nor does Plotinus's *Nous*, simply. Thomas notes that "there is in some way always an infinite distance between being and absolute nonbeing (*non entis simpliciter*)" (*DP*, 3.1.ad.3) and so "to draw something from nothing to being belongs to an infinite power, on account of the infinite distance" (TMC, 13.) In short, only infinite pure actuality has the power necessary to cross an infinite distance, that is, to create *ex nihilo*, or simply, to create.

38. *MTTA*, 80.

fullness—which is God—and therefore all of creation participates in his existence.[39] *Esse* is that which makes this kind of participation possible. The issue, succinctly put, is to acknowledge "the intelligibility of being and the unity that follows therefrom, while also wishing to defend the reality of multiplicity or diversity (the many)."[40]

First, we need to understand that *esse* is not itself a thing or an entity (indeed, to say "itself" of *esse* is improper, but our language somewhat fails us here), but rather that which is most universal. *Esse* thus cannot participate in anything, rather can only be participated. Another way to put this is that *esse* is not the subject of being, but rather the act of being.[41] This is what Thomas means when he describes *esse* as the "act of all actualities." *Esse* is that which enacts, everything else is enacted by *esse*.

What then is the subject of being? In terms of creation, it is things themselves—that is, substances. Indeed, says Wippel, metaphysics, or the science of being as being, considers substance first and foremost, precisely because substance is the "highest in its claim to being."[42] A substance then participates in being but is not being itself; it participates by virtue of *esse* as its *actus essendi*, it is not the *actus essendi*. This means that all substances then must be composed, since *esse* itself is infinite and one. Substances are finite and participate in *esse*, which indicates that *esse* is limited by substance and, therefore, some metaphysical constituent of substance. Since *esse* is not a "thing," it does not take on a concrete formation: this service is rather provided to *esse* by substance. *Esse* admits of nothing extrinsic to its formal content, since it already is the fullness of actuality, and therefore it must be the case that substances are composed beings. The composite cannot be identified with its *actus essendi* because *esse* itself is not composed. All creatures are composite, and all have an *actus essendi*.

Creatures are therefore composite beings, which participate in *esse* and do so analogically. It would be, however, wrong to say that creatures participate

---

39. Of course here we encounter the problem of pantheism, which Wippel addresses with Thomas's understanding of analogy. In his commentary on Boethius, Thomas makes it clear that being is never predicated univocally, only analogically, and this is necessary not only to maintain the absolute transcendence of God or *esse subsistens*, but also the true diversity of the things we encounter in creation. Being is not a genus; it is said in different ways of different things. However, as Wippel points out, "if being is said in different ways, this is always by way of reference to something that is first" (*MTTA*, 80), so it is not simply that being means nothing. Beings do participate in being itself, in an analogical fashion.

40. *MTTA*, 94.

41. *MTTA*, 98.

42. *MTTA*, 80.

directly in *esse subsistens*, as this is God himself. Thomas thus introduces the concept of *esse creatum*, which is neither an abstract universal concept nor God. What then is it? Language partially fails us here, for *esse creatum* is not an "it"—that is, not a substance nor any instance of a particular concrete being. Thomas notes in his commentary on the *Divine Names* "that nothing can be described as an existent unless it is has *esse*,"[43] which implies therefore that *esse* is common, and this is how we arrive at another name Thomas often uses, *esse commune*: "It is that intrinsic principle, that act of being, found in every existing entity, that is, which accounts for the fact that it actually exists."[44]

However, we must note that Thomas refuses to identify *esse commune* with *esse subsistens*. The latter simply is God, and the former is that in which all creatures participate (analogically) for their existence. This distinction is a fine one.[45] Again, Thomas takes his cue here from Dionysius, who shows that God is the cause of *esse commune* itself. We cannot, however, make *esse commune* into some sort of mediator or demiurge. Rather, Dionysius shows that because God is the universal cause of being, "he is the cause of all particular beings, including the various levels or degrees of beings."[46]

The next step is then to understand the relationship between *esse subsistens* (i.e., God), *esse commune*, and all creatures. *Esse commune* is not a mediator between God and creation because it is neither "thing" nor "self." The question of the relation between the two terms then arises. Wippel continues here his analysis of Thomas's commentary on the *Divine Names*, stating that Thomas spells out three differences between the relation of *esse commune* to God and to existents. The first and perhaps most obvious difference is that creatures depend on *esse commune*, while God does not. In fact, the opposite is true—*esse commune* depends entirely on God. The second difference is that all creatures fall under *esse commune*, while God does not. Again, the inverse is the case: "*esse commune* itself falls under God's power. For God's power is more extended than is created *esse*."[47] Last, as stated above, all creatures participate in *esse commune*, while God does not.

Thomas spends some time with this third point, explaining that created *esse* is a kind of participation in God and a likeness of God.[48] Wippel writes that

43. Quoted in *MTTA*, 114.

44. *MTTA*, 115.

45. Though it is one that we need to guard if we are to avoid pantheism, or, as Avicenna feared, the co-mingling of God with the world. See on this point Etienne Gilson's *Being and Some Philosophers*, 79–84. See also n39 above.

46. *Commentary on the Divine Names*, c. V, lect. 2, n655. Quoted in *MTTA*, 115.

47. *MTTA*, 115.

48. *DV*, 22.2.2: quod ipsum esse creatum est similitudo divinae bonitatis; unde inquantum aliqua desiderant esse, desiderant Dei similitudinem et Deum implicite.

"this is Thomas's way of explaining Dionysius's statement that *esse commune* 'has' God. He means that it, i.e., the entities that fall under it, participate in a likeness of God."[49] So *esse commune* is what allows existents to participate in and therefore—analogically—in some sense be a likeness of God, without themselves being God. The correct understanding of participation is then important for our understanding of creation.

God is surely both first and final cause of all creatures, but creatures participate in God's likeness by way of *esse creatum*. Every creature participates in *esse creatum*, which means that every creature has *esse*, but none is identical to the act of being. "Every individual created existent may be viewed as only sharing in or participating in *esse*, with the consequence that the *esse* (act of being) which is intrinsic to it is only a partial sharing in the fullness of *esse commune* when the latter is simply considered in itself." *Esse commune* is not media*tor*; rather, considered in itself, it is pure media*tion*. A creature has divine likeness only and because it participates in *esse commune*, which in turn has no "self," and thus cannot subsist or be God. Remember that Thomas has said that *esse commune* falls under God's power. This means that creatures only exist insofar as God is their cause; *esse commune* has no creative power. "Hence, in participating in the *esse* which is efficiently communicated to it by God, the creature may also be said to participate in God, that is, in his likeness."[50]

All creatures do then participate in *esse subsistens*, but only by way of *esse commune*. Wippel points out that there are occasions in which "Thomas refers even more directly to the participant as participating in its source or in God rather than in *esse commune*";[51] when Thomas does this, he is referring to the analogical cause or agent, and this agent is neither the same as the divine cause nor the same as the creatures that it causes analogically. *Esse commune*, as likeness of the divine goodness, is pure mediation between God and creatures.

The shape of creatures' participation in *esse commune* is also revelatory of the divine goodness. As mentioned above, Thomas understands multiplicity in terms of reflecting and representing the divine goodness: one creature can never on its own demonstrate and reflect the whole of God's radiant goodness, and as such multiplicity is in some sense required in creation.[52] We have shown that creatures, in their very being—that is, their being caused by God and their participation in being itself—have some degree of divine likeness. This participation can be parsed in three different ways, though all three are

---

49. *MTTA*, 115.
50. Both this and the previous quotation are from *MTTA*, 116.
51. *MTTA*, 116.
52. See n5 above.

coincident with each other. As we have already stated, creatures participate in *esse commune*, that is to say that they share in it without possessing its fullness. Second—again, by way of *esse commune*—every creature is similitude of the divine likeness. Third, each creature's particular act of being, while logically distinct, simply is its participation in *esse commune* and reflection of the divine likeness. Wippel notes that in the order of philosophical discovery, the first understanding of participation leads to the second, but in the order of nature, the second is the metaphysical foundation for the first. "If finite natures or substances do in fact participate in *esse commune*, this is ultimately because they participate in *esse subsistens*."[53]

Now, *esse* is infinite actuality, and as such, Thomas states, can only be one, but we live in a world of diversity and multiplicity. We again encounter our main question: How is this infinite actuality limited by what is finite? Put another way: Whence limitation? Wippel offers two explanations: (1) by appealing to the intrinsic composition of being or (2) by appealing to the fact that the *esse* of every such being is only a limited and deficient imitation of divine being. Wippel does away with the second appeal quite quickly: creatures are not fallen-away *spermatikoi*, but rather subsisting revelations and reflections of God. Wippel notes that "Thomas insists that act as such is not self-limiting. If one finds limited instances of act, especially the *actus essendi*, this can only be because in every such case the act principle *esse* is received and limited by a really distinct potency principle."[54] We must look to the compositional nature of creatures in order to understand limit.

The real distinction: *esse* and essence

This leads us to essence, of which substances are composed along with *esse*. It is the study of the composition of being that leads Thomas to articulate the real distinction between *esse* and essence.[55] Wippel outlines five main arguments Thomas makes for the real distinction between *esse* and essence; here it is only necessary to discuss two. The first, he calls the *intellectus essentiae* argument, which comes from Thomas's *De ente et essentia*. There is some disagreement about this argument,[56] especially as presented in the *De ente*,

53. *MTTA*, 121.
54. *MTTA*, 128.
55. Wippel is careful to note that while Thomas is fairly consistent across his oeuvre in identifying the participated principle in non-divine entities as *esse*, he has many names for the principle that participates, including *ens*, quiddity, form, and *res*. Each has a slightly different meaning, though we will use essence for the most part.
56. See Gilson, *History of Christian Philosophy in the Middle Ages*, esp. 420–27;

but Wippel's reasoning is convincing and sound. In chapter 4 of the *De ente*, Thomas discusses essence as it is found in separate substances, rather than material creatures. The question here is whether there is composition at all in separate substances. Thomas replies that there is no matter-form composition in separate substances, but this does not rule out composition of any sort. Rather, a separated substance will be composed of essence and existence.[57] The argument is a fairly simple one: separated substances are not pure actuality—they have potency and so must be composed in some fashion. Thomas explains further that we can understand the essence or quiddity of a substance without necessarily understanding or proving its existence (*esse*), whereas there is no way to understand something without understanding its essence. This indicates a real "otherness" or distinction between *esse* and essence.

Thomas continues, explaining that because *esse* is the principle of actuality itself, nothing can be added to it, and therefore in only one being is it possible that *esse* and essence are identical. More than one being whose existence is identified with its essence is a logical impossibility because this would be to say that there is more than one being who is simple actuality. This cannot be the case.

As a way to demonstrate his point, Thomas names three different ways that substances can be multiplied: (1) addition of difference, as genus is differentiated into species, (2) the same form is received into different instances of matter, and (3) one of its kind exists in separation while any other instance is received in something else. The first and second cases cannot apply to *esse*; the third can and in fact does. Thomas goes about demonstrating this next, which is to say that Thomas goes about demonstrating that there is a being whose essence and *esse* are identical, that is, what we refer to as God. Thomas writes that everything that belongs to something is either caused by the principles of its nature or comes to it from without. Wippel adds here a third possibility: "that which belongs to a thing might be identical with the thing itself."[58] However, existence itself cannot be caused (efficiently) by the form or quiddity of a thing, for the simple reason that this would mean that a thing has caused itself, which is impossible. "Therefore it is necessary for every such thing, whose existence (*esse*) is other than its nature to derive that existence from another."[59] Last, as he has already established in many places, Thomas

---

Sweeney, "Existence/Essence in Thomas Aquinas's Early Writings"; MacDonald, "Esse/Essentia Argument in Aquinas's *De ente et essentia*"; Bobik, *Aquinas on Being and Essence*.

57. In a material substance, essence includes both form and matter, while in a separated substance, essence or quiddity is simply equal to the form itself.

58. Wippel, "Aquinas's Route to the Real Distinction," 291.

59. Wippel, "Aquinas's Route to the Real Distinction," 291.

explains that because that which exists through another must be traced back to that which exists of itself, there must be something that serves as the cause of all existence such that it is itself existence.

Therefore, in *De ente*, Thomas demonstrates both the real distinction between *esse* and essence and the fact that this real distinction helps prove the existence of God and what his nature must be. Wippel notes that he does this both more or less to complete his argument, but more importantly—and more to our point—"to establish the point that existence is related to essence as act to potency."[60] So Thomas shows that separate substances are composed, and through their composition, that *esse* is to essence as act is to potency. Again we encounter our question of limitation: If *esse* is to essence as act is potency, how can potency (essence) limit actuality (*esse*)? A further question: Whence potency? *Esse* is infinite, essence is not: How does that which is not infinite arise from and limit what is infinite? Additionally, given Thomas's articulation of the real distinction, we must note that not only does essence come from *esse*, but it is also really distinct from it—this would indicate that essence somehow both comes from *esse*, and is also outside of it. These are all implications of the question of the limitation of act by potency.

Thomas makes several arguments[61] for the real distinction based on the fact that all created being exists by participation. We know that *esse* is not composed because it participates in nothing else; rather, everything that is participates in *esse* (to be precise, in *esse creatum*). We also know that *esse* itself is unlimited, and so the natural question is then what allows the limited substances we encounter to be just that: limited. The answer is a substance's essence. *Esse* is unlimited, yes, "but participated *esse* is limited to the capacity of that which participates in it."[62] The real distinction between *esse* and essence,

---

60. Wippel, "Aquinas's Route to the Real Distinction," 294.

61. The second argument Thomas uses to prove the real distinction we have more or less covered above, though it differs slightly, because rather than proving God's existence, as he does in chapter 4 of *De ente*, Thomas takes it is as given (see *MTTA*, 150). Still, the philosophical principle is the same: it cannot be the case that more than one being exists whose essence is identical to its *esse*. Wippel draws our attention to chapter 52 of *Summa contra gentiles* II, where again Thomas is trying to show that though separate substances do not have matter, this does not mean that they are not composed. "*Esse* insofar as it is *esse* cannot be diversified. It can only be diversified by something that is other than *esse*" (*MTTA*, 151). Therefore, if there is such a thing as subsistent *esse*, there can only be one such being. Similarly, "if any genus were subsistent, then it could not be the case that species proper to it could be included within it" (*MTTA*, 152). The species, or any other difference, would be impossible to add to something already subsistent.

62. *MTTA*, 164.

and the composition of creatures thereof, is then in some sense responsible for there being finitude at all.

There is more here than just an argument for the real distinction, or rather, the articulation of the real distinction contains within it the questions of finitude and limitation. Wippel comments, "because unreceived *esse* is unlimited, appeal to some distinct receiving and limiting principle in the participant will be required to account for the limited presence of *esse* in that participant." Wippel points us to Thomas's commentary on the *Liber de causis* to develop this point. Proposition 4 states that the first of created things is *esse*, which Thomas takes to mean not a universal or separated *esse*, but *esse*, "as it is participated in at the first (and highest) level of created being, the level of intelligence and soul."[63] This is multiplied because of the diversity of its participants, not because of any diversity found in its own nature. This is important for two reasons: (1) a diversity within *esse* would mean *esse* is a type of genus, or a concept, rather than real, and (2) if *esse* has no diversity in itself, it must mean that the diversity we encounter must be due to different natures or essences which each have varying capacities for *esse*.

Wippel once again brings up the possibility that this distinction between *esse* and essence is not real, but only logical. He then offers substantial evidence that Thomas in no way and likely never thought this. "As Thomas has explained in a number of other contexts, *esse* insofar as it is *esse* is not divided." And yet, of course, we do encounter a multiplicity of beings. This must then mean there is a real diversity between different natures, but also "requires real diversity within every such being between something which receives and diversifies *esse* (the act of being) and the received and diversified act of being itself."[64] If *esse* is of its nature unlimited, there must be something—in reality, not just in thought—to account for the diversity of beings which we encounter.

Wippel gives yet another reason for this being not merely a conceptual distinction, this time having to do with the fact that *esse* is not self-limiting. Insofar as *esse* is subsistent in individual creatures, it is limited because creatures participate in it, they do not contain it. "If one is to account for the limitation of that which is not self-limiting, one must postulate within such a participant an intrinsic principle which receives and limits *esse* (the act of being), and a really distinct act of being which is received and limited."[65] Therefore, if we are to understand creatures' participation in the act of being as real and not merely conceptual, then there must be a really other essence or quiddity as

---

63. *MTTA*, 165.
64. *MTTA*, 167.
65. *MTTA*, 167.

well. Participation requires composition; composition requires really distinct principles.

The real distinction helps us understand the metaphysical composition of creatures, but it does not in itself explain how *esse*, which is perfect and complete, is limited by that which is seemingly below it. Wippel notes that *esse* is not self-limiting, which means that essence must be its limiting principle. How this composition and limitation comes about, however, we have yet to explain. We have already proven that creatures are composed of *esse* and essence, and we know that *esse*, as considered by Thomas, is the actuality of all acts. Thus, says Wippel, we must consider essence in this respect as a certain kind of nonbeing. Indeed, this reaches all the way back to Parmenides, who thinks multiplicity must be rejected because there is no sense in which nonbeing may be said to be or be real. However, neither Thomas nor we can reject multiplicity, and therefore it seems that we must affirm nonbeing in some sense.

The question of course is in what sense we mean this. "Nothing is divided from being except nonbeing,"[66] writes Thomas, and yet, as was mentioned above, *esse* has no diversity in itself. Thus, we must account for the diversity and multiplicity in beings through, it seems, nonbeing. Obviously, we must be careful with our language here. It is difficult not to refer to nonbeing as if nonbeing were an "it" that has agency. Still, we must use the language available to us, even if it at times falls short of the reality. Wippel points out that while Thomas does not think of nonbeing as reified in any way, he does admit "that in some way the negation of this being is included in that being. In other words, Thomas is willing to admit that in some way nonbeing is."[67] The undeniable multiplicity and diversity of this world requires it.

Starting very simply, we can observe that the negation of one being is included in the being of the next, and we can say that this negation is not bad; indeed, we might say that this negation is even a good. To the first part, we can see that when x is not y, being non-y is included within x's being. How can we say this is good? Let us take ourselves as an example: I think it is good that I am not another person, but this means that the other's negation, the non-other, is therefore included within my being, in a positive sense.[68] Thomas recognizes and pursues this avenue of thought in his arguments about multiplicity.

66. *ST* I.5.1.c.

67. *MTTA*, 178.

68. It would be interesting to pursue Thomas's understanding of *aliquid* and *aliud quid* as a transcendental in connection with this point on negativity. *Aliquid* is named a transcendental by Thomas in *DV* 1.1 (dicitur enim aliquid quasi aliud quid; unde sicut ens dicitur unum, in quantum est indivisum in se, ita dicitur aliquid, in quantum est ab

Having established that composition is necessary for diversity, we turn our attention to nonbeing: Wippel writes, the "most fundamental opposition between being and nonbeing will be enough for [Thomas] to distinguish a first created effect from God, the uncreated cause. And it will also be required for him to distinguish any creature from another."[69]

Nonbeing is not an "it" and has no subsistence. And yet, nonbeing plays a part in the structure of reality. Thomas never addresses nonbeing as such in a thematic way, but he must address it when dealing with the metaphysical structure of creatures. Wippel points out that according to Thomas, there are two kinds of creatures: complete and incomplete beings, the former of which we have already addressed: "There is a kind of creature which enjoys complete being (*esse*) in itself, such as the human being or anything of this sort."[70] These creatures, though they are complete in themselves, are not entirely simple—as is God—because they still receive their being, that is, they are composed. Thus, every complete creature is composed of *esse* and essence.

There is, however, another kind of creature, which Thomas addresses in his commentary on Peter Lombard's *Sentences*. These creatures do not enjoy complete being in themselves, but only in something else. Thomas uses prime matter, or any form, or any universal to try and illustrate what he means here.[71] None of these principles of reality are subsistent in their own right, only as they come together with another principle of being. But, Wippel asks, if these creatures really are creatures and they are not composed, then how is it the case that they are not God? They seem to be at least imitating divine simplicity; what then distinguishes them from that simplicity? Another, perhaps more pointed way of asking the question: How is it the case that *esse commune*—most universal of universals—is not simply God?

Thomas's answer is fairly straightforward: such creatures are not simple in the way God is. Wippel summarizes: "because [they] are potentially divisible or divisible *per accidens*. Such is true of prime matter, of form, and of a universal. Or it may be that [they] can enter into composition with something

---

aliis divisum). A being in its distinction from other beings is an *aliquid*, and some form of negation is present in its being distinct from other beings. Wippel unambiguously affirms that *aliquid* as *aliud quid* is a transcendental property of being for Thomas in *MTTA* (192–94). For more on this point see Rosemann. "*Aliquid*." This article is a summary of the argument Rosemann presents in *Omne ens est aliquid*.

69. *MTTA*, 183.

70. *MTTA*, 184.

71. Est etiam quaedam creatura quae non habet esse, in se, sed tantum in alio, sicut materia prima, sicut forma quae libet, sicut universal. Book I, d.8, q.5, a.1.

else."[72] We know that God does not enter in composition with anything else; this would be contrary to divine simplicity.

These distinctions are important because these incomplete creatures—perhaps most directly prime matter and *esse creatum*—do, in a sense, "look like" God. This is to say, they are not composed beings, nor are they something we can put our hands on—a creature at which we can look, identify, point. As such, there may be a danger of giving them semi-divine status, as Thomas believes many ancient philosophers have done before him.[73] The co-eternality of divinity and matter perhaps falls under this schema. Or, as in the case with a certain kind of pantheism, we could simply think that the existence all creatures share is God's subsistence. When looked at from the point of view of simplicity and composition, this seems a tempting mistake; however, though these principles of being are creatures, it is clear that they are not creatures like most others.

Esse creatum is then a special sort of creature, along with others of this status, which Wippel calls "creatures that do not enjoy complete being."[74] This means that though *esse creatum* is the key to anything existing at all, in order to subsist, *esse creatum* must be divisible and come into composition with essence. At the same time, as we have already established, essence is something really other than *esse*, which is actuality itself. How is it the case that the perfection of being can come into composition with something that is truly distinct, really other from itself? Remember that Thomas has affirmed that "nothing is outside of being except nonbeing."[75] Here, Wippel explains, is where we must explore Thomas's affirmation of relative nonbeing.

Wippel points us to question 52 of Thomas's *Summa contra gentiles*. Thomas is here arguing for the real distinction between *esse* and essence, and, Wippel writes, "in one of these arguments he comments that *esse* insofar as it is *esse* cannot be diverse. It can only be diversified by something which is other than *esse*."[76] Therefore, in every finite being there is something other than *esse* which allows it to be. This "something" is what diversifies and divides *esse*, making the creature limited, and subsistent. This "something" is of course essence. And yet *esse* is being itself. So if essence is other than *esse*, it must be nonbeing, at least in a certain sense.

Obviously essence cannot be *absolute* nonbeing: this would be nothingness. In the third question of *De potentia*, Thomas explains that "whatever

72. MTTA, 185.
73. See ST I.44.2.c.
74. MTTA, 185.
75. ST I.5.1.
76. MTTA, 187.

receives *esse* from another is said to be nonbeing when it is considered in itself if it is distinct from the *esse* it receives from another."[77] Essence then, considered in itself, is nonbeing; however, considered in relation to *esse*, essence is being. Wippel provides more evidence to this point, turning to Thomas's *Treatise on Separate Substances*, wherein Thomas explains that the term "nonbeing" (*non ens*) can be said in many ways, including negating a substance's act of being. If we negate a substance's act of being, then what is left is its essence. In this sense, essence is *non ens*. Pushing this even further into material being, Wippel explains that "we may negate the form by means of which [the substance] participates in *esse*. If we describe what remains as *non ens*, the expression 'nonbeing' will now refer only to matter."[78]

Thus Wippel explains how Thomas both deals with the Parmenidean objection to multiplicity and multiplicity itself:

> Being cannot be divided from itself by itself, to be sure; it can only be divided by something that is different from itself. But this does not mean that what is different from *esse* must be identified with absolute nothingness or absolute nonbeing. Thomas is defending an alternative—relative nonbeing. Therefore in every complete finite being or substance, there is a composition of and a distinction between its intrinsic principle of relative nonbeing (essence) and its act of being (*esse*).[79]

Relative nonbeing then helps us explain the multiplicity of creatures and the diversity that *esse commune* enables. However, it is important to remember the "relative" qualifier here: essence does have some sort of positive content.

Relative nonbeing: essence and matter

As to what that positive content is, we may turn shortly to Cornelio Fabro, who Helen James John rightly claims as one of the fathers of existential Thomism, along with Etienne Gilson. John points out that Fabro was one of the first in the twentieth century to recover Thomas's understanding of *esse* as the perfection of all perfections, and also as the hermeneutical key to Thomas's work. *Esse* is not a brute fact of existence, but the root of all actuality. Indeed, Fabro's basic understanding of metaphysics is a reflection on "the proportional relation of essence and the act of being,"[80] which is, of course, the real distinction.

77. DP 3.4.ad.4.
78. MTTA, 188.
79. MTTA, 189.
80. Fabro, quoted in John, *Thomist Spectrum*, 89.

The mind is struck by the fact that all beings are different from each other, and by the fact that all beings are the same insofar as they exist. Reflection on this point, says Fabro, leads one ultimately to the real distinction between *esse* and essence.[81]

Fabro understands being to be the fullness of actuality and therefore intelligibility as well. This means that all other modes of being "appear as restrictions and partial negations,"[82] which includes essence. However, within the dialectic of the real distinction, each essence, concretely considered, "is seen to represent a particular, indeed, unique perfection."[83] This perfection cannot really be seen from the point of view of *esse*, but must be looked at from the point of view of the concrete substance.

Considered in itself, essence is nothing; essence needs *esse* to be. However, the opposite is also true, albeit asymmetrically: *esse* cannot subsist without essence. Both have a relative perfection vis-a-vis the other, while *esse* always maintains ultimate perfection. Still, when it comes to individual substances, we do not "see" their *esse*, but rather their essence: in the order of knowledge, essence comes first. This is why, according to Fabro, we can only "see" *esse* when set over against essence. When considered in the abstract, being is only *esse maximum formale*, or the plenitude of perfection, whereas when considered in the concrete, individual substance, *esse* is simply the act proper to a particular formality. Interestingly, Fabro calls this a particular being's "share of the divine splendor,"[84] which recalls Wippel's formulation of *esse creatum*, above.

Still more interestingly, Fabro names essence as a kind of image of the divine as well: it manifests "some aspect of divine perfection, is in itself intelligible; but however great its perfection, of itself is never *real*."[85] Note that it is not the case that either essence or *esse* is an image of God, but that both are, albeit each in a different fashion. Indeed, we might even say that both principles in the real distinction each image something about divinity separately, and each in their unity—which Fabro calls "a kind of indwelling"[86]—add yet

---

81. There is no need here to rehash Fabro's tracing of Thomas's arguments for the real distinction, as Wippel's work hews closely to them. Indeed, Wippel makes it clear that Fabro greatly influences his understanding of Thomistic metaphysics. See *MTTA*, chapter 5. As we will see in the next chapter, Fabro also influences Ulrich's work.

82. John, *Thomist Spectrum*, 90.

83. Fabro, quoted in John, *Thomist Spectrum*, 91.

84. Fabro, quoted in John, *Thomist Spectrum*, 91.

85. Fabro, quoted in John, *Thomist Spectrum*, 92.

86. Fabro, quoted in John, *Thomist Spectrum*, 94.

another distinct way of imaging God. Just as different creatures image God differently, each part of the structure of reality does so as well.

Fabro takes the real distinction to reveal at the same time both the fragility and solidity of the creature. The latter because the root of every substance's reality comes from that which is most real and actual—being itself—but the former because the creature always comes in some sense from nothingness. Here we encounter, in a different form, Wippel's understanding of essence as relative nonbeing. *Esse* is the fullness of all being and must be, according to Thomas, diversified by something in some sense outside of itself, which, relative to it, is nonbeing. Thus substances have within themselves an opposition of being and nonbeing—not in fact accidentally, but as constitutive to each being itself.

We have hinted at this already above, but it is the Christian doctrine of creation that allows Thomas the intellectual room and flexibility, as it were, to have an insight into both the act of existence (*actus essendi*) and the meaning of nonbeing, or nothingness. Fabro writes that "the nothingness from which God by his creative act brings forth the creature is precisely that which the creature is, the *that-which-is-not*, before and apart from the creative act of God."[87] In light of creation, nonbeing is not simply unintelligible, or simply incomprehensible,[88] but part of the very structure of creation. It is with this fact that we can begin to answer our ultimate question about the limitation of the infinite.

Matter

Of the many kinds of nonbeing, matter in a certain sense seems most relevant to us. We are, after all, material creatures that subsist in a material world. Of course, matter is not absolute nonbeing, but in a certain sense, and considered in itself, it looks more like absolute nonbeing than any other metaphysical principle. This is because of, if we can put it this way, matter's proximity to absolute nonbeing: matter is the lowest of all created effects—there is literally nothing "after" matter. And yet, as we have been pointing to all along in this chapter, matter seems to have a monumental role in the metaphysics of creation: it is ultimately matter that limits infinite being. Infinite actuality is somehow defined by potency, even as it must be the case that potency cannot be wholly outside of being, otherwise matter would be absolute nonbeing:

---

87. Fabro, *Participation et causalité*, 29, quoted in John, *Thomist Spectrum*, 100.

88. Though I think Augustine and others would agree that nothingness also does have those characteristics; it depends on the kind of "nothingness" we are addressing.

"nothing is outside of being except nonbeing." In order to understand how the limitation of act by potency is possible, we now turn to the structure of matter in Thomistic metaphysics.

Matter, like *esse*, is difficult to write about, insofar as matter, like *esse*, is not an "it," and also has no real existence in and of itself. Recall too that Thomas draws a comparison between matter and *esse* when he speaks of what Wippel calls "incomplete creatures."[89] So again we use our language analogously here.

Matter, writes Wippel, is defined by potency, or exists in potency; it is that which can exist but does not. In *De principiis naturae*, Thomas distinguishes between the kind of matter that is in potency to accidents, which is the matter *"in* which" or *in qua*, and that which is in potency to substantial existence, which is the matter *"from* which" or *ex qua*. Strictly speaking, only the matter *ex qua* is matter in the proper sense, though it is the case that everything in potency can be called matter.[90]

Composite beings are made up of form and matter, and we know this at least in part because of the phenomenon of generation and corruption. Things change, and when they move in the direction of actualizing their form, this is called generation, whereas when things move away from the actualization of their form, this is called corruption. This leads Wippel to outline three distinct principles required for explaining beings: (1) form: that by which something is made to be in actuality, (2) matter: being (*ens*) in potency, and (3) privation: "nonexistence in actuality."[91]

Privation is interesting to us here, if only because it looks the same as matter, so to speak. This is to say that both matter and privation are nonbeing in a certain sense, though when it comes to substance and interaction with form, privation and potency are very different. Matter, we might tentatively say, is the capacity or the readiness for form. It is that which will be informed, and is always at work in a substance. Privation, on the other hand, is nonexistence proper (or "in actuality" as Wippel puts it), and thus is responsible for corruption of substances, or a moving away from actuality. Matter, we might say, is preparation, while privation is a lack. Additionally, privation is always accidental, while this is not the case with matter. Still, "matter and privation are one and the same in the subject, but differ in nature,"[92] writes Wippel.

Though they are different in nature, we should note that matter is always subjected to some privation in this world. Wippel writes, "while it is informed

---

89. See *MTTA*, 184.
90. *De principiis naturae* (hereafter=*DPN*) 2.
91. *MTTA*, 297. See also *DPN*, 7–12.
92. *MTTA*, 297.

by one form, it lacks another, and vice versa. . . . [P]rivation is the absence of a form in an appropriate subject. It is not mere negation. Thus we do not say of a stone that it undergoes privation because it cannot see. But we do assign blindness as a privation to a subject which is designed by nature to see."[93] So, at least this in this world, privation always plays a part in materially composite substances, though when we speak of their being, we need only speak of form and matter.

Every being is therefore made up of form and matter, but to speak of matter in itself is to speak of prime matter. "Prime matter," writes Wippel, "is matter in the unqualified sense." This means that prime matter includes neither form nor privation in its nature, rather prime matter "serves as the ultimate subject for form and privation."[94] Again, we must be careful here: prime matter is not some sort of first substance in which all other forms inhere; this would be to say that prime matter has some sort of subsistence in itself. This is not the case. In fact, prime matter may only be seen, so to speak, from the point of view of actuality. Form gives all definition and understanding of being, and thus matter can only be looked at from that point of view. That does not mean that we can say matter simply does not exist, or that it is only a logical concept. Rather, its existence is different from that of form. We have of course already named this existence—that is, potency—but it is worth retreading here.

In *De principiis naturae*, Thomas writes that "it should also be understood that prime matter is said to be one in number in all [natural] things."[95] To be one in number, Thomas explains, could mean two different things. The first explanation is that something could be one among many of the same type, but this would result from a division, and we have already seen that prime matter is not divisible in itself. Divisibility comes from substantial form, and prime matter has no substantial form. So this cannot be how prime matter is one. However, there is another way of being numerically one, which is, "if it is without the dispositions which cause things to differ in number. And prime matter is said to be one in number in this way."[96] Prime matter is numerically one because there is nothing else like it.

This first helps to demonstrate the difference between matter and privation, even though, again, they can look the same or are the same in a subject. Prime matter "is" in a way that privation is not. That is to say, privation cannot be said to be numerically one, because it is not anything at all. Privation only

93. *MTTA*, 298.
94. *MTTA*, 298.
95. *DPN*, 13.
96. *DPN*, 13.

occurs where there is already a composite being, and only occurs in the process of becoming, not in being, properly speaking. On the other hand, "in generation, the matter ... is there throughout, whereas the privation is not ... the matter which does not include privation is something permanent."[97] Therefore we can say that matter in some sense exists, even if we cannot perceive it without form. Indeed, later in *De principiis*, Thomas writes, "since it has no form as an ingredient of its nature, prime matter does not have actual existence, since actual existence is only from a form."[98] Though prime matter exists, it can only be known through form. The same cannot be said of privation.

The second reason it is important to show that prime matter is one is to demonstrate some interesting parallels between prime matter and *esse*. Above, Wippel has already drawn our attention to one of the parallels between *esse* and prime matter: he calls both "incomplete creatures." Remember that this says nothing about *esse*'s perfection—only that *esse* has no substantial existence on its own. It is the same with prime matter, though of course we would not say that prime matter is the perfections of all perfections. Likewise, in *De principiis* II, Thomas notes that prime matter cannot be known through itself. Joseph Bobik writes that prime matter "cannot be known *through itself* since it has no form; nonetheless, it can be known *through the form* which is *in it* without being *of it*."[99] Almost the same exact sentence could be written of *esse*, save that form is in it (rather, *esse* is in—or actualizes—form). Additionally, *esse* is numerically one in the same way that prime matter is numerically one, that is, such that nothing else is like it. Remember that *esse* too is indivisible in itself; it too is "without dispositions which cause things to differ in number."[100]

This is not to say that the two are the same—we only wish to draw attention to the parallels at the moment. It should be mentioned that Thomas does not himself draw the parallels in *De principiis*. It is of course the case that prime matter can only enjoy being insofar as it is in potency to form, while this is not at all the case for *esse*. Prime matter, says Wippel, is pure potency, and therefore in the exact opposite place on the Porphyrian tree as *esse*.

As stated above, we know prime matter primarily through the phenomenon of change. Wippel writes that "Thomas (and Aristotle) appeal to privation, matter, and form in order to account for change, and to prime matter in order to account for that radical kind of change we know as substantial. ... Moreover, when commenting on *Meta* VII, c. 53, Thomas remarks that

---

97. DPN, 10.
98. DPN, 14.
99. Bobik, *Aquinas on Matter and Form and the Elements*, 27.
100. DPN, 13.

matter cannot be known sufficiently except through motion."[101] This does not mean that matter is an unchanging substance through which forms pass in and out—that would mean prime matter had actual existence, which Thomas is always careful to preclude. "Thomas's personal view [is] that prime matter is pure potency. The new substantial form which is to be introduced into it in a given case does not preexist in any actual way in the matter, not even as an *inchoatio* or incipient actuality."[102] If motion is how we know matter, then matter is the first subject of motion, and so must differ from all substantial forms and their privations. Matter does therefore have some sort of identity in itself and one that we can identify by paying attention to the metaphysical structure of composed beings.

Prime matter, then, helps us account for change because it is potency. As form is the principle of act in a composed being, it would be impossible to explain change or motion based on form alone. Motion is to move from potency to act; therefore there must be some principle of potency in beings if we see them change, which we manifestly do. Every material creature is then composed of both matter and form. Prime matter, according to Thomas, is a potency which cannot be got behind, so to speak; it is the ultimate subject of both form and privation, though considered in itself, matter has neither form nor privation in its nature.[103] It is, says Wippel, pure potency. Thus, prime matter is different from nonbeing, but different from nonbeing differently than form differs from nonbeing.

This is not to say that form and matter are building blocks, which, when added together construct a whole being. It would be a mistake to conceive of beings in this way. Thomas always has the concrete substance in front of him when thinking metaphysics—that is, the whole.[104] Therefore, we can affirm that prime matter never exists on its own, but at the same time is a principle of being. That is to say, matter is within the definition of natural substance. If this

101. *MTTA*, 301–2.

102. *MTTA*, 301.

103. *DPN*, 14: Et est sciendum quod, licet materi prima non habeat in sua ratione aliquam formam vel privationem, sicut in ratione aeris neque est figuratum neque infiguratum, tamen numquam denudatur a forma et privatione. Quandoque enim est subuna forma, quandoque sub alia. Sed per se numquam potest esse, quia—cum in ratione sua non habeat aliquam formam, non habet esse is actu, cum esse in actu non sit nisi a forma. Sed est solum in potentia. Et ideo quiquid est in actu, non potest dici materia prima.

104. Bobik addresses this in his commentary on *DPN*, writing that Thomas asks the question at the end of *DPN* about the numerical sameness of matter, form, and subject in order to emphasize that the primary subject of metaphysics is the substance itself, not the principles thereof. Bobik writes, "matter and forms of different sorts are the principles of natural things and not vice versa" (98).

is the case, we also must say that form and matter have one single act of being, and "it is by reason of this single act of being [*esse*] that a composite substance subsists."[105] Form gives this act of being to matter, says Thomas, but if this is the case, form itself cannot be the act of being (*esse*). Thus we encounter the tripartite metaphysical structure of corporeal beings: matter, form, *esse*. Matter is the principle of potency, *esse*, actuality itself, and form, as the principle of actuality, communicates act to matter. Thus form with respect to matter is active, but with respect to *esse* is receptive.

The question of the limitation of actuality is then a question of nonbeing, which, as we have seen above, can be said in different ways. Considered in itself essence is nonbeing, though it is not absolute nonbeing; considered with respect to *esse* we can see that essence both is and substantializes *esse*. Similarly, matter considered in itself is nonbeing, but not absolute nonbeing. Matter is potency, and this potency is responsible for the limitation of infinite actuality such that more than one individual of a species can subsist. That matter is the principle of individuation seems to be widely accepted by most Thomists in the English-speaking scholarship,[106] but the discussion never addresses what is significant about limitation in itself. That a principle of individuation—that is, some principle that ultimately limits infinite actuality—should exist at all, is not a point for reflection in much Thomistic scholarship.

105. *SCG* II.78.

106. It is so well-accepted that it is often inserted into discussions of Thomas's work, even where Thomas has not had recourse to the principle. For example, in *The Thomist Spectrum*, John writes that "matter is the condition of multiplicity" (91), without any accompanying citation from Thomas. Similarly, in his commentary on Thomas's *De principiis*, Joseph Bobik writes, commenting on no. 34, in which Thomas addresses the relationship between matter and form, that when we are able to count two individuals of the same species, "each has its own designated matter, which is the principle of individuation." This is a bit curious, since Thomas does not even address individuation in this section (91). See also Haggerty, "Principle of Individuation According to St. Thomas Aquinas" and Kent, "Prime Matter According to St. Thomas Aquinas." Additionally, see McMullin, *Concept of Matter in Greek and Medieval Philosophy*, a collection of papers from a conference of the same name which is taken as authoritative to this day. Though not all the papers concentrate on matter as the principle of individuation, all those that discuss matter in relation to Thomist philosophy do. See especially John J. Fitzgerald's "'Matter' in Nature and the Knowledge of Nature: Aristotle and the Aristotelian Tradition," esp. 69–74; Joseph Owen's "Matter and Predication in Aristotle," and the accompanying Comment by N. Lobkowicz; Norbert Luyten's "Matter as Potency," esp. 105–10, and the accompanying Comment and Response; James A. Weisheipl's "The Concept of Matter in Fourteenth Century Science," esp. 147–56; and Joseph Bobik's "Matter and Individuation," and the following Comment by Milton Fisk.

Looking forward, we can say that asking the question of matter in itself seems to have at its heart a difficulty conceiving how things are created, specifically, *ex nihilo*. It is in some ways easier to think of a pre-existent and pseudo-substantial matter that receives forms imparted by God; were this the case, we would not have to face the nothingness whence the world comes in quite so radical a way. But the revelation of the doctrine of creation *ex nihilo* forces us to do just this: if creation really does come from nothing, then when thinking about substances, we are constantly thrown back to the Creator, he who brought us out of nothing.[107] If we are constantly thrown back to the Creator, then we are also constantly faced with the radicality of what he has given in creation: the gift of being.

The radicality of the gift of being then leads us to ask the question of limitation—or perhaps better put, the gift of being *is* a question about limitation, since creation itself is limited.[108] God gives through *esse creatum*, but

107. In *ST* I.45.5, Thomas addresses why it only belongs to God to create. In the reply to third objection ("only a finite power is needed to produce a creature by creation. But to have a finite power is not contrary to the nature of a creature. Therefore it is not impossible for a creature to create" *ST* I.45.5.ob.3), he shows that although the world is finite, it has also come from nothing. Therefore an infinite gap has been bridged, so to speak, and an infinite power is necessary to make this bridge. "For if a greater power is required in the agent in proportion to the distance of the potentiality from the act, it follows that the power of that which produces something from no presupposed potentiality is infinite because there is no proportion between *no potentiality* and the potentiality presupposed by the power of a natural agent, as there is no proportion between *not being* and *being*. And because no creature has simply an infinite power, any more than it has an infinite being, as was proved above (*ST* I.7.a.2), it follows that no creature can create."

108. There are two major exceptions to this trend of Thomist indifference toward the meaning and signification of limitation. One is Wippel, "Thomas Aquinas and the Axiom That Unreceived Act Is Unlimited." There Wippel traces *esse* and its limitation in Thomas's work and eventually concludes that if one agrees with Thomas that what he calls *esse*, the act of being, is indeed the actuality of all acts and the perfection of all perfections, wherever one finds it realized in only limited fashion, one must account for its actual realization, to be sure, but one must also account for its limitation, for the fact that it is not realized according to its full power or plenitude in this particular instance. "For Thomas, appeal to an extrinsic cause is necessary but not sufficient to account for this. He is convinced that a distinct intrinsic limiting principle is also required, in order to account for the limitation of that which is not self-limiting" (564). The second is W. Norris Clarke's seminal article "The Limitation of Act by Potency: Aristotelianism or Neoplatonism." In it, he demonstrates that the principle *actus non limitatur nisi per potentiam*, which had long been held as coming more or less directly from Aristotle, is actually a reception and transformation of Neoplatonic principles. Aquinas, as we have pointed out in this chapter, rejects neither tradition in favor of the other, but instead offers a synthesis in light of the doctrine of creation, which, we could say, allows each tradition to be truer to itself than it was by itself. Aristotle's insight of act and potency, a central tenet

what God gives ultimately is subsistence, which *esse creatum* does not have in itself—indeed needs limitation in order to subsist. If, then, our metaphysics of creation is to be sufficient, it must account for the goodness of creation—a goodness that reaches all the way down, so to speak, even to that which limits actuality, which would at first glance seem only to be impediment.

This lacuna shows that our thinking about matter is not yet deep or radical enough. Matter is not just something necessary in order that creatures in this world may be individuated, but precisely because it is part of the order of creation, matter must reveal something of the divine goodness that nothing else can, stumbling block though it has been and may be. Matter must then be some privileged image of the Good—the key to understanding matter is then understanding how this is the case. It is at this level that Ulrich approaches thinking about matter.

To perhaps anticipate what follows in the next two chapters, we will point out that thinking matter radically requires a thinking of the whole of creation radically, and for Ulrich, this means understanding creation in terms of a metaphysics of being as gift. The gift of being is given so radically that it seems from the creature's point of view almost as if the receiver was always already there to receive the gift,[109] when in fact, the capacity to receive at all is part of the original gift.

---

of his metaphysics, and one of the most incisive explanations of change ever given, was expanded to account for the participatory structure of beings, which ultimately protects the unity and identity of individual beings. Neoplatonic principles were similarly expanded: with Aristotelian act and potency grounding Neoplatonic participation "all the intelligible essences below the One now appear as limited and hence imperfect participations of this supremely perfect and absolutely simple first principle, which somehow embraces within itself the perfection of all the lower determinate essence but is none of them particular" (176). The Neoplatonic understanding of participation helps explain the fundamental generosity and plenitude seen in the hierarchical order of the universe, but is also filled out, as it were, by act and potency, which strengthens the understanding of composite unity in every individual being.

Though Clarke's article begins to point to the importance of this principle, it does not delve into why limitation of act by potency is significant—that is to say, what this principle reveals about the nature of God (though to be fair, the article's intent is not this, but rather to show that the principle, and therefore all of Thomas's thought, has deep roots in the Neoplatonic tradition). This point remains to be argued.

109. In this sense we might say that the Greeks really did see something true when they identified matter (or *chôra*, from Plato) as "always existing" (*Timaeus* 52A, see n1 above). The gift of being is given so radically in the act of creation that it can obscure, in a certain sense, that creation has a Creator. But this should be a clue to the nature of creation and its Creator: the Creator allows creation to be so freely that it can forget its origin.

Ulrich not only highlights, but we could say, plunges into, the radicality of the gift of being: being is given so radically by God that it is also given the power to generate matter, which is wholly other from it, and it gives this wholly other power over itself—that is, the capacity to receive and individuate being.[110] If we do not understand this deeply enough, then we cannot really understand matter because we cannot understand that substances are given to themselves wholly and radically. Seeing the radicality of the gift of being is then the key to situating matter properly in a metaphysics of creation. Therefore our task in the next chapter will be to unfold Ulrich's metaphysics of creation, a metaphysics of being as gift.

---

110. It should be noted that Rudi A. te Velde, in a section about causality, has a couple of interesting pages on matter and its relation to—and what it might reveal about—God in his *Participation and Substantiality in Thomas Aquinas*. He says that when Thomas writes of the first effect of the universal cause, it is not always clear whether he means *esse* (being), which is the first effect, or whether Thomas is referring to matter, because it is presupposed by all secondary causes (that is, all created causes). It seems to me te Velde views this as a fruitful ambiguity, leading us to contemplate what Thomas means when he says "*proprius effectus*" of the universal cause. Te Velde ultimately affirms that the *proprius effectus* is in fact being, however, te Velde also writes that "matter is the effect proper to the power of the universal agent" (179), by which he means matter can be brought into being only by creation, which of course is an action only possible to God.

Te Velde goes on: "Even matter, though not yet actual, has some being, as it is not entirely nothing. Therefore the first cause, whose power extends formally to being as such, includes even matter in its effect which reveals most clearly the difference between the first cause and all other causes" (180). Thus, it seems to me that for te Velde, matter in a sense is the best indicator of creation. Though this line of thought seems intrinsically open to Ulrich's development of Thomas on this point, te Velde does not develop it in this or another work, nor does this seem to be taken up in any of the recent discussions on Thomas and matter.

2

The Basic Structure of Ferdinand Ulrich's Metaphysics of Creation

Esse non subsistens and the fundamental temptation of thought

THE QUESTION OF MATTER is, in some sense for Ulrich, the question of creation. Its meaning and its role in the meaning of creatureliness is not a tangential subject for him, but indeed, a through-line of the entirety of his metaphysics. However, in order to see and understand this golden thread throughout Ulrich's work, it is first necessary to familiarize ourselves with his understanding of metaphysics as a whole, which is at the same time both distinctive from and in continuity with Thomas's metaphysics of creation. Thomas's metaphysics is the foundation of Ulrich's approach; however, Ulrich does not simply reproduce Thomas's arguments. Ulrich's metaphysics is rather an interpretation of Thomas's work, which, as mentioned in the previous chapter, focuses on Thomas's insight about created *esse*: *esse* is *completum et simplex sed non subsistens*.[1] We will follow Ulrich's first book, *Homo Abyssus*, quite closely here, as this is where he systematically lays out his metaphysics of creation. It is important to note that while Ulrich takes his metaphysical categories from Aquinas and the tradition, it is also the case that his language develops these categories in significant ways.

1. *DP* 1.1.

Ulrich, like Fabro[2] before him, sees the interplay between *esse* and essence as one of the most important questions for metaphysics. Also like Fabro, Ulrich takes Thomas's articulation of the principle of *esse* and everything implicated therein to be Thomas's most fundamental and important contribution to thought. Obviously this principle of being itself does not stand alone or apart from metaphysics, but influences our entire conception and understanding of the world. *Esse*—"to be," the act of existence—lies at the center of Ulrich's thought; just as we turned our attention last chapter to nonbeing in order to account ultimately for creation and multiplicity, so too does Ulrich. Being is always the focus of metaphysics, but in order to account for anything beyond *esse subsistens*, we must also address nonbeing. Wippel helps us to see that positing nonbeing is necessary in order to account for the world; this is true, but Ulrich's attention to nonbeing throughout his work, and especially in *Homo Abyssus*, reveals that perhaps there is more to understanding the issue of nonbeing than as something simply necessary to work through: as we will see, Ulrich shows that it can reveal something positive about the nature of being itself.

Homo Abyssus begins with Ulrich stating that "being and man belong together in a primordial way and that being reveals its *superessentiality* in this very relation to man even and precisely with respect to man's *essence*."[3] Ulrich's metaphysics is never thought abstractly, even in its difficulty; rather, the concrete question of man is always, we might say, both behind and in front of Ulrich's thinking of being.[4] We should also note this word "superessential," which Ulrich uses about being, as this is key to Ulrich's metaphysics: being is superessential; that is, it is above essence; essence owes everything that belongs to it to *esse*.[5]

One last note before moving into systematically addressing Ulrich's metaphysics: Ulrich's absolute and unwavering emphasis on the non-subsistence of

---

2. Ulrich only mentions Cornelius Fabro once explicitly in *Homo Abyssus* (German: 148, English: 142), but his influence on Ulrich is clear, even if mostly implicit: Fabro's contribution to the "rediscovery" of the Thomistic principle of *esse* as the act of existence makes Ulrich's insights possible. For more on Fabro's contributions see John, *Thomist Spectrum*, esp. chapter 6, "Fabro, Participation and the Act of Being," 87–107. For more on Fabro's influence on Ulrich, see GA, 266, esp. n353.

3. HA, 1.

4. Bieler writes: "Der Mench ist *durch* das Sein, das sich zu ihm als Substanz wie der Akt zur Potenz verhält" (FG, 232).

5. We will explain this more completely below, but Thomas refers to *esse* as "the act of all actualities" and the "perfection of all perfections" (*DP* 7.2.9). *Esse* can only be so if it transcends essence, which provides the principle of actuality (i.e., the form) for substances. *Esse* could only be "the act of all actualities" if it is not itself essence; this is why Ulrich refers to *esse* as "superessential."

created being itself. We have of course already encountered this fact in our review of a Thomistic metaphysics of creation, but Ulrich understands that not regarding this point seriously enough, or indeed outright denying the non-subsistence of being, is what ultimately leads to every disordered way of thinking about the world or creation, and therefore about God as well. Ulrich calls these "temptations of thought." These temptations, as we will see, may begin with confusion about differing metaphysical categories, but all lead to the same end: the pseudo-hypostasization of being, which is ultimately a denial (implicitly or explicitly) of creatureliness, and thus, a rejection of God.[6] To attribute any subsistence to *esse* is to deny that *esse* proceeds from God and affirm that *esse* is the origin of substances. Thus, the non-subsistence of being is irrevocably tied to our understanding of what it means to be creature, and therefore, of God himself. Because God is the source of being, our thinking about being will end in God, a fact that Ulrich finds neither contradictory nor hindering to metaphysical thinking.

Indeed, being's non-subsistence is what allows anything to be at all, according to Ulrich. We will flesh out this point much further in this chapter, but, because *esse* is non-subsistent, it can, according to Ulrich, pour itself out into substances, thus giving finite creatures their own *esse*, or act of existence. Were *esse* subsistent, this handing itself over or pouring itself out to that which is ontologically after would be impossible. Thus, it is the hypostasization[7] of being itself, in many different forms, that represents for Ulrich the main and most fundamental temptation to reason. He writes:

> Being can never be fixed in itself, not even in the moment of a mere determination of reflection, in order *then* to empty itself,

---

6. Marine de la Tour puts it this way: In these temptations of thought, the substantiality of being "is purchased at the price of the superessentiality of being; the destination of the event of being is the closure of the ontological difference in the absolutely formal, known and articulable (logicized) actuality. Ideality and reality are absolutely identical in the end, the achievement of their mediation is the repeal of mediation (i.e., of superessentiality) itself" ("Die Vollendung des Seienden wird mit dem Verschwinden der Überwesenhaftigkeit des Seins erkauft; Ziel des Seinsgeschehens its der Schluss der ontologischen Differenz im absolut formhaften, gewussten und auswortbaren (logisierten) Wirklichen. Idealität und Realität sind im Ziel absolut identisch; der Erfolg ihrer Vermittlung ist das Aufheben der Vermittlung (d.h. des überhaften Seins) selbst" GA, 313).

7. Hypostasization: to attribute substantiality to created being. Only God is *ipsum esse subsistens*—that is, being subsistent in itself—and so to hypostasize being is to place it alongside of God (or indeed, to replace God with *esse creatum*). The hypostasization of being makes being's mediation impossible because being must hold on to itself, as it were, rather than leaving it free to give away everything it receives to creatures. Obviously we cannot actually hypostasize being, and so Ulrich often calls this temptation of thought "pseudo-hypostasization."

or in order to make possible the unfolding of the ontological difference for reason. Self-diffusive being, which is *gift* [*Gabe*] through and through, does not start out "contained in itself" in this self-donation. If it did, being would not be given away without remainder.[8]

Being, according to Ulrich, follows the "little way": it claims no subsistence for itself, but precisely because of this, can give existence to everything else. This is what Ulrich identifies as the coincidence in being of wealth and poverty, a theme to which we will return.

The path of the ontological difference

We have already anticipated our entrance into Ulrich's metaphysics with the introduction above of the ontological difference. In the previous chapter, we saw that Thomas was concerned over the course of many works and through different proofs to show that there is a real distinction between *esse* and essence. It is not that Ulrich discards this distinction, nor does he take it for granted; however, his focus in *Homo Abyssus* and his own metaphysics is rather on the ontological difference: the principle difference between being as such [*Sein*] and beings [*die Seienden*].

According to Ulrich, the ontological difference, at first glance, and according to some thinkers,[9] seems to be defined by contradiction. That is to say that the ontological difference is being versus beings, as if somehow the two compete against each other for pockets of subsistence, or as if by concrete beings having subsistence, it takes away from the wealth and majesty of being itself. To posit a contradiction, however, between being and beings is to hypostasize being itself, whether it be actually reified or given some kind of

---

8. *HA*, 20.

9. Heidegger seems to go in this direction. In his "Postscript to 'What Is Metaphysics?'" he writes that being lets beings emerge from it, and also that "sacrifice is the departure from beings on the path to preserving the favor of being" (256) in *Pathmarks*. The ontological difference seems then like an either/or in a Heideggerian metaphysics. While Ulrich accords just as much importance to the ontological difference, for him the ontological difference is not a contradiction, but the fruitful tension that allows both being and beings to be (and thus, to be good, true, and beautiful). Marine de la Tour writes that the "ontological difference . . . is for Ulrich the 'place' of the givenness of being" ("ontologische Differenz . . . ist für Ulrich der 'ort' des Gegebenseins des Sein," *GA* 59). Heidegger sees contradiction as the basis for dynamism, which is why the ontological difference is an either/or for him, whereas Ulrich understands it to be the difference rooted in a prior (and higher) unity that allows anything to be at all.

THE BASIC STRUCTURE OF FERDINAND ULRICH'S METAPHYSICS

pseudo-subsistence.[10] Either way, we fall into error. Looking for the moment at just the relationship between being and beings, this error would result in placing the two terms in the same order, thereby leaving us with no actual difference.

To give being even a pseudo-subsistence "would mean nothing more than the unilateral extension of beings, a sublimation that would make genuine transcendence impossible,"[11] writes Ulrich. This expresses itself in one of two directions. The first is that beings are an extension of being which itself has no depth precisely because it has no "self." If this were the case, the end could give us access to nothing but image: the end, having no substance itself, cannot communicate itself to the knower (for there is no "self" to know) nor can it allow the knower to transcend it for the sake of knowing being because it is not really an image, but a facsimile of being. This facsimile, while at first seeming to point to the fact that only being exists (thereby exalting it), is soon exposed in its incapacity to communicate anything at all—whether about being or about itself. Thus, we are left with nothing at all. This is why Ulrich says that if in this case "one then took seriously the '*non subsistens*' [of being], all existing being would be sacrificed to the nihilistic 'nothing.'"[12]

The second direction the hypostasization of being can lead us is the dissolving of being itself into beings. In this case, being itself, or *esse*, is nothing. The finite creature is conceived "as the ultimate, crystallized and concretized extension of a universal being that pours itself out in an undifferentiated way."[13] Being then would always already be subsistent and thus there would be no giving over of being to beings. Indeed, all of reality would be closed in a certain sense, because there can be no ontological difference through which beings receive their subsistence, that is, themselves. Finite reality is closed off from any transcendence, being already perfect in itself. The closing off of the ontological difference results in the closing off of the world to mystery and transcendence. Being and beings are not opposed, explains Ulrich, "the finite is nevertheless not extinguished in this sublation [in the infinite]; instead, it is for the first time affirmed in its finitude by the intimacy being is now able to have with it."[14]

---

10. This is all, of course, in thought. The metaphysical structure of reality does not ultimately depend on how man thinks of it. However (and this is not in the purview of this book), Ulrich's thought does help demonstrate in what ways being does depend on man's thought, given that "being and man belong together in a primordial way."

11. *HA*, 36.

12. *HA*, 36.

13. *HA*, 37.

14. *HA*, 32.

The ontological difference then must be real, though the foregoing in no way explains exactly what it is, and how the two sides of the difference, as it were, relate to each other. Ulrich is quite explicit in his taking up of Thomas's definition of being or *esse* as *actualitas omnium actum* and *perfectio omnium perfectum* in addition to its characterization as *non subsistens*. Ulrich also again takes up Thomas's understanding of substance as the proper subject of being.[15] Ulrich describes the relationship between the two as a "path." "Thus one can say that esse is itself in the substance and that the ontological difference unveils itself as the 'path' by which esse comes to subsistence: in an ever more profoundly grasped return to its 'own' [*Eigene*]—that is, to itself—in the finite entity."[16]

Before, however, moving directly into what Ulrich means by this path, we should note an additional danger in the hypostasization of being itself, which is the making of being into God. This is of course not unrelated to the two temptations mentioned just above; because of its status as perfection of all perfections, we can easily slide into the mistake of making being into God. The hypostasization of being itself makes being into everything, both beings and God. As we saw in chapter 1, the difference between God and *esse non subsistens* is the subsistent nature of being. If we hypostasize being, we inevitably set it over against God himself. It could be that we conceive of being itself as one step lower than God, or as mediator of God's divine will, but ultimately, it would always lead to either *esse* as that which gives existence to beings or God. Again, our metaphysics would be founded upon a contradiction rather than an affirmation.

Notice too that every road down which this temptation of thought leads brings us ultimately to the annihilation of one aspect of the metaphysical structure of reality or another. If we hypostasize being such that beings are all merely a function of being itself, then we get the annihilation of beings. If we instead dissolve being itself into beings, we are left with the annihilation of being itself. And last, if we hypostasize being and set it over against God, we annihilate God. If being itself becomes the ultimate source of existence, then God is unnecessary. We see then, in a preliminary way, that founding our metaphysics upon a contradiction always leads to the annihilation of something real in this world. And we also see why it might be that Ulrich calls this a "temptation": in annihilating any one part of reality, it may seem easier to think the rest. That is to say, somewhat over-simply, we have less about which

---

15. *DP* 7.7: substantia est ens tamquam per se habens esse, and *SCG* 2.55.2: Forma enim manente, oportet rem esse: per formam enim substantia fit proprium susceptivum eius quod est esse.

16. *HA*, 37.

to think. It is like going through a math equation and "canceling out" all that we deem superfluous to solving the problem. However, when our thought and our metaphysics are built upon the most foundational "yes" possible—a "yes" to the entirety of reality[17]—it will be much more comprehensive and truer, even if much more difficult (perhaps even impossible) to grasp. That may, however, be the point.

Nothing, then, can be left out of our question of being, according to Ulrich. But what about nothing? In the previous chapter we began to address the metaphysical issue of nothing with regard to how Thomas answers Parmenides' charge of there being no such thing, so to speak, as nothing. In fact, according to Thomas, there must be a way in which we can speak of that which is outside of being, so that we can account for change and movement among other phenomena. And yet, and as Ulrich also often draws our attention to, Thomas makes it clear that there is "nothing outside of being except nonbeing."[18] It might then be the case that nothing and nonbeing are not exactly the same, but rather, that nothing can somehow be held within being itself, while this is not the case with nonbeing. We began to see this with Wippel's explanation of relative nonbeing.

The marks of being

Being is "nothing"

Ulrich acknowledges the necessity of addressing nothing early in *Homo Abyssus*. He warns that we must be guard against hypostasizing or reifying nothing similar to the temptation of hypostasizing being itself. But we must address nothing, because, as Ulrich avers, nothing and being are in some sense convertible. This is a rather bold statement. But in it is an acknowledgement of the importance of thinking—and thereby in some sense affirming—nothing in our metaphysics, while at the same time not substantializing nothing.[19]

17. The radicality of this "yes" will be unfolded in what follows, but for now we can say that this foundational affirmation is God's "yes" to being nothing himself in a certain respect.

18. *DP* 7.2.9: Nihil autem potest addi ad esse quod sit extraneum ab ipso, cum ab eo nihil sit extraneum nisi non-ens, quod non potest esse nec forma nec materia.

19. Though this book is written with an eye toward Ulrich's continuity with Thomas, it would be irresponsible not to mention that it is clear that Ulrich writes in response to modern philosophers—specifically Hegel and Heidegger, though of course others as well. Ulrich writes early on in *Homo Abyssus* that "modern nihilism has its roots precisely in the substantializing of being as such" and "the 'nothing' (non subsistens) has also been brought to 'subsistence' along the same path" (*HA*, 29). The "substantializing of being" is

Being can be said to be convertible with nothing, according to Ulrich, precisely because of being's character as *esse non subsistens*. Being itself is not a thing, not a being, has no subsistence in itself. Ulrich remarks that "being does not remain stuck in itself. . . . Being is not an effective actuality in the sense of *efficiens*."[20] Rather, he continues, quoting Thomas, "being itself has the character of the good,"[21] which means that being simply is self-diffusive. Being is not a being, being is a non-being.

Ulrich warns us not to think being as potency either; just because being itself is not a being does not mean it is potency. *Esse* is the fullness of actuality, as Thomas understood, but being is not a reified thing. Ulrich writes, "Not only should we say that to be is a nonbeing, but we should say that it *is* 'nothing'! There is therefore no contradiction in calling esse, as a *completum et simplex*, 'nothing,' if we are thus simply bringing to expression its 'non-subsistent' character."[22]

Ulrich advocates no nihilism here: in fact, just the opposite is true. It is precisely in highlighting being's nothingness that we avoid nihilism—that

---

Ulrich's accusation against Heidegger. Being is given subsistence—even if it is somewhat mythical or supertranscendental—and thus being and beings are always in the end pitted against each other. We saw just above that this leads to nihilism. Ulrich thinks the substantializing of nothing occurs in a similar way, but interestingly enough he takes Greek thought as a precursor, so to speak, for this occurring (though it is important to note that Ulrich distinguishes between Greek philosophy in its origins and the "reviving" of Greek philosophy in the post-Christian era). He writes that in Greek metaphysics "The non-subsistence of being got lost from view of speculative reason. The 'nothing' (non subsistens) was then introduced in order to bring being out of this new, abstract identity" (HA, 34). I am not sure it is entirely fair to say that being's non-subsistence is "lost" as it seems to me it can only be found with sufficient radicality when one has access to the doctrine of creation *ex nihilo* (in this however, I suspect Ulrich takes his cue from Thomas: see ST I.44, a.2, corpus); however, the point for Ulrich is that when one sees form as "the whole of a thing's being" (HA, 33) then the contingency that we encounter in this world can only be the result of that which is *not* being—i.e., matter, or substantialized nothing. Ulrich writes that "otherness" here can not only be outside of being, but, "the otherness or the negation of being's positivity takes on a different meaning in light of being as being, as it is liberated and opened to thought by the 'fullness of time.' Being as being negates negation in a complete way. The other is no longer left 'outside.' Being left outside occurs when the power to be does not extend beyond the Platonic idea that still clings to itself and persists in its abstract and unmediated identity. But now the other is 'taken up into being' in the mode of nonbeing, though of course not as something that would affect or determine being from the outside. The category of 'otherness' gets reconceived here" (HA, 33).

20. HA, 28.

21. ST I.5.4.2: quod bonum dicitur diffusivum sui esse, eo modo quo finis dicitur movere.

22. HA, 29.

is, we avoid the hypostasization of being itself and the resulting annihilation of either being, beings, or God. It is in fact in our denial of nothingness that nothing becomes reified or even deified. Acknowledging nothing in affirming being's convertibility with nothing also—and crucially, at the same time—affirms the reality and goodness of being, beings, and their ultimate source, God. It is the pseudo-subsistent *ipsum esse*, according to Ulrich, that destroys reality and elevates unreality, because the pseudo-subsistent *ipsum esse* "possesses only a pseudo-fullness, since it cannot in fact exist in reality."[23]

Our acknowledgment and affirmation of nothing even somehow within the boundaries of being itself will then be crucial to our understanding of the whole of reality, and even more important to our unfolding of Ulrich's metaphysics. Indeed, this may be the key to Ulrich's understanding of reality: that being affirms and comprehends even that which at first glance seems excluded. But nothing is outside of being except nonbeing. There is no contradiction at the foundation of reality, and therefore neither can there be in the foundations of our thought. We must then in some way acknowledge nothing with the deepest (and seemingly most ironic) "yes" possible. The question is, of course, in what way, and what this could mean.

Above we mentioned the ontological difference between being and beings and the "path," as Ulrich calls it, between them. Following this path will help us better understand what it is to affirm nothing. There may at first glance seem to be a contradiction in being, but we must be careful to affirm that contradiction is not the foundation of being itself. The seeming contradiction of being lies in its nature, which is the fullness of actuality, while at the same time non-subsistent. Being also has the nature of the good insofar as it is self-diffusive.[24] Being does not hold onto itself, as it were; indeed, there

---

23. *HA*, 30.

24. *DV* 22.2.2: quod ipsum esse creatum est similitudo divinae bonitatis; unde in quantum aliqua desiderant esse, desiderant Dei similitudinem et Deum implicite, and *ST* I.19.3.c: Deus non solum se vult, sed etiam alia a se. Quod apparet a simili prius introducto. Res enim naturalis non solum habet naturalem inclinationem respectu proprii boni, ut acquirat ipsum cum non habet, vel ut quiescat in illo cum habet; sed etiam ut proprium bonum in alia diffundat, secundum quod possibile est. Unde videmus quod omne agens, inquantum est actu et perfectum, facit sibi simile. Unde et hoc pertinet ad rationem voluntatis, ut bonum quod quis habet, aliis communicet, secundum quod possibile est. Et hoc praecipue pertinet ad voluntatem divinam, a qua, per quandam similitudinem, derivatur omnis perfectio. Unde, si res naturales, inquantum perfectae sunt, suum bonum aliis communicant, multo magis pertinet ad voluntatem divinam, ut bonum suum aliis per similitudinem communicet, secundum quod possibile est. Sic igitur vult et se esse, et alia. Sed se ut finem, alia vero ut ad finem, inquantum condecet divinam bonitatem etiam alia ipsam participare, and *ST* I.5.4.2: quod bonum dicitur diffusivum sui esse, eo modo quo finis dicitur movere. It should be noted that the principle *bonum*

is no "self" on which to hold. Still, this presents us with a problem, both in thought and in reality. "Being seeks itself as being," writes Ulrich, by which he means that being does seek some unity with itself. Another way we might put this is that being seeks subsistence. A moment's thought helps to orient ourselves: if, as Thomas, Wippel, and Ulrich all affirm, the substance is the proper subject of metaphysics and the proper recipient of being,[25] that is, where we concretely and primarily encounter being, then it is logical that being would desire subsistence. In fact, because of the convertibility of being and nothing, being either "is" God or finite beings—that is to say *esse non subsistens* does not exist somewhere beside God or beside beings; it is nothing in itself. But to be is good! And because of this, being, if we may put it this way, seeks to be—seeks subsistence.

This already-and-not-yet character of being is what Ulrich calls "the crisis of being." We should take "crisis" here in all of its senses: there is the more common connotation of a situation in which one is in trouble and must figure one's way out of the problem. But there is also the more fundamental—and not unrelated—meaning of crisis, coming from the Greek: a decision, and moreover, one that will profoundly affect all other actions and events that come thereafter. We will return to this crisis, but for now let us say this: the crisis consists in being's being able to give itself away—the decisiveness of being in pouring itself out (*Entäußerung*) to beings, in love. Better put: being's crisis reflects the decisiveness of love. It could be, Ulrich points out, that being clings to itself, reflecting something opposed to love, a relation in which one term does not give itself away freely, but instead makes the other into a function of oneself.[26] This clinging to itself would be the opposite of being's real crisis,

---

diffusivum sui in Thomas is somewhat debated, though Ulrich takes it to be thematic in Thomas's work (see *HA*, 28). For a summary of the contemporary debate about this principle, see Blankenhorn, "Good as Self-Diffusive in Thomas Aquinas." Blankenhorn traces W. Norris Clarke's and Norman Kretzman's work on the argument both to introduce and explain why this principle is in question, ultimately concluding that *bonum diffusivum sui* is in fact a principle throughout Thomas's work. Blankenhorn also notes at the end of the article that though the good as self-diffusive "is key to [Thomas's] understanding of the act of creation, the interrelated nature of the universe, and theory of operation," and is a rich area in Thomas's corpus, it is an "almost ignored aspect of his metaphysics and philosophical theology" (837).

25. *DP* 7.7.

26. This is the principle at stake in the section of *HA* entitled "The Theological A Priori in the Pseudo-Speculative Unfolding of Difference in God" (*HA*, 56–60). There, Ulrich explains that "If the Father is not 'able' to divest himself of the entire divine essence to the Son in the Son's procession, then there would remain, so to speak, a 'not yet' communicated remainder of the divine essence, which from the perspective of the Son in relation to the Father manifests itself as a remainder of a not yet obtained divine nature"

and intrinsically connected to the hypostasization of being. It would therefore imply the destruction of the ontological difference.[27]

The ontological difference between being and beings then is premised upon and circumscribed by the crisis of being. Indeed, without being's reflection of the decisiveness of love, individual beings could never come about. "After all," writes Ulrich, "the concretion of the res comes as a result of being's non-subsistence."[28] Here we encounter another phrase unique to Ulrich: the *Subsistenzbewegung*,[29] or being's movement into subsistence. The *Subsistenz-*

(HA, 57). The Son would therefore remain a function of the Father, always waiting, so to speak, for the Father to give him "the rest" of his divinity. This is also one of the main themes of GV, in which Ulrich meditates on the parable of the prodigal son and shows that in each of the two sons' respective relation to his father, there is an element of either (a) the father not giving his son everything and therefore making him a function of the father's self, or (b) the son grasping at what has not been given, and therefore making the father into an impotent giver (see esp. 186–94). A true gift requires that the giver give everything all at once—to hold nothing back, as it were—and the receiver, in freedom, to consent to being given everything. In some sense, Ulrich is attempting to assess modern metaphysics according to this logic of an impotent frozen giver and a grasping receiver. He writes in HA that "The fate of modern metaphysics is made possible by this 'impotence of God's fatherhood'" (HA, 57).

27. Ulrich calls the opposite of being's crisis the "ideal vacillation [*ideale Schwebe*]." This vacillation is what would occur should being not be decisive, as it were, as always already pouring itself out to beings. Ulrich introduces the word "Schwebe" in the preface to HA, writing, "This experience of being in the world at the disposal of the 'advent of being' that needs to be actualized in thought at every moment, however, dissolves if it is not grasped on the basis of God's positivity, next to which being cannot hold itself in suspension [*Schwebe*] in order subsequently to 'hand itself over' as hypostasized being to the existing thing [*dem Seienden*]. Indeed to the extent that being is hypostasized, it becomes utterly incapable of surrendering itself since the hypostasis thus negates the fissure [*Durchriß*] that passes through the ontological difference; in this way, being has already anticipated its mediation to concrete subsistence in an ideality that claims absolute validity" (HA, 3). Were being to refuse its necessary sense, it would hold itself in a pseudo-hypostasization, vacillating between God and beings. In reality, being either is God or finite beings, and "is" not anything in between. In his "Lexicon" to HA, D. C. Schindler describes the ideal vacillation thus: "Created being does not exist apart from existing things *nisi in intellctu solum*, 'except in the intellect alone' (SCG 1.2.6.5); if being is thus separated as its own reality, so to speak, and so 'suspended' in itself, is at the same time absorbed into the intellect or in the subject; the hypostasizing of being and the reduction of being to ideality occur simultaneously (HA, 499). Ulrich also uses the term *Seinsschwebe*, or "vacillation of being" to describe something similar: if being were to "cling to itself," it would be held in suspension between God and beings rather than have subsistence in God or in beings.

28. HA, 47.

29. Though I cannot here discuss this fully, it should be noted that Ulrich's work is greatly influenced by the philosopher Gustav Siewerth. Siewerth makes the

bewegung is another name for the act of creation, though Ulrich's terminology here highlights not the Creator or giver, but what this act looks like, so to speak, within being itself. It is the *Subsistenzbewegung* that allows the ontological difference and individual beings to be. However, we must be careful not to think being here as if it already had an identity with itself or some kind of pseudo-subsistence before it empties out in the movement into subsistence. "To speak of being's movement into subsistence is never to suggest that an ens *in-completum* follows a path into its subsistence, *because* esse is no ens, but rather a non-subsistens."[30] Rather, because *esse non subsistens* is never subsistent, it is both always already pouring itself out to individual beings and always already pure mediation of God. Or better: the former *because* the latter.

One more note about what the movement into subsistence is not: it is not a *motus*. That is to say that there is no motion from potency to actuality in being's path to subsistence. Remember that *esse* is already the actuality of all actualities. Therefore, what Ulrich means by "movement" here we cannot identify simply with intra-worldly motion. Rather, it seems that Ulrich uses the term movement to indicate a dynamism in the ontological difference and in the relationship between being and beings. Though there is no motion from potency to act in this relation, there is, as Ulrich puts it, an "unfolding." This unfolding helps us realize that this difference between being and beings is not a static opening that merely occurs on some metaphysical plane other than

---

Verendlichungsbewegung, or movement into finitude, a centerpiece of his metaphysics. Both movements (that is, into subsistence and into finitude) describe the same act, but Ulrich introduces the term *"Subsistenzbewegung"* to emphasize being's being either God or being—and nothing in between. Additionally, Siewerth introduces the categories of ideality and reality (which we will eventually meet in this chapter), which both become touchstones in Ulrich's metaphysics, but Ulrich adds the category of Bonität, bonicity; the *Subsistenzbewegung* highlights the Good as being's origin and telos. For more on this point, see Bieler's *FG*, 264.

Another point in which Ulrich and Siewerth differ is their understanding of the convertibility of being and nothing. Siewerth assigns "Nichts" an almost transcendental state, which Ulrich criticizes because it would ultimately make the self-exchange between being and nothing impossible, leading to a self-enclosed being (see *HA*, 322). Marine de la Tour writes on this point, "For Siewerth the nothingness of potential reason arises out of the positivity of being, so that it excludes this nothingness and itself is witness to the positivity of reason, whereas for Ulrich, the 'nothing' of reason has a fundamentally different meaning" ("Während für Siewerth die Nichtigkeit der potentiellen Vernunft aus die Positivität des Seins entspringt, damit es diese Nichtigkeit ausschließt und sich als Positivität in der Vernunft bezeugt, hat im Grunde für Ulrich das "Nichts" der Vernunft eine ganz andere Bedeutung" *GA*, 140). For Siewerth, nothingness becomes the transcendental of pure receptivity while for Ulrich it is important that there be a coincidence of poverty and wealth in being itself. For more on this point, see *GA*, 12–136.

30. *HA*, 46.

our own concrete reality, but rather a coming to light of what an individual being's being actually is—that is, that each being has within itself the ontological difference. This Ulrich calls the "horizontal dimension" of ontological difference. The vertical dimension of the ontological difference "comes into focus in an original way within the horizontal dimension of the concrete self-actualization of the finite substance, that is, in its externalizing self-presentation (appearance) and its internalizing return to itself."[31] If the horizontal dimension of the ontological difference makes it clear that individual beings are not self-enclosed, static blocks of substance, the vertical dimension helps us see the similar truth when it comes to being itself: being empties itself out into beings. By emphasizing both the horizontal and vertical dimensions of the ontological difference, Ulrich warns against applying a hollowed-out stasis to any term within the ontological difference. Being empties itself out into beings: this is the vertical dimension of the ontological difference; but neither are substantial beings static blocks: there is also within each being a (horizontal) ontological difference between their being and their appearance, which is not necessarily motion (that is, a moving from potency to actuality), but rather an unfolding of the *res*'s being into the spatio-temporality it inhabits. In both cases, the ontological difference appears as being appears.

To say that the ontological difference appears as being appears is itself no small claim. Appearance is an accident, and yet it is in and through appearance that we encounter being. As Balthasar writes in *Theo-Logic I*, "*being* appears," and "being *appears*."[32] Though appearance is accidental—that is to say, the appearance of each individual being could be another way—being is always communicated by these accidents of appearance. Thus, the ontological difference itself is communicated by mere appearance. We can see then in the appearance of the ontological difference, through the appearance of an individual being, that already what is metaphysically higher allows itself to be expressed by that which is lower—indeed, that which it itself has caused. This expression of the higher by the lower is one of the keys to Ulrich's metaphysics.

According to Ulrich, being has what he calls a "sense" [*Sinn*]. This sense means both being's meaning and its direction. This latter part of the sense of being—that is, its direction or movement—should be somewhat clear given what we have covered above: being moves in the direction of subsistence, in the direction of pouring itself out to beings. Being's meaning, however, is not yet entirely clear. Certainly, being's direction must come from its meaning: why does being, the perfection of all perfections, empty itself out into individual beings? It was said above that being seeks subsistence, and this is true,

---

31. *HA*, 49–50.
32. Balthasar, *Theo-Logic I*, 37.

but it is perhaps not sufficient to answer the question of the *Subsistenzbewegung* fully. Rather, the answer lies in something else mentioned above: being's meaning comes from that of which it is the likeness, namely, divine goodness.

Being's likeness to the divine goodness is what explains its self-diffusion. "It is the nature of the good to be self-diffusive,"[33] writes Thomas. Thus being's sense, as Ulrich calls it, is founded entirely upon this, namely, the divine goodness. Being's meaning and direction of movement are not two different moments stacked on top of one another, but coincide perfectly in the Good.

We must reiterate that without the *non subsistens* of being, none of this would be possible. Indeed, it is better said that the non-subsistence of being is a direct expression of being's likeness to the divine goodness. At no point does being vacillate or cling to itself, but rather it is always already emptying itself out to that which is in some sense other than itself. Thus, being's non-subsistence, its no-thingness, helps us see the substance, so to speak, of the Good. The crisis of being has in some way always already been decided; because of the nature of the Good, the nature of being is decisive. But notice: being's being nothing (that is, *non subsistens*) is entirely affirmed here! It is the no-thingness of being that allows it to be *similitudo divinae bonitatis*. The hypostasization of being is a refusal of the self-diffusion proper to the Good, and thus a refusal to image the Good.

This play between being's absolute perfection and fullness and its nothingness Ulrich names the wealth and poverty of being. This theme is woven throughout his work and thus we will encounter it repeatedly; let us offer a brief explanation here: On the one hand, being is the wealthiest of created effects, for it is the perfection of all perfections. On the other hand, being is the poorest of created effects, since it has no subsistence in itself. But this coincidence of wealth and poverty is no accident. Being's nothingness—its poverty—is what allows it to be the wealthiest of all created effects because being has no limit: because being has no subsistence in itself it can receive infinitely. This infinite reception is then the source of being's wealth. But being's receiving infinitely (its wealth) is entirely for the sake of giving itself away infinitely to beings. Were this not the case—were being to hold even the tiniest part of itself for itself, so to speak—then being's receptivity would not be infinite: it would be limited by even this small withholding. Whatever being is given it gives away completely. Indeed there is no "self" to hold on to what being is given; its nature is mediation. Thus we can say that it is only because being is poor that it is rich, and its richness is entirely for the sake of its poverty. Indeed there is no oscillation between the two poles, as if one moment being is rich

---

33. *DV* 22.2.2. See n24 above.

and the next poor, but rather the dynamism of being itself is a result of this coincidence of wealth and poverty.

Being's nothingness, then, is for Ulrich the key to understanding the radicality of the gift of being. Nothingness is not an-other to being itself, not outside of being, but most radically a property of being itself.

Being's "necessary sense"

Ulrich understands being to have a "necessary" sense, the *notwendige Seinsinn*. We have already mentioned his somewhat enigmatic use of the word *Sinn*, and his use of *notwendig* is no less so. *Notwendig* is generally translated as "necessary," coming from the Latin *necessarium*. Ulrich writes: "'Necessary' in Latin means the ne-cessarium, that which cannot be avoided. For being's movement into subsistence, this means accordingly that being comes unavoidably out of its crisis into subsistence, or in other words, being in its being-ness arrives at the *res*."[34] Again: being seeks subsistence and does so necessarily. But this is not the only meaning of *notwendig* for Ulrich; he also further mines the word's etymology:

> In the German word *not-wendig*, another aspect of the crisis of being comes to expression, namely, the "whence," the resource that fills the need of assumed subsistence. Here we cannot fail to mention explicitly the "distress [*Not*] of contradiction"; for the Need must be there if it is going to be filled. The necessary in a certain sense "requires" the need that it fills. Without this need, it itself "is" not, as it were.[35]

This interpretation of the necessary, that is, that it is need-relieving, is perhaps less clear than the former. Ulrich points out that the Latin sense of necessary brings to mind—indeed, almost relies upon—the fact of an already existing entity, the *res*. This sense of necessary "always already has being's movement into subsistence as such behind it in a certain respect."[36] This is certainly not incorrect, for there is something true about being able to assume being's movement into subsistence. We should be able to take subsistence for granted, because it is given! However, Ulrich notes that this is not the whole story, so to speak. "*Ipsum esse* does not subsist *actu*, even though it is *actus actuum*"[37] The *Subsistenzbewegung* relieves being of what would otherwise

---

34. *HA*, 61.
35. *HA*, 61–2.
36. *HA*, 62.
37. *HA*, 63.

turn out to be a contradiction within itself, relieves being of the "need [*Not*]" of subsistence. This need is always already within being itself. *Ipsum esse non subsistens* precisely by its being *non subsisten*s (nothing!) is constituted in part by this need. *Ipsum esse* is at once everything and nothing, and its necessary sense is the movement that has always already saved being from this contradiction.

Interestingly, if being were not to make this move into subsistence—or if reason does not see or understand the necessary sense of being—being clings to itself and does not follow its crisis through to its end. And in this indecisive position, being loses both its everythingness and its nothingness, and thereby loses itself, so to speak. Left in a state of distress, without a movement into subsistence, *ipsum esse* becomes a static block of ideality in which the *res* partakes in order somehow to gain reality. But if this were the case, the *res* itself becomes static block of being, not that in which being fulfills its necessary sense, not the *capax entis*, but rather a function of the pseudo-subsisting *ipsum esse*. In the vacillation of being, we lose everything: being itself, *non subsistens*, and *res* in its proper place as *capax entis*. Being becomes something such that *ens* cannot be anything but an extension of this reified being.

This brings us back once again to the ontological difference and to being's necessary sense, that is, its movement into subsistence. We have so far been dancing around this path, not quite going down it yet, trying to explain with Ulrich the meaning of being and its relation to beings. But the time has come explicitly to shed light on being itself in relation to its ultimate source: that is, God. Being has no meaning without creation (and by creation, we mean here both the act and the telos of the act). I argued last chapter that Thomas's great contribution to metaphysics—his understanding of *esse*—comes out of his understanding of the doctrine of creation, and Ulrich's exploration of the meaning of being is similarly grounded in an attempt to understand the world as created in as radical a sense as possible.

It is only within the context of creation that being can have any sense. Again, it is important to remember that Thomas's insight about being comes out of his understanding that creation is *ex nihilo*—that is, nothing precedes it, and it comes entirely from God—and yet creation is *not* God; every *ens* is entirely itself and yet also entirely from God. Ulrich's understanding of the necessary sense of being also helps us see the difference between the real distinction and the ontological difference, which are of course related but ultimately not the same. Oster writes that Ulrich finds "a deep correspondence"[38] between the two. Ulrich writes in *Homo Abyssus*,

---

38. "eines tiefen Gesprächs" (*MMS*, 62).

> Only when being's transnihilation has been carried out to the point of the positively existing res—that is, when the difference holds sway no longer between being and essence [*Sein und Wesen*], but now as the difference between being and the subsisting entity [*Sein zum subsistierienden Seienden*], which overtakes the previous difference—is the ultimate rigor of being's movement of finitization made visible.[39]

Ulrich understands the ontological difference both to ground and encompass the real distinction, even as the real distinction in some sense allows the ontological difference to be. Were the ontological difference to close, it would result in being absorbed into beings, or vice versa. However, with the ontological difference held open, there is room for there to be a real distinction between essence and *esse*—that is to say, being does not overtake beings. At the same time, the real distinction ensures that *esse* has a place to substantialize—that is, essence is real and it receives being. It is "the necessary sense of being," writes Ulrich, "that orders being into finitude,"[40] which is where we encounter both the real distinction and the ontological difference.

Though we can argue to being itself from intra-worldly evidence, the ontological difference and the necessary sense of being cannot hold themselves up, according to Ulrich. Like Thomas, Ulrich understands *ipsum esse non subsistens* to be not media*tor* (for this would be to give *esse non subsistens* a kind of pseudo-subsistence), but pure media*tion*. The role of the act of all acts is simply mediative: to give being to beings while itself having no status of *res*. This is what Ulrich calls the *Subsistenzbewegung*, which occurs because of the necessary sense of being.

This explanation of *esse* and its role in creation is logical for Ulrich, but not sufficient. In order really to glimpse the radicality of creation, it must be seen and explained not only in light of how, but the more radical question: Why? We mentioned an answer to this—skimmed over too quickly, in fact—in the previous chapter. God creates in order to show forth his own glory and share it. The question of being is not asked well unless proposed in this light, namely, in the light of creation and all that results therefrom.

Thus, for Ulrich, the key to the question of being only reveals itself when asked in light of God's love for creation: this is in fact the ultimate and best answer to the question "why?" posed just above. What this love means concretely and what light it sheds on the meaning of being will be unfolded more in the rest of this chapter, but for now it suffices to say that the necessary sense of being is only necessary—can only be necessary—if God has always already

---

39. *HA*, 86.
40. *HA*, 67.

revealed himself as love, and thus, Creator. Being can only give itself to beings because it is the *similitudo divinae bonitatis*. The necessary sense of being only arises because of the one whom being mediates. "The necessary sense of being," writes Ulrich, "orders being into finitude,—that is, into the self-finitizing of the act of subsistence—in 'obedience to the Spirit' [*Geistgehorsam*]."[41] Being "must" move into subsistence because of he who is the source of being.

So too the ontological difference can only be fully explained and understood in light of creation. The temptation of hypostasizing being and thereby substantializing nothing in one way or another can only come if one does not see properly that it is ultimately God who holds up, or holds open, as it were, the ontological difference. Being has no "need" for pseudo-subsistence because it is always already attaining subsistence in obedience to its source. "The Spirit of God pervades [*durchwaltet*] the ontological difference," writes Ulrich, "he affirms the crisis of being and holds open the ontological difference."[42] It is in the ontological difference, then, which appears as being appears, that the meaning of both creation and being start to appear: to let beings be, not as a function of what comes before, but as themselves.

Moreover, we mentioned at the beginning of this chapter that for Ulrich, as for Thomas, in order for our metaphysics not to be built on a contradiction, we must affirm even nothing: not as substantialized, but as, somehow, not entirely outside of being itself. Ulrich points us to this when he explains that the meaning of being can only be elucidated in terms of love. Yes, being's necessary sense drives it to finitude, but finitude in a certain sense must include nothingness. If finitude is to be understood ultimately as a good, and not simply a descent or fall from infinite actuality or goodness, then being's necessary sense must include an affirmation of nothingness. The question is what this could mean.

According to Ulrich, being both is and has an *Aufgabe*, or task, and this task is intimately connected with being's necessary sense, in which potency is included. Being's task, it may be said simply, is to let finitude be. This should not be confused with saying that *esse non subsistens* is the efficient cause of finitude. Rather when Ulrich uses the word "task" he means that being's nature is simply to give itself away, and its task is to do just that. Ulrich writes that there is a twofold sense of this task, which is the archetypal beginning of the *Subsistenzbewegung*. Ulrich's description of being as task helps us to articulate better what we mean when we call being dynamic. Again, being's dynamism is not a *motus*. De la Tour explains the two-fold task of being in this way. "Task means simultaneously on the one side complete gift and on the other side

41. HA, 67.
42. HA, 67.

something that is still being completed or done."⁴³ Being as complete gift or completely given indicates being having always already given itself away. De la Tour writes that in the first sense of being's task we see that the *Subsistenzbewegung* does not aim at its own hypostasis or subsistence "but at the being of beings, at their subsistence."⁴⁴ In this we see that the non-subsistence of being cannot be separated from its being *completum et simplex*. Being could not be "completely given" if it was not in itself non-subsistent.

The second aspect of being's task is its abiding superessential presence in beings themselves. The gift of being is not given once and then cut off, as it were, from the giver. Being abides in beings, not as a tyrant that directs beings' acts such that the individual being is really just an extension of being. Rather, being abides in beings precisely to let beings be. Its presence allows the being to be seen. Ulrich writes, "Being is a giving up of self as a task given to itself. That which is gets thus swept up more and more into being's self-gift and movement of finitization, which opens it up more and more to being."⁴⁵ De la Tour sums up this twofold task quite nicely when she writes,

> The emptying of being into beings as "task of being" in the first sense is not a downfall, but precisely the way and manner by which the actuality which is the task in the second sense can inhere—in which this task is "fulfilled." As the task is understood more deeply in the first sense, the more seriously being is given to beings in the second sense, as what is most intimate: the essence of their essence.⁴⁶

---

43. "Aufgabe meint zugleich einerseits restloses Gabe und anderseits etwas, was zu vollziehen oder bestehen ist" (*GA*, 161).

44. "In diesem ersten Sinn bedeutet die Aufgabe des Seins auch, dass die Subsistenzbewegung—oder die Vermittlung des Seins—nicht auf das Sein selbst als Seinhypostasis zielt, sondern auf das Sein des Seienden, auf sein Subsistenz" (*GA*, 161).

45. *HA*, 70. The German is worth quoting here since there are some shades of meaning that do not come across in translation, especially in the first sentence: "Das Sein ist sich selbst Aufgabe in der Selbst-auf-gabe. Aus der Verendlichungsbewegung und Aufgabe des Seins steht daher das Seiende solchermaßen im Zug auf das Sein hin, daß es vom Sein her zur je größeren Offenheit... zu sich hingeführt wird" (*Homo Abyssus. Das Wagnis der Seinsfrage*, 71).

46. "Die Entäußerung des Seins in das Seiende als ‚Aufgabe des Seins' im Ersten Sinn ist kein Untergang, sondern gerade die Art und Weise, in der es der Wirklichkeit als Aufgabe im zweiten Sinn innewohnen kann, in der sich ja diese Aufgabe ‚erfüllt'. Je tiefer die Aufgabe im ersten Sinn gedacht wird, desto ernster ist auch das Sein dem Seienden im zweiten Sinn aufgegeben, als sein Eigenstes sein Wesen—sein Wesen—aufgetragen" (*GA*, 162).

Whence, though, this sacrificial nature of being? It would seem that all things desire to be and we might say, to be themselves. Why, then, this handing over? Here we must look at being's structure. When we say that all things desire to be, we can also add that all things desire to be themselves; every thing has some sort of unity whereby it can be recognized.[47] Being does not have this kind of unity, according to Ulrich. "*Ipsum esse non subsistens* does not have the structure of an essence in a sense that would allow it to concretize itself into substantial entity and unity."[48] Were being to grasp, so to speak, after this kind of concretized unity by not moving into subsistence, or staying within the ideal vacillation, this would again only result in pseudo-subsistence, or a pseudo-wealth. Were this the case, there could be neither finite beings nor could there be *in actu* a hypostasized being. Being would have a shadow existence.

However, we know that being does hand itself over, and we know this because we do encounter finitude, in the form of finite beings. This handing over of itself is not, however, an annihilation of being; Ulrich calls it rather being's transnihilation.[49] Being is not annihilated in the handing over of itself to finite beings, but rather, seeing as being as such is always already no-thing, this sense of the task (*Aufgabe*) simply points to being's nature. Being cannot concretize or substantialize itself, and thus it must ("necessary sense of being") hand itself over in order to gain the unity and identity that everything desires. Here then, we come to the second sense of the task of being, in which being is actually given to itself precisely in its handing itself over. In the first sense, being surrenders itself to the poverty of finitude; being does not grasp after itself in pseudo-subsistence and thus cannot "stay" infinite. However, in this handing itself over, being gains a wealth it could never achieve under its own power, as it were. Being gains subsistence in its pouring itself out to concrete beings.

Thus, we see that the task of being is never one-sided—never a simple poverty or a simple wealth—but always a dual movement in which being gains the wealth of subsistence by accepting the poverty of finitude. Bieler describes being's wealth and poverty this way: "Being is always already *given in this unity*. Its non-subsistence is given not in concurrence with its act-fullness, but belongs to it."[50] Here too we see that being is neither slave to beings nor tyrant

---

47. *Morphe*: the look of a thing gathered up in speech (*Physics*, 193a31).

48. *HA*, 69.

49. The word is *Durchnichtung*: a nothingness (*non subsistens*) transferred *through*. We will cover transnihilation more completely in chapter 3.

50. "Das Sein ist immer schon *in dieser Einheit gegeben*. Die Nicht-Subsistenz steht also nicht in konkurrenz zur Aktfülle des Seins, sondern gehört zu ihr" (*FG*, 267).

over them. There is always already a both/and structure in the relationship between being and beings that emerges in the fundamental difference between them. This, Ulrich says, is again the necessary sense of being showing itself: "being's going *away* from itself is a coming *toward* itself as task, insofar as being makes itself into its own task *on the way toward itself* as the very giving up of self that it is."[51]

Thus, the ontological difference between being and beings never indicates an absolute separation of the two: in other words, this is not a fundamental contradiction upon which creation is founded. But it is also the case that the ontological difference does point us to being's being no-thing and its necessary sense: a movement into a subsistence.

Ulrich writes that the relation between *esse* and essence—that real distinction—only comes into proper focus when looked at through the necessary sense of being. Being's task is self-gift (both its giving-of-itself and its giving-itself-to-itself), and this is why it "must" move into subsistence. However, we said above that it is not in the structure or nature of being as such to gain the unity of entity. Ulrich puts it thus: being "cannot mediate this unity (or act of subsisting) itself, because it is 'nothing.' It is therefore in a certain sense dependent on its mediation to finite subsistence."[52] But here we encounter a stumbling block: what can mediate this substantial unity to being as such without already being included simply within being?

Being's "obedience": the procession of essence

We have of course already named this mediating principle: essence. However, Ulrich's description of the coming-to-be of essence, while grounded in Thomistic principles, may help us better understand why essence and *esse* are not simply opposed to each other. Ulrich writes that essence "must itself proceed from being," though he also writes that "as the 'other' to being, the essence considered in itself is fundamentally *non ens*."[53] These two statements about essence seem almost contradictory. Though Ulrich does not take the real distinction to be the foundational difference within creation, it is still important, especially with respect to being's necessary movement into finitude, for finitude is not possible without essence. Thus, this issue must be more deeply explored.

51. *HA*, 70.
52. *HA*, 71.
53. *HA*, 72.

In order to help frame what follows, let us state explicitly what the obedience of *esse* is, especially with regard to essence: essence's procession is the self-gift of being. As we will see shortly, essence, even as it proceeds wholly from being, is entirely different from being and thus is only possible in the obedience of being to the logic of love, to that of which being is the image. The deepest meaning of self-gift is allowing an-other to be, and to be freely. Indeed, love means not just allowing an-other to be but also, as Ulrich puts it, "presupposing" the other such that one acts, so to speak, as if the other is always already there.[54] Essence's procession from *esse* is just one example of this logic of self-gift that runs throughout all of creation.

Nothing is outside of being except nonbeing, Thomas tells us, and therefore it is not proper to say that essence is not included within being as such. And yet it is essence that mediates—or we could say, gives—substantial unity to *esse*, so essence must be other than *esse*, at least in some sense. "This 'other,'" writes Ulrich, "which proceeds from being must at the same time be already given, or posited as *really distinct* from being."[55] That both things are true is not contradictory, though perhaps how it avoids contradiction is not immediately clear. Ulrich clarifies that essence is not merely a "linear extension" from being, nor a "deduction" from it; to posit either of these is to destroy the reality of the real distinction. Rather, Ulrich points again to the ontological difference in order to explain the real distinction: we can see the real distinction precisely because of the more primordial difference between being and beings, which itself we can see only because of the non-subsistence of *esse*. The nature of *ipsum esse non subsistens* is to be nothing but the giving away of itself (which in turn, is an affirmation of itself) to finitude in the form of finite, concrete creatures. Thus, says Ulrich, "We see that the real distinction between esse and essence becomes manifest most profoundly from the perspective of the convertibility of being and 'nothing.'"[56]

This does not exactly explain what essence is and whence it comes; it does demonstrate how important being's nothingness is for Ulrich: the real distinction is more or less unintelligible, according to Ulrich, if not seen in the light of concrete creatures, which is impossible without recognition of being's nothingness. It makes no sense to speak of the real distinction abstractly; it only emerges when holding creatures in view. Ulrich affirms again that essence must come from being as such, for being is fullness, though essence is "posited as really distinct from being." It can be so because being "'comes' to

---

54. See the introduction, esp. nn23, 24.
55. *HA*, 72.
56. *HA*, 73.

itself by means of the essence, which is determined as potency."[57] The only way essence can be posited as something really distinct from being, but still come from being itself is if it is in potency with respect to being, which is the act of all acts. Thus, we see that the crisis of being gives rise not just to substantial, concrete beings, but in order to do that (in order to affirm itself[!], in other words), being generates potency, which emerges from being but cannot be identified with it. Potency then for Ulrich seems to be a key for understanding both essence and being's *Subsistenzbewegung*.

Again we turn to de la Tour for help in explicating this. She writes that "being's movement into finitization has no real stopping point in the sense of terminus. It is more precise to say that it does have a real resting place: the finite substance, which, however, thought cannot capture absolutely."[58] What does this mean? That thought cannot "capture" the finite substance? Though the finite substance is real, its substantiality contains more, we might say, than the substance's essence or even its actuality. In other words, accidents of a substance, though only having existence because of the substance to which they belong, also radiate something more than just the substance's essence. Material accidents are just that—accidents—and yet material substances are always expressed in and through their accidents.[59] The finite substance, as de la Tour puts it, is more than essence, and the expression of the concrete thing through its accidents is evidence of this. All of this is to say that materiality (and therefore matter) is in some sense the resting place (*Zielgrund*) of the movement into finitude. Matter, however, is in some sense below substance—it is potency,

---

57. *HA*, 73.

58. "Die Verendlichungsbewegung des Seins hat keinen realen Zielengrund im Sinne eine festen Terminus. Genauer gesagt hat sie einen realen Zielgrund: die endlich Substanz, die aber das Denken nicht absolut festhalten kann" (*GA*, 162).

59. Ulrich writes: "The things that appear to us actualize themselves in 'their other.' This is why they 'appear.' The appearance is different from their essence, even though their essence exhibits itself in the appearance. Thus the tree's essence makes its appearance through and in what is not that essence, for example, in 'this' tiny leaf. If the vast abundance of leaves, the root, the branches, the specific differentiation of cell structure did not exist, then the essence of the tree itself could never become actual. But it *is* in *actuality* only in the multiplicity of appearance, which is in a certain sense undetermined with respect to its unity. The essence of the tree actualizes itself in 'its other' and becomes manifest therein. The superessential 'to be,' however, mediates the essence into the appearance, indeed, the appearance comes to light as a result of being's mediation in a certain sense as the '"to be" of the essence,' insofar as what unveils itself therein is precisely the fact that the substance is not appearance; for it affirms itself in and through its accidents and is co-affirmed in them" (*HA*, 398). Though each accident considered in itself is not necessary, accidents as a whole are in fact necessary for material substances to be at all. Something similar could be said of the relationship between *esse* and substances.

while substance is in act. This means that the *Verendlichungsbewegung* of being must aim below (or beyond) act; de la Tour puts it this way: "The emptying [of being] into matter as 'non-essential ground of possibility' overtakes essence as resting place."[60] The *Verendlichungsbewegung* or *Subsistenzbewegung* of being—in its aim at the concrete material substance—generates potency as the result of this aim. Potency is the condition of possibility for any concrete material substance and thus is included in the *Subsistenzbewegung*.

That being generates potency may at first sound strange, but this must be the case. Otherwise, whence potency? If somehow always "existing," we fall into an oversimplified dualism, and if somehow coming to be not by mediation of act, then we fall into an idealism, which we will address in the next chapter. Of course we must be careful in our wording: when we say potency is "generated" by being, we do not mean that potency is a thing that can stand, as it were, on its own. Rather, because being's task is creation, and creation is the multiplicity of material, finite substances, then potency somehow comes out of being's *Subsistenzbewegung*—and not, we must note, as unwanted byproduct, but as condition of otherness at all.

That potency—which at first glance seems opposite to act and therefore being—comes from being's movement into subsistence needs to be explored. If we say that the "resting place" or "aim" (*Zielgrund*) of the *Subsistenzbewegung* is the finite entity—its concrete subsistence—and matter is included within that very subsistence as the "last step," so to speak, of the *Subsistenzbewegung*, it may look at first as though the movement into subsistence has, strictly speaking, nothing as its end. But rather than looking at this end as sheer nothingness (or nonbeing, which is outside of being itself), perhaps the better term is "abyssal." For Ulrich, the term "abyss" never indicates a sheer, sterile, nothingness, but rather that which we cannot fully grasp or conceive. The abyssal "resting place" of the *Subsistenzbewegung* of being that is matter is itself only possible because of being's abyssal beginning. Neither the *Subsistenzbewegung*'s origin, nor this "last step" (i.e., matter) is an essence (though the former is superessential, while the latter is non-essential) and therefore neither is definable. Potency is thus intrinsically connected—and indeed springs from—the superessentiality of the beginning. De la Tour puts it this way:

> In its enactment of the movement into finitude being's absolute gift/task [*Aufgabe*] (or in Ulrich's words: transnihilation) consists in the necessity *and* the em-powering of essence as an-other to being: the necessity of otherness because "nothing occurs or happens" [*HA*, 71] in being itself, which is neither essence nor

---

60. "Die Entäußerung in die Materie als ‚nichtwesentlichen Ermöglichungsgrund' überholt das Wesen als Zielgrund" (*GA*, 163).

hypostasis, so the mediated principle [i.e., essence] is necessarily "an-other"; the em-powering of otherness because the transnihilation of superessential being does not constitute a negation—it is rather the enactment of being itself, the manifestation of the completum et simplex in the procession of "an-other" from being (the essence).[61]

Being's *Subsistenzbewegung*—and therefore too, essence—cannot then be understood in its fullness without looking at creation, that is, the multiplicity of essences (and therefore, beings) which exist therein. We must keep in mind how important it is for Ulrich that being itself remains no-thing (*non subsistens*); it seems multiplicity is a constitutive element, as it were, of the ontological difference. Otherwise we would end up once again with a pseudo-subsistent *esse* set over against the *actio ipsum esse subsistens*—that is, God. Multiplicity is then also key to understanding essence.

Perhaps we come dangerously close here to a caricatured Platonism, in which matter is responsible for a fall away from unity into multiplicity. This is not the case for Ulrich, but this temptation is important to keep in mind. According to Ulrich, essence must proceed from *esse*; therefore there can be no potency or matter which pre-exists being itself.

In the discussion of the real distinction and its relationship to multiplicity, Ulrich introduces the category of love. Recall the introduction: Dionysius too ultimately has recourse to this category to explain multiplicity. We must remember that any subsistence given to being (or grasped at) by being itself is always a pseudo-subsistence because there is already *ipsum esse subsistens*. Being's nature is the *similitudo divinae bonitatis* and as such is pure mediation of being. The only reason being need not hold onto itself, as it were, is because it is image of that which is at the same time most united and most generous. *Per impossibile*, were being to grasp at pseudo-subsistence, it would no longer be image of God and thus no longer be *ipsum esse*. The

> experience of God's always already perfected absolute positivity of love compels reason to determine the "self-emptying" of being as an act that has always already been superseded in finite

---

61. "Die absolute Aufgabe (oder mit Ulrichs Worten: Durchnichtung) des Seins ist im Vollzug der Verendlichungsbewegung zugleich Notwendigkeit *und* Ermöglichung des Wesens als eines dem Sein anderen: Notwendigkeit der Andersheit, weil im nicht essentiell strukturierten und nicht hypostasierten Sein selbst ‚nichts gescheiht oder an ihm nichts passiert', das vermittelnde Prinzip also notwendig ein ‚anderes' ist; Ermölichung der Andersheit, weil die Durchnichtung des überwesenhaften Seins keine Vernichtung darstellt; sie ist vielmehr Vollzug des Seins selbst, Manifestation des completum et simplex im Hervorgang des dem Sein ‚Anderen' (des Wesens)" (*GA*, 166).

beings. If God therefore is absolutely One, then the ipsum esse is "subsistently itself" in the many, in the multiplicity and variety of beings, insofar as what comes to expression is precisely not (!) the fragmentation of being but its *unity*, which reveals itself in the act of subsisting.[62]

Ulrich here indicates that multiplicity, rather than being a falling away from unity, or a betrayal of being, in fact is only possible because being's nature is to image God, and God's nature is the absolute positivity of love. Any other explanation of multiplicity ultimately falls short of the nature of being and the nature of God.

Multiplicity, then, is intrinsically connected to—indeed arises out of the nature of—the divine as good. This should not surprise us, as this comes directly from Thomas. He writes in *Summa contra gentiles*: "Therefore, just as the first rational principle of divine providence is simply the divine goodness, so the first rational principle in creatures is their numerical plurality, to the establishment and conservation of which all other things seem to be ordered."[63] That last part is remarkable because it can be said that *esse* and essence (and the real distinction between them) are in fact ordered to multiplicity—that is, in the service of creatures themselves. Creation is meant, in its very multiplicity, to manifest the glory and goodness of God and can do so because the nature of God is love.

We must now return to essence's role in all of this. Ulrich, with Thomas, has made clear that essence cannot be outside of being, but at the very same time, affirms that essence is not the same as *esse non subsistens*. Rather, essence arises out of *esse* as potency, and can therefore mediate subsistence to *esse*. Notice here the somewhat ironic role reversal: *esse non subsistens*, the act of all acts, is in some sense subservient to potency. In its *Subsistenzbewegung*, *esse* "must" submit itself not only to potency—that is, what is below it—but to that which it itself has generated. Ulrich therefore calls essence here "the decisive authority"[64] in both the *Subsistenzbewegung*, and therefore, the multiplicity of creatures.[65]

62. HA, 75.
63. SCG, 3.20.
64. The phrase Ulrich uses is "Die entscheidene Instanz" in *Homo Abyssus: Das Wagnis der Seinsfrage*, 79.
65. This is not to say that essence is not also naturally obedient, we might say, as if set over against *esse*'s obedience. However, given each principle's distinct character, the obediences look different. "From being's perspective, the essence is an 'open space,' which rises up to meet being. Such an 'openness' is nothing other than 'obedient listening to being' ['*Seinsgehörigkeit*']" writes Ulrich (HA, 82). However, an obedience of that which is lower on the hierarchy of being to that which is higher is less surprising.

The procession of essence from being is the presupposition of otherness by being. To presuppose another means already to take for granted not only that the other exists, but also what is implied therein: if the other exists then it already has a claim. This is what it means for essence to have an authority over *esse*, even as it proceeds from *esse*: essence is presupposed by being such that being allows essence to put claim to being even though it does not pre-exist being. Stefan Oster writes that when the giver gives,

> the receiver already has a uniquely defined form. It is already "there." . . . [The giver] himself gives the actuality of the other, which indeed, on the one hand he *has presupposed (spontaneity, subsistence)*, and which however, as such, and at the same time, he has presupposed *already* as really distinct from himself and therefore can simultaneously return to him. . . . He "releases" his presupposition from his grasp [*Zu-Griff*] from the beginning of his existence [*Setzens*] as different from himself; he gives this difference freely and recognizes thereby that it is always already there.[66]

The emergence of essence in the *Subsistenzbewegung* is then the first presupposition of otherness we encounter (metaphysically) in the act of creation. This is a pattern we will continue to see: the presupposition of the other, and coincident claim the other has on what is prior. In fact, this is what allows an-other to be at all. Were this not the case, essence would be an extension of *esse*, and always subject to its tyrannical presence. When being presupposes essence in its movement into subsistence (i.e., the act of creation), however, it not only allows essence to be (and to be its own), but precisely in allowing it to be, being allows essence to exert a claim. Otherness would be inconsequential (or result in slavery) without this coincident claim.

We will see this pattern of presupposition throughout Ulrich's metaphysics, but for now let us look a little more closely at the relationship between *esse* and essence. We know that essence must come from being, but we also know that being cannot obtain subsistence for itself—therefore, Oster says that there "*must* be a principle that is *presupposed* as really different";[67] however, before

---

66. "Der Empfangende hat schon eine je eigene, bestimmte Gestalt. Er is schon ‚da' . . . Er gibt sich der Wirklichkeit des Anderen, die er sich zwar einerseits *vorausgesetzt hat (Spontaneität, Setzung)*, die aber als soche zugleich in realer Verschiedenheit von ihm schon vorausgesetzt da ist and die ihm nun deshalb zugleich zu-kommen . . . Er ‚entlässt' seine Vorassetzung aus dem Zu-Griff eines anfängliches Setzens, in eine Differenz zu ihm selbst; er gibt diese Differenz frei, und anerkennt dadurch, dass sie immher schon da ist" (*MMS*, 240).

67. "sondern dem Willen des Schöpfers gehorcht, *bedarf* es eines Prinzips, das ihm zugleich real unterscheiden *vorausgesetzt* ist" (*MMS*, 241).

receiving being, essence is properly nothing. Thus we can say at one and the same time that essence is nothing without being and that essence's reality and otherness is entirely presupposed by being. Essence's procession from being in the *Subsistenzbewegung* is nothing else than being's presupposition of another. This allows essence both to be and to have an authority or claim over being itself, even as it is metaphysically inferior. This is why, writes Oster, "Thomas can say that being *follows* form, that form *gives* finite subsistence being."[68] Thomas is not violating the basic metaphysical principles of act and potency, but he can see the implications of being poured out as radically as it is in the act of creation.

Essence is therefore neither passive cavity nor metaphysical void, but the fruit of being's *Subsistenzbewegung*, its self-emptying. And precisely as being generates essence or allows essence to proceed as really other from itself, it simultaneously gives essence its own task [*Aufgabe*], or claim on being. We see this in being's obedience to essence. "Being belongs to essence—which is really different from being—it harkens to [*ge-horcht*] essence," writes Oster, "because it itself gives essence and at the same times lets essence give."[69] As a result, looked at from the point of view of the creature, it can be said that essence gives the causality of substance, as if essence initiated it. But this is only possible because of how radically being gives itself away. Oster confirms this when he writes that being gives itself away so completely that "seen in a certain light, the principle of finite beings [i.e., essence] gives birth to being itself because it brings it to itself, helps being to subsistence. Beings are—in a certain sense—the cause of being because in receiving being they *enact* it."[70]

We recall that Ulrich introduces the category of love to begin a metaphysical explanation for multiplicity, or perhaps we could say more simply, creation. What Ulrich means by love is unfolded throughout his oeuvre as well as specifically in *Homo Abyssus*, but we might begin by saying it is intrinsically linked to obedience. Indeed, this obedience of being to essence is, according to Ulrich, another indicator of that which being images: God himself, and specifically the nature of God's love. Thus, in paying attention to and drawing out

---

68. "kann Thomas auch sagen, dass das Sein der (Wesens-)Form *folge*, dass letzlich die Wesensform der endlichen Substanz das Sein *gibt*" (*MMS*, 243). See *ST* I.9.2: esse consequitur formam and *ST* I.14.2.ad.1: forma enim inquantum perficit materiam, dando ei esse.

69. "Das Sein gehört dem—von ihm real unterschieden—Wesen, es ge-horcht ihm, weil es sich je diesem Wesen gibt und zugleich sich je dieses Wesen geben lässt" (*MMS*, 245).

70. "Die Prinzipien des endlich Seienden bringen in gewisser Hinsicht das Sein selbst hervor, weil sie es zu-stande bringen, ihm zur Subsistenz verhelfen. Sie sind—in geweisser Hinscht—sogar Ursache des Seins, weil sie das Sein im Empfangen: *tun*" (*MMS*, 246).

being's *Subsistenzbewegung* in his metaphysics of creation, it seems that Ulrich is pointing out something often missed in such discussions: that creation is possible only when and if that which is higher submits itself—is obedient to—that which is lower, out of love.

Ulrich then lays out three points with regard to being's obedience to essence, while also keeping in mind that essence proceeds from being. In the first point, Ulrich thinks it important to note that "being is not annihilated [*vernichtet*] 'through' the essence, but is instead transnihilated [*durchnichtet*]." The distinction is subtle, though crucial. If being were simply to disappear when it gives itself over to finitude through essence, this would mean two things: (1) essence is actually superfluous—that being had within itself the immediate power of substantializing itself all along and just needed to enact it—and (2) that by implication, being always already had some sort of hypostasized existence. *Trans*nihilation, on the other hand, indicates that being offers its own no-thingness up in such a way that it allows what is below it to be. This is what Ulrich means when he writes "the superessential power of being thus opens itself up to the 'space of essence.'" This openness that is itself essence is not possible without the proper nothingness of being. In turn, essence has the capacity to receive being. "Being's coming together with the essence is therefore determined as the reception of what has been transnihilated; being's transnihilation out of the crisis of its circumincession with the 'nothing' bears witness to itself in being's being received."[71]

Secondly, we must be careful about the temptation to subsume *esse* into essence. Ulrich calls this "a radicalized essence metaphysics," and points elsewhere to thinkers who have done exactly this.[72] At first, this may seem like a move to elevate the finite by elevating essence over and above *esse*. However, it does the opposite: by thinking of essence as the ultimate term in metaphysics, we then lose essence's mediation of what is "ultimately infinite"[73]—that is to say, we lose the beauty and dignity given to essence precisely in its being given the capacity to mediate, substantialize, and affirm being in being's transnihilation. It also loses the inherent dignity of allowing being to appear, that is, of revealing being.[74] A radical essence metaphysics therefore evacuates not only being itself of its content, as it were, but the essence's as well.

Thirdly, though in the *Subsistenzbewegung* undetermined being is determined in and through essence, we must again be careful not to think of

---

71. All quotations from this paragraph are from *HA*, 82–83.

72. *HA*, 83. Ulrich takes Scotus to be the paradigm of this, and explains his reasons at length in "Inwiefern," which I will address in the following chapter.

73. *SCG* 1.43.

74. "It is essence that unveils the truth that being holds nothing back" (*HA*, 62).

the movement into subsistence as two "things" coming together to form finite creatures, thereby reifying both *esse* and essence and recognizing none of what each reveals about the metaphysics of creation. In the true interplay between *esse* and essence, in which *esse* submits itself to essence to be limited, we see that *esse* never totally secures itself in itself (that is, its subsistence) and thus always has its "task" at hand. This has two implications: (1) the task (*Aufgabe*) of *esse* never comes to an end—that is, *esse* is always giving itself—and (2) insofar as creatures participate in *esse*, so too do they never fully secure themselves. Though creatures are subsistent, they are not infinite, and thus they too are always dependent, just as *esse non subsistens* is. Thus, according to Ulrich, we can catch a glimpse of the *ex nihilo* of creation simply by drawing out all of the implications of the real distinction.

It would be easy to construe this dependence negatively; it could seem, given the schema we have just laid out, that nothing is ever really given itself, nothing really possesses its own being. This construal is possible, however, only if we lose sight of the positive reality in which the real distinction inheres: the thing itself, the *res*, the creature. When thinking the real distinction, we must try and simultaneously think about the reality of the creature, which does in fact subsist, as neither *esse* nor essence does. "The consideration of the real distinction between being and essence terminates in the 'positive reality' in which being and essence are always already unified and blended into one."[75] Thus, the *res* in some way has an existence independent of—while simultaneously entirely dependent on—*esse* and essence. And it is this "substantial independence," Ulrich writes, that "is a witness to the fact that to be as *non subsistens* has always already 'given itself over,' that it does not cling to itself, but is always already concrete entity."[76] Substance is then a concrete sign of being's obedience in the *Subsistenzbewegung in love*, rather than an extrinsic necessity.[77]

Perhaps we could put it this way: if the concrete substance in its proper autonomy is not in view, it seems as if the real distinction is simply a mechanism to prevent any one part of creation from becoming too much like God. However, when looked at through the lens of the creature, the real distinction instead becomes a further revelation of the logic of creation—that is, to let be that which is not God. Even as we parse the metaphysical structure of

---

75. HA, 87.

76. HA, 68.

77. Obviously Ulrich uses the word necessary in conjunction with the *Subsistenzbewegung*, but that kind of necessity is one proper to love: when one loves, one simply must give a gift to the beloved, etc. When I attach the qualifier extrinsic to necessity here, I mean to indicate a kind of necessity that derives from a tyrannical authority.

substance, there is no moment in which an individual substance is not fully itself, as if *esse* (or essence) could remove itself from the equation[78] at some point in order to demonstrate to the *res* just how utterly poor and dependent it really is.[79] Rather, *esse* really gives itself entirely to the substance—as mediated by essence—and holds nothing back,[80] as it were. *Esse*'s *Subsistenzbewegung* is in some sense complete in each individual substance;[81] no *res* could be substantial were this not the case.

Here we encounter in the *res* a similar interplay of wealth and poverty we have already seen in *esse*. It is true that the *res* really does possess its own substantiality; it really exists concretely in the world. At the same time, however, substance is entirely dependent on *esse* and essence for its being substantial. The *res* is poor in that it cannot give itself substantiality, but it is wealthy because it has substantiality. In fact, we would never know *esse* without the *res*. It is only through patient and careful attention to reality that we come into a knowledge of being.

This then points us once again to the relative primacy of substance. It is the substance that is the proper subject of metaphysics; metaphysics is always in the service of understanding reality as we encounter it, not a creation of a system into which we try and fit reality. There is, then, some sense in which the real distinction disappears in the encounter with a concrete substance. We need to be careful here, for it is not the case that Ulrich denies the real distinction, nor does he say that it is only a logical distinction; however, if the *res* really is given itself—that is, its own substantiality—then it must be the case that the distinctness of the principles of *esse* and essence fall away in this respect in the face of the substantial unity of the *res*. And this is appropriate: *esse* and essence unite in order to let another be; without their disappearance, as it were, the *res* would always be haunted by the presence of the principles that make it up. The substance could never be itself; it would be the puppet

---

78. The issue of death needs to be addressed here, but is not within the scope of this project. We should however note that death is not a cruel joke—a time when either *esse* or essence is removed from the creature so as simply to expose its utter dependency—but rather a mercy given the post-lapserian world which creatures inhabit. We should also note that even in death the creature still exists, though not of course in the exact mode we know it in this world.

79. Though of course, looked at in different light, the creature is in fact utterly dependent.

80. We could read this phrase in two senses: *esse* gives everything it "has" to the creature, but also that *esse* holds back the creature's fall into nothingness—that is, *esse* uses its own nothingness to prevent the creature from being nothing itself.

81. That is to say, complete qua *esse* in the creature. See Bieler's *FG*, 232.

of *esse* and essence. Ulrich puts it succinctly: "in the ontological moment of reality being and essence are always already fused in a unity."[82]

The unfolding of the *Subsistenzbewegung* in the ontological moments of reality, ideality, and bonicity

The movement into subsistence of being itself occurs because of the necessary sense of being in which being finds both its gift and task. This *Subsistenzbewegung* has three ontological moments, which Ulrich names reality, ideality, and bonicity. It is important to keep in mind as we move through these moments with Ulrich that this is not a temporal unfolding, or a series within time. The unfolding of being in the moments of reality, ideality, and bonicity is an event that is occurring all the time—and always already has occurred—and it is not a process that will someday reach its final destination. We cannot help but present them in some way as a series, but this is not the reality.

We have affirmed with both Thomas and Ulrich that substance is the proper subject of being (*substantia est ens tamquam per se habens esse*), and that the unfolding of the *Subsistenzbewegung*—that is, the outpouring of *esse*—is entirely for the sake of beings. This does not mean, however, that the movement into subsistence stops, as it were, in superficial or static substance. Rather, according to Ulrich, everything we have described thus far in this chapter is in a sense always contained within every individual being. Our metaphysical situation is not one of building blocks stacked on top of each other, but rather a whole: a dynamic reality that is united in its participation of being and reflection and radiation of the Good. The ontological moments, as Ulrich names them, are always being expressed and appearing in substances all the time, if we have eyes to see this dynamism. The ontological difference (so too the real distinction) appears with the appearing of every substance, and this is no less true of the movement into subsistence. Each of the ontological moments describes creation as a whole, but each is also taking place, as it were, in each substance.

The three ontological moments of reality, ideality, and bonicity are thus ways to describe what it means and how it is that being pours itself out entirely for the sake of beings, but they are also each "moments" of every individual being. Each moment reveals something unique and indispensable about being's movement into subsistence, and therefore also about what every individual substance reveals about the nature of being, and therefore too the nature of God. The ontological moments are thus another way to articulate what it

82. *HA*, 94.

means for God to create, and specifically, to create in the way that he has—that is to say, to create material being.

Reality, ideality, and bonicity correspond to the *res*, *esse*, and the *ens*. The first regards the substance with respect to its essence, the second with respect to *esse* or being, and the third is their unity. Each moment is necessary for both understanding the individual substance and our entire metaphysical reality in its proper dynamism, which is to say, how substance participates in being and manifests the Good. The moment of bonicity is then, fittingly, the telos of the *Subsistenzbewegung*: it is the *ens* that is both the point, so to speak, and the end of the movement into subsistence. The Good is both origin and aim. The moments of reality and ideality are not superfluous, however, since in and through their mediation, the creature is really given to itself.

As is often the case for Ulrich, he thinks through and describes these moments by also thinking through the temptations that come with them: this can be summed up as isolating any of the moments, though this temptation expresses itself most clearly in the moments of reality and ideality, as we will see shortly. When either reality or ideality is isolated, either essence or *esse* becomes the only and entire interpretive horizon for our metaphysics, leading, ultimately, to the fundamental temptation of thought presented in the first part of this chapter: the substantializing of being and resultant rejection of the Creator. When thinking being, all three ontological moments must be held together, and this is only possible in light of the Good. Indeed, Ulrich's contention is that only the Good has the capacity, as it were, to uphold these three moments in a fruitful tension, which ultimately allows both the Creator and creation to be, so to speak, themselves.

Indeed, we might say that in the articulation of *Subsistenzbewegung* and the three ontological moments, Ulrich is attempting to understand and articulate in the most radical way possible just what creation means: that being is given. Each of the moments, corresponding to a different metaphysical constituent of substance, both secures and helps explain this astonishing fact, and each puts a different accent, as it were, on what it means that being is given. With regard to reality, the accent is on the givenness of being, whereas in ideality, the accent is on what is given—that is, being. So we might say somewhat oversimply that the ontological moments of reality and ideality both describe the same truth—being is given—but describe it from two different sides. Being is *given*, and *being* is given, as it were. In order to see why this is the case, let us first address the moment of reality.

Reality

Oster writes that "Ulrich names 'reality' the concrete, enduring, finite substance which has concretized (con-crescare) out of the essential form and matter with what has already been received, i.e., the already finitized being."[83] The ontological moment of reality is first, according to Ulrich, precisely because our metaphysics must remain rooted there; without the *res*, we could see nothing about being, and all metaphysics becomes mere concept. Another way to put this is that being would be stuck in the moment of ideality, though we will address this shortly. The ontological moment of reality, as incarnated for us in the *res*, guides being's *exinanitio*—its giving itself away in its task—insofar as in a certain sense the *res* is at least the proximate telos of the *Subsistenzbewegung*. Being transnihilates, writes Ulrich, "in the direction of the finite res," which in turn means that the obedience of being demonstrated in the *Subsistenzbewegung* "also has to hold with respect to reality."[84]

The ontological moment of reality is most closely associated with essence because it is that which allows all of the metaphysical principles to "concretize." Essence is where an individual being or creature is really given itself, where it *belongs* to itself—essence is the capacity of the creature to be itself, to be a substance.

The temptation that comes with the ontological moment of reality is to isolate it, thereby ultimately evacuating essence of its given power. Ulrich writes, "The absolutizing of the positive reality into a determinative horizon of the speculative unfolding of being necessarily leads to the notion of existence as 'permanence.'"[85] If the ontological moment of reality is isolated, and all that can be seen, so to speak, is essence, the *res* is not given to communicate anything beyond itself, but rather isolated within its own existence. This in turn means that the *res* cannot in fact be *given* anything: there is nothing but the essence. Essence does not mediate anything greater than itself, which also means that essence has not been given this power by *esse*. Again we see that in the attempt to elevate something, it is actually depotentiated. Ulrich writes,

> The positive reality can never be isolated, it can never, so to speak, be exclusively "posited" within the realm of the self-unified essence without destroying itself, just as being becomes enfeebled into a mere potency-to-be if it is suspended in the static crisis of ideality.

---

83. "‚Realität' nennt Ulrich die konkrete, währende endliche Substanz also zusammen gewachsen (con-crescare, konkret) aus Wesensform und Materie mit dem schon empfangenen, d.h., schon verendlichten Sein" (*MMS*, 262).

84. *HA*, 130.

85. *HA*, 93–94.

It is only with respect to a constantly renewed obedience to the necessary sense of being, which is rooted in bonitas, that we overcome the distress in ideality and the essentializing of being in reality.[86]

Isolating the ontological moment of reality only results in making the essence effectively nothing.

Ideality

In the ontological moment of ideality our emphasis shifts: *being* is given. "In 'ideality,'" writes Oster, "Ulrich refers to being insofar as it contains everything in itself, is *non-subsistent* fullness and actuality, insofar as it is really different from concrete beings."[87] This moment is most closely associated with the metaphysical principle of *esse*. We might ask why, then, we began our explication of these moments with reality and the corresponding principle of essence—after all, essence proceeds from *esse*, and therefore in some sense, essence is second. Ulrich reminds us here that "because of the non-subsistence of being, ideality begins not in ideality but reality"; that is to say, "reality is the proper beginning of ideality."[88] With this Ulrich calls to mind yet again that being itself "is" nothing and that most properly speaking being is either God or beings.

The ontological moment of ideality is a recognition of what is given: being itself, which—since *esse creatum* is not mediat*or* but pure mediat*ion*—is in a sense the being of God himself, but always and only as mediated by *esse non subsistens*, which is *esse creatum*. Looking at creatures with regard to their *esse* thus helps us to recognize that substances participate in and are granted subsistence by that which transcends them all, and simultaneously that being has always already been mediated to the finite creature. If the moment of reality helps us to see *that* creatures are really given to themselves and given to reflect and refract the Good by virtue of their essence, ideality helps us understand *why* creatures are given to themselves: so that in their subsistence they may participate in that which transcends them.

Recognizing the ontological moment of ideality in the *Subsistenzbewegung* thus allows us to recognize that (1) the creature comes from nowhere but God himself, (2) the creature *is* nothing other than God himself, except

---

86. *HA*, 97.

87. "Mit 'Idealität' wird bei Ulrich das Sein bezeichnet, insofern es die alles in sich führende aber *nichtsubsistente* Fülle und Aktualität ist, insofern es aber auch vom konkreten Seienden real unterschieden ist" (*MMS*, 261–62).

88. *HA*, 147. Ulrich cites here Félix Ravaisson's *Essay sur la métaphysique d'Aristote*, vol. 1 (Paris: L'Imprimerie royale, 1837), 573: "The real is the beginning of the ideal."

as *radically given away*, (3) the creature is *radically given to itself* insofar as it and all of creation subsists, and (4) even as the creature is really given itself, this is only accomplished by virtue of the pure mediation that is *esse non subsistens*, which transcends all beings. Thus the moment of ideality helps us to understand just what it means to say that God creates in and through *esse non subsistens* or that *esse non subsistens* is pure mediation.

It is difficult to hold together the moments of ideality and reality at once, because it is difficult to see how essence, which follows *esse* metaphysically but at the same time gives subsistence to *esse*, can come from *esse*. However, as Thomas writes in *De potentia*: "God simultaneously gives *esse* and produces that which receives *esse*."[89] Recall that the *Subsistenzbewegung* "occurs" because of the necessary sense of being, which itself is a result of the crisis of being: being subsists, and subsists as either God or beings. Being "must" pour itself out, and this outpouring is described as the movement into subsistence by Ulrich. There is, however, another side, as it were, of the movement into subsistence, which Ulrich calls transnihilation. If the movement into subsistence is the outpouring of being with respect to *esse*'s fullness and actuality, transnihilation is that same movement, so to speak, with respect to *esse*'s non-subsistence. Transnihilation is, we could say, the *Subsistenzbewegung*'s underside. This means that transnihilation is a communication of the perfection that is *esse*'s nothingness to what emerges from it. Essence emerges from *esse* precisely as potency—as Wippel calls it, relative nonbeing—but essence cannot come from outside of being ("nothing is outside of being except nonbeing"), and so when Ulrich writes that being transnihilates, he means that it gives itself away so radically that essence, which is in potency to being itself, can emerge from being, but as really other to being. In describing the movement as *Subsistenzbewegung*, we see that being gives its actuality, but in using the term transnihilation, we see that, in a sense, being gives even that which it does not "have": potency, or relative nonbeing, emerges from *esse* in the form of essence. This is what Ulrich means when he uses the verb "presuppose" (*voraussetzen*): in the movement into subsistence, an-other—in this case, essence—is presupposed even though the other does not already exist. Recognizing that the *Subsistenzbewegung* is simultaneously transnihilation helps us see this presupposition of essence by *esse*—that is, the simultaneity of their givenness—is only possible when neither the moment of ideality nor the moment of reality is isolated.

Ulrich writes,

---

89. *DP*, 3.1.17.

We thus see that the thinking that would follow being in its crisis in an abyssal way has to co-enact and undergo openness to its transnihilation that being has by virtue of the essence. It is only on the basis of the necessary sense of being, which pervades the ontological difference, that the "relationship" between being and essence is able to unfold: as the "self-sameness" of the positing of essence and its procession from being.[90]

In the act of creation, both essence and *esse* are given; *esse* is metaphysically prior, and yet essence is given the task of giving *esse* subsistence. Again we see here that the higher allows itself to be expressed by the lower. Without both *esse* and essence at once, we lapse into a metaphysics in which either the *res* or *esse* is the only thing that really "is."[91] Each temptation is in truth a temptation to do away with mediation: on the side of reality, to do away with the mediation of existence to the creature by *esse*; on the side of ideality, to do away with the mediation of subsistence to *esse* by essence. Each attempt to elevate its respective moment ultimately destroys the moment. Ulrich maintains that the only way these moments can be thought together correctly is in light of that which enables mediation in the first place: the Good.

Bonicity

If the ontological moment of reality is most closely associated with essence, and the moment of ideality is most closely associated with *esse*, then bonicity is their unity, which both encompasses the previous two moments and transcends them. Bonicity makes the ontological moments of reality and ideality possible even as it is also the telos of the *Subsistenzbewegung*. If the accent on "being is given" was in different places in the moments of reality and ideality, then in the moment of bonicity we can catch a glimpse of the whole, of the truth of creation: being is really given to the creature. *Ens* best represents bonicity because it is in the *ens*, that is, the creature with respect to *esse*, that we see both the individual creature in its subsistence and the transcendent and fruitful *esse* that allows the creature to be.

We saw above that there is a danger of isolating the moments of reality and ideality: if we halt the *Subsistenzbewegung* at reality, essence is absolutized, and if we do the same at the moment of ideality, *esse* is conceptualized,

---

90. *HA*, 135.

91. Ulrich points out that these mistakes are committed by Suárez and Scotus, respectively, and shows briefly in *HA* how each leads to a breakdown in how we understand creation. See *HA*, 138–39. This is also a major theme in "Inwiefern," which we will address in the next chapter.

with both mistakes leading to a destruction of God or the world in thought. This danger does not exist in the moment of bonicity because it is the nature of the good both to unite and be fruitful. It is not in the nature of the good to isolate; rather, the nature of the good is constantly and continuously to point to the other, and therefore its very nature is to unite without collapsing.

The moment of bonicity[92] then guarantees that neither being nor beings is forgotten: we might say that the good holds open the ontological difference, as it were, ensuring that neither is subsumed into the other.[93] Oster writes that "in and through the bonicity of being, the ideality and reality of being are communicated and united to each other without being identified with one another or absorbed into one another."[94] The telos of the *Subsistenzbewegung* is then the allowing of an-other to be, which is only possible in the fruitful unity of the good.

Ipsum esse non subsistens is the *similitudo divinae bonitatis*. Thus, in a way, it should not be surprising that the telos of the *Subsistenzbewegung* is

92. See n29 above, as well as *GA*, 178–87. Bonicity is another point at which Ulrich diverges from Siewerth. Though in his *Der Thomismus als Identitätssystem*, Siewerth first articulates the moments of reality and ideality, Ulrich introduces the moment of bonicity because he saw that the *Subsistenzbewegung* could not terminate in reality without producing a dialectical relation between ideality and reality. De la Tour writes, "Ulrich emphasizes [the moment of bonicity] over Siewerth, for whom the ontological moment of reality represents the terminus of the *Subsistenzbewegung* (really: creation). If reality is the terminus of the movement into subsistence, then the good is not the *causa finalis* and the *Subsistenzbewegung* loses the unity and intelligibility it has in light of being's [necessary] sense. Therefore, Siewerth encounters contradiction at every point in his speculative depiction of being's movement into finitude, which he can solve only unsatisfactorily because for him the unifying and sense-giving perspective of absolute bonitas is decisive only in the sense of a speculative goal . . . but it does not determine and guide thought's every step" ("Ulrich betont dies gegen Siewerth, für den das Seinsmoment der Realität den Terminus der Subsistenzbewegung darstellt. Ist die Realität der Terminus der Subsistenzbewegung, dann fällt das bonum als causa finalis aus und die Subsistenzbewegungverliert die Einheit und Intelligibilität, die sie im Licht des Seinssines hat. Deshalb stößt Siewerth an jeder Stelle seiner spekulativen Darstellung der Verendlichungsbwegung des Seins auf einen Widerspruch, den er nur unbefriedigend lösen kann, weil bei ihm die vereinheitlichende und sinngebende Perspektive der absolute bonitas nur in einem bestimmten Sinn entscheidend ist: Die Positivität des Seins ist wie das Ziel der Spekulation bzw. das, was es spekulativ nachzuvollziehen gilt, sie bestimmt und leitet aber nicht jeden Denkschritt" *GA*, 183).

93. We could also put it this way: The ontological moments of reality and ideality help us identify the real distinction, but understanding the ontological difference is only possible in light of the moment of bonicity.

94. "In der Bonität des Seins und durch sie sind Idealität des Seins und Realität des Seins zueinander vermittelt und zusammengeschlossen, ohne zugleich miteinander zur Decken zu kommen und ohne ineinander aufgehoben zu werden" (*MMS*, 263).

the ontological moment of bonicity. As the image of God's goodness, *esse*'s unfolding into subsistence cannot but be guided by and aim at goodness itself. The question is exactly what that means or looks like. We might now suggest a tentative answer. We have seen just above that speculatively halting the *Subsistenzbewegung* at either the ontological moment of reality or ideality effectively attempts to substantialize *esse non subsistens*, evacuating *esse* of its very nature by ignoring its non-subsistent character. This in turn halts *esse*'s natural activity, which is simply mediation. Put another way, endowing *esse non subsistens* with pseudo-subsistence destroys its very nature and turns it into a perverse "self" which cannot give itself, cannot mediate being. Both its wealth and poverty are inverted: *esse* is no longer the richest of all creatures; in its pseudo-subsistent state, it is tyrannical, only wealthy because ungenerous, and poor because friendless, and most tyrant-like of all, profoundly unfree. Neither the moment of reality nor ideality alone is enough to allow being to go beyond itself—that is, neither has the capacity to allow being always already to give itself away. In this, we see that *esse*'s imaging the divine goodness is not *a part* of its nature, but, as Thomas says, simply *is* the nature of *esse non subsistens*. "Bonicity," Ulrich writes, "represents the moment in which being consolidates itself out of ideality and reality, without clinging to these two moments in themselves as 'sublated' or as 'needing to be sublated.' In the bonum, being opens up its very heart."[95]

In short, it is the ontological moment of bonicity that allows being to transnihilate, or allows being to presuppose an-other. Ulrich calls being wealthy because it is the act of all acts, but in talking about being and beings—i.e., the ontological difference—we come up against the same question time and time again, as we did with Thomas and Wippel, which is, if nothing is outside of being except nonbeing, how does anything else come to be at all? It is of course true that essence has something to do with this, but again we emphasize that essence must not be conceived as coming from outside *esse* such that the two are part and counterpart. Rather, as was said above, essence is a result of being's transnihilation, a surrendering of *esse*'s very nothingness such that that nothingness can be other to being itself: essence. If essence were to act as counterpart, there would be no original unity and all of reality would be founded upon, at the deepest level, contradiction. Transnihilation is thus intrinsically linked to—indeed, only possible because of—the ontological moment of bonicity.

This is important for both the individual creature and for creation as a whole for two reasons. (1) Without understanding that being transnihilates

---

95. *HA*, 151.

(rather than simply nihilates, as is the case with Heidegger),[96] we cannot see the original unity upon which creation is founded. This would result in many metaphysical difficulties, but our main concern is the unity between act and potency. If potency is completely outside of actuality, if it is not somehow generated by it, we are back to a similar problem as the ancients had, in addition to there being no true unity in individual substances. (2) Without the moment of bonicity allowing being to go beyond itself, the nature of individual beings would also be "stuck" in themselves. Ulrich writes that "what becomes clear in the moment of being's bonicity is precisely the fact that the concrete entity can never make absolute perfection its aim *in actu*; it therefore never achieves itself in an absolutely 'single' step, in the sense that being would have included and actualized in its self-affirmation every possibility ascribed to it as finite being."[97] This would imply (a) there is no real difference between being and beings, and (b) beings cannot themselves go beyond themselves, cannot give themselves away; in a word, cannot be fruitful. But beings are fruitful, just as being itself is. And thus we begin to see that every individual being carries within it something analogous to being's transnihilation.

What this points to, says Ulrich, is that all creatures are in some sense *in via*: no creature can remain in itself and still paradoxically be itself. The coincidence of the wealth and poverty of being is also true for all finite entities in an analogous sense. Were this not the case, the finite substance "would cling to itself in a manner that corresponds to the elimination of the not-yet of the ontological difference when being is absorbed into the res."[98] This halts the *Subsistenzbewegung* at the ontological moment of reality, the problems of which we have already seen. We must also note, however, that this *in via* character of being does not mean being is constantly giving itself to beings so that it can then remove itself, ensnaring individual beings in some sort of Sisyphean enterprise in their desire to be themselves.

> [The] self-affirmation of the act of being in the concrete, finite substance... does not occur in a movement into subsistence that constantly begins anew, as it were in a continuous *giving* and a continuous *withdrawal* of being. In this case we would have overlooked the positively-persisting reality, the moment in which the substance "always already" abides [*west*] in actuality and *perdures*, prior to any movement into subsistence.[99]

---

96. See nn9, 19 above.
97. *HA*, 151–52.
98. *HA*, 152.
99. *HA*, 152.

Being does not give itself to then withdraw; rather, its always "already" giving nature[100] comes from its non-subsistence, which it can only have, so to speak, because it is the *similitudo divinae bonitatis*. Its no-thingness, its non-subsistence is the condition of its being the image of the divine goodness. Therefore, for anything to image God, which is itself a perfection of being, every creature must in a certain sense carry the perfection that is the *non subsistens* of *esse*. It is in transnihilation that being passes this perfection on to every creature, and thus a certain kind of no-thingness is present throughout creation, albeit in an analogous way.

Ulrich draws our attention in this regard to the accidents of an individual substance, writing that "Being's self-achievement in finite subsistence can thus give proof that it is a valid enactment of the crisis of being only insofar as the finite substance pours itself out into the accidents and affirms itself in and with them or 'beyond itself.'"[101] This is an analogous continuation of the transnihilative character of being into beings themselves. If accidents are something in themselves—that is, if they are at all meaningful—then they must be in a certain sense other than essence. And indeed, we know that they must be, since two men are humans even if one has a snub nose and one does not. At the same time, however, accidents do not arise entirely outside of essence, otherwise, essence could not be expressed in the accidents. So the accidents are other than essence, and yet it is essence that has created the possibility for accidents to come to be in the first place. This is not incidental to the *Subsistenzbewegung*, but indeed in some way the very reality of it as a "horizontal" expression of it. Ulrich writes that the "necessity of the accidents' procession from the heart of the finite substance—that is, the bonum—thus results from the moment in which the speculative enactment of being's movement of finitization terminates in this heart," and later,

> The procession of the accidents is the concrete result of being's self-mediation to itself, a mediation that first became apparent in the vertical dimension of the movement of finitization. The substance yields itself and affirms itself by externalizing and internalizing in, through, and with, the accidents. The bonum makes evident in an exceptional way that substance becomes *what* it always already was.[102]

---

100. This also implies an always already *having given*, i.e., the act is *also* already complete in the *ens*.

101. *HA*, 152.

102. *HA*, 152–53. See also n59 above, as well as this passage from *HA*: "To be sure, there is just a single movement into subsistence in which being comes to itself in the infinite variety and multiplicity of beings. If this pull toward finite subsistence, however,

Thus we see that in an analogous way, essence transnihilates as well, except in this case in a horizontal direction. It gives itself up to be expressed by the accidents of the substance, and as with being and individual beings, cannot be seen without those accidents. Essence allows itself to be seen by that which is ontologically lower than it. This is impossible without the primordial fruition that the ontological moment of bonicity reflects.

Here Ulrich again circles back to the relationship between act and potency, writing, "the ontological moment of bonicity prevents possibility and actuality from being simply external to one another."[103] Accidents and essence are not opposed to one another; rather, the accidents reveal the substance. But these same accidents cannot be without the substance. Considered in themselves, accidents are nothing; they reveal what was always already there in substance, even though substance cannot be revealed without them.

> The unity of possibility and actuality comes to light . . . from the perspective of the necessary sense of being, so that what *becomes* actual is what always already *actually is*, without it being a matter of the mere repetition of a fixed entity or of all possibilities being always already actualized. The substance flows out, to be sure, into its accidents; that is, the accidents flow from substance.[104]

---

is speculatively separated out into its "phases," if the entity enters into the *resolutio* back to the *actus ultimus*, then what is shown on the speculative return path energized by the necessary sense of being is the fact that *what comes about* in the teleological movement into subsistence, in being's convergence out of the moment of ideality and reality into bonicity, is *the kenosis of the finite substance in its accidents*. What comes to light here is the co-affirmation of the posited ground of the substance in the multiplicity of the acts in which the substance (not *esse*) comes toward itself. This does not mean, however, that the substance would be identified with the accidents. The contrary is the case. It is precisely the substance's self-expression in the dimension of the accidents that would indicate its self-affirmation in the negation of this externalization. The accidents would be an extension of the substance if the essence were *not* disclosed in the externalization of the accidents through the superessential act of being" (155). In the first chapter of HA, Ulrich quotes Thomas: "Under the accidents lies hidden the substantial nature of reality. . . . The truth lies hidden under the likeness and figures that signify it (because the intelligible world is enclosed within as compared with the sensible world, which is perceived externally), and *effects lie hidden in their causes, et e converso*" (ST II-II.8.c), and comments on this, writing, "This *et e converso* is worth noting because it says that the accidents, too, in which the essence of things affirms itself in a productive and expressive way, have sort of a concealment within the substantial nature of the thing" (HA, 14). Ulrich understands accidents to be a manifestation of the ever-more of being, which essence is given to express, and at the same time, accidents allow, so to speak, essence to reconfirm itself (that is, its self-unity) in its very expression in and through the accidents.

103. HA, 153.
104. HA, 153–54.

Ulrich calls the accidents a "mediating dimension": they mediate a substance's innermost being even though they themselves are nothing.

Ulrich cautions against collapsing the difference between substance and accidents. Indeed, the difference is necessary for the accidents to be themselves as mediators. We see then, in the appearance of material creatures, "being's convergence out of the moment of ideality and reality into bonicity" which Ulrich identifies as "the *kenosis of the finite substance in its accidents*."[105] Again we see the translation of being's necessary sense into the finite creature; every creature bears the mark of being, yet differently. Thus, Ulrich is able to say: "In the heart of bonicity, the reality thus preserves its openness to the crisis of being (transnihilation) and is nevertheless wholly reality, without being able to dissolve the secondary acts of its actualization into the single track of the duration of persistence. On the basis of bonicity, however, being itself is also manifest in the crisis as non subsistens."[106]

In the ontological moments of reality, ideality, and bonicity—i.e., the path of the *Subsistenzbewegung*—we can more clearly see what is at stake for Ulrich in a proper understanding and articulation of the metaphysics of creation: understanding the nothingness of *esse non subsistens* as radically as possible. It is this nothingness that Ulrich shows is a perfection of being itself, that keeps open the ontological difference, and allows that same ontological difference to be in the first place. We have asked several times in this chapter how anything other than *ipsum esse* can come to be in the first place, and we have returned again and again to the non-subsistent character of being. Because it is the *similitudo divinae bonitatis*, being does not grasp at pseudo-subsistence, but rather gives itself over to be substantialized by that which is both other and ontologically lower than itself. Not only that, but when being hands over even its very nothingness ("being holds nothing back") in its transnihilation, it hands over that which it does not possess for itself in order that something other may come to be. And thus, all of creation has this character of being—the image of the divine goodness—that is, being able to give that which it does not possess, of being able to pass on its perfection so that another might come to be.

However, if the transnihilative character of all creation is true, then it must be true down to the smallest, or perhaps better said, it must be true of even that which is metaphysically furthest from being. This we know to be matter, which we will explore in the next chapter.

---

105. *HA*, 155.
106. *HA*, 155.

3

Ferdinand Ulrich's Understanding of Matter

THE THREE ONTOLOGICAL MOMENTS—REALITY, ideality, and bonicity—are an articulation of the radically given nature of creation, and they help explicate what it means that *esse creatum* is the first of all created effects and that being is given in creation. The ontological moments as articulated by Ulrich represent a development in our understanding of *creatio ex nihilo* insofar as when thought together; they help us to think the subsistence of the creature in light of God's presupposition of creation. We saw this presupposition in the previous chapter with respect to the emergence of essence from *esse*: essence must be both really other from *esse* and be released by *esse* (because nothing is outside of being). Thus the emergence of essence in being's transnihilation must be because *esse* presupposes essence as always already there to receive it and, in this very presupposition, essence is given to be. We will see that this same logic exists throughout creation, because it is in a sense the logic of creation itself. In short: that being is gift is only possible if everything—that is, *esse*—is given by God and given so radically that, even though created, God presupposes the other—in this case, creation—is in some sense already there to receive.[1] Every stage, as it

---

1. See Schmitz, *Gift*. This small book is in a way a setting up of precisely this point. He writes there that the "drama of creation" is "the conferring of actual existence *ex nihilo*" (97); Schmitz writes, "Now, within the creational context, the creatureliness of the creature,—its being-a-creature,—is not a received condition which it *has*; nor, strictly speaking, is being-a-creature even a received condition that it *is*; rather the received condition

were, of the *Subsistenzbewegung* is guided by and represents in a different way this radical presupposition of the other. The ontological moments as articulated by Ulrich help bring this radicality to light.

In this chapter, we will explore with Ulrich what happens to our metaphysics of creation when not viewed in this light of radical gift. If *esse creatum* is given as radically as Ulrich affirms that it is, it must be the case that this gift-nature runs all the way through creation—goes all the way down, as it were. This is why we now turn to matter: as the lowest of created effects, it is Ulrich's test-case, so to speak, for the radically given nature of creation. A metaphysics of being as gift is founded upon the principle that the higher presupposes the lower: the higher allows the lower to be in itself (i.e., the higher) in some sense "before" the lower exists in actuality. If then, a metaphysics of being as gift is true, matter, the lowest of all created effects, must also be presupposed.

It is perhaps then no surprise that Ulrich's dissertation is dedicated to this point—that is, how our understanding of being will affect our understanding of matter. Entitled "Being and Matter: To What Extent Is the Structure of Substance Decisive for the Concept of Matter in Suárez, Duns Scotus, and Thomas?," the dissertation presents Suárez and Scotus as foils for both each other and for Thomas in order to demonstrate that our metaphysics of matter will show the deficiencies in our metaphysics of creation as a whole: "at length the truth will out."

Ulrich understands Suárez and Duns Scotus also to be exemplars, we might say, of metaphysicians who stop the *Subsistenzbewegung* too soon, or, perhaps better put: metaphysicians who interpret creation within the horizon of only one of the ontological moments, reality and ideality, respectively. Neither places the good at the center of his metaphysical schema, or in other words, each makes something other than bonicity an integrating point, and so both end up with an erroneous understanding of matter. We will see that in a sense, because of the restriction of the horizon in which each interprets

---

itself is *it*" (73–74). Later, he writes that the "modest task" of the book is "to clarify the nature of the absoluteness of creation *ex nihilo*; and to rebuild a sufficiently rich texture of causality as an aid towards understanding better the nature of creative activity. These two themes have come together in the conception of creation as absolute gratuity of the gift undertaken by the creator in endowing the act of being and its conditions. . . . For in giving and receiving we find a moment of absolute gratuity that points towards act in its purity, and a moment of absolute receptivity that points towards—nothing. So that giving and receiving, understood as the communication and reception of act, points towards creation *ex nihilo*, once the inherent absoluteness of radical presence and radical absence has been translated into original act (*esse*) and original potency (*praeter esse*) in the creative communication that founds the ontological composite unit, the creature" (127–28).

creation and being, neither has room, so to speak, to account for matter *as matter*. Each makes it to be something it is not. By comparing these thinkers to each other and then to Thomas, Ulrich sheds light on the radical implications of Thomas's assertion that being is the first of all created effects, that it is *simplex et completum sed non subsistens*, and finally, what matter helps to reveal about being.

In what follows, we will first sketch out a general outline of both Suárez and Duns Scotus's metaphysical schema. Ulrich's dissertation includes no exposition of these thinkers; his dissertation is an interpretation—which itself is not entirely obvious—that presupposes a basic understanding of Suárez and Scotus. Therefore, I will shortly—and with the help of Etienne Gilson—summarize Suárez's and Scotus's thought. I will then circle back, following Ulrich,[2] in order to draw out the implications of their understanding of being for matter (which will in turn redound back upon being itself). Last we will, again with Ulrich, return to Thomas's metaphysics of creation and show that only in light of the radicality of *esse creatum* as Thomas understands it is there a metaphysical "place" for matter.

Suárez and Scotus

Suárez, says Etienne Gilson in *Being and Some Philosophers*, does not begin his metaphysics with the principles of being; rather, he is concerned with "the very things (*res ipsa*) with which metaphysical knowledge is concerned."[3] This leads Suárez to regard the concrete thing, which he calls the *ens*, above all else. Suárez understands *ens* to be said in two different ways: a present participle—that is, the state of currently existing or be*ing*—and as a noun—that is, the thing which is. This leads Suárez, for clarity's sake, to introduce the term *essentia realis* for the *ens* as a noun, or the "real essence." The *essentia realis*, however, prescinds from actual existence—meaning that whether or not a thing actually exists has no bearing on the reality of the *essentia realis*.[4]

Gilson points out that the *essentia realis* is the building block, as it were, of metaphysics for Suárez. This is somewhat problematic because the actual existence of the *essentia realis* does not make a difference to an essence's being "real." Essence, insofar as it is, is the perfection of reality; existence then

---

2. I do not intend in what follows to interpret either Suárez or Scotus in themselves, nor assess Ulrich's interpretation of either of these thinkers, as each of these tasks would constitute an entirely different work. My aim is to present Ulrich's interpretation in order to gain insight into his understanding of matter and what implications for matter our conception of being has.

3. *BSP*, 97.

4. *BSP*, 98.

is a mode of essence, rather than the essence's act of existence, in the way that Thomas understands *esse creatum*. This means that essence precedes existence, and indeed this precedence ultimately reduces existence to essence. It also means that for Suárez, there are or could be "real essences" that do not actually exist. This in turn implies that the *essentia realis* includes possible being (i.e., the real essence that does not yet exist). "Actually existing being," i.e., the *ens* as participle, writes Gilson, "represents a restricted area of being in general which . . . includes both possible and actual being."[5] Actuality is then a particular case of being, which includes both possibility and actuality, and indeed in some sense this seems to give priority to possibility. Thus, Suárez's introduction of the *essentia realis* as what is really real, we might say, not only results in existence's being identified as a type or mode of essence, but also results in a subtle inversion of act and potency.

Because for Suárez essence is what is real (whether it be actually existing or being in general), it is difficult for him to conceive what existence means, or more pointedly, what it is. In fact, Suárez asks the question, *quid existentia sit* (what is existence?);[6] and indeed, as we have said above, being *is* nothing. But far from the way Ulrich means this, Suárez interprets existence as a property of the *essentia realis* in certain situations. Existence is achieved by the *essentia realis*, it is not always already given, and is certainly not a cause. Thus, for Suárez, essence actualizes qua essence, rather than essence actualizing through the outpouring of *esse*. "In his own notion of being," writes Gilson, "Suárez has no room for existence as such."[7]

Suárez then, in Gilson's estimation, reduces existence to essence, thereby eliminating the real distinction between *esse* and essence. Essence is what is really real, according to Suárez, and *esse* thus becomes a condition that the real can take on—or not. Additionally, Suárez, in his desire to regard the *res ipsa*, identifies the *res* with the *essentia realis*—that is to say, the *res* simply *is* the essence in a certain mode. The *res*—that is, the substance with regard to essence—is then in a certain sense the only thing a Suarezian metaphysics can see.

In this sense, Duns Scotus is Suárez's dialectical opposite. Scotus also ends up identifying *esse* with essence, but does so in what Ulrich will identify as the horizon of ideality rather than that of reality. Gilson calls Scotus's understanding of essence "Avicennian" or "Greco-Arabic."[8] Scotus understands

---

5. *BSP*, 98.

6. *Disp.*, XXXI, I, 13, p. 177 (quoted in *BSP*, 105).

7. *BSP*, 103.

8. *BSP*, 84. Ulrich calls Scotus's understanding of essence "Greek" ("Inwiefern," 82). I will address this in the third section of this chapter.

essence, or as he calls it, nature, to be that which will eventually come into existence. He receives this notion, says Gilson, from Avicenna, but Scotus has a problem to contend with here, which is the doctrine of *creatio ex nihilo*. Avicenna, says Gilson, understands essences to be necessary, but this cannot be the case for Scotus, as this would impinge upon the freedom of God.

In order to deal with this issue, Scotus comes up with a schema that allows this understanding of essence or nature to be compatible with the Christian doctrine of *creatio ex nihilo*. The natures at their origin are nothing other than objects of the divine intellect—that is, the divine ideas. These natures then enjoy the being of an object, that is, the being that an object of the divine mind would enjoy. Notice then that these natures somehow pre-exist the actually existing concrete being. The natures may become actually existing concrete beings by the divine will. As possible beings that may be created, Scotus names the natures *possibilia*; as beings producible by the divine will, Scotus calls the natures *creabilia*; as actually existing beings, Scotus calls the natures *creata*. We already see a difference between Thomas and Scotus: for Scotus the natures pre-exist the actually existing creature. Another difference seems to be the emphasis, with regard to creation, of the divine will over the divine goodness: if a nature is made into an actually existing creature, "it is an effect of God's free will" writes Gilson; indeed, "the will of God is in no way bound by the intrinsic necessity of the essences . . . the very possibility of actual existences hangs on God's free will."[9]

The nature then enjoys some sort of being in the divine intellect and then enters into a second stage of sorts as a *creabile* when it will be made into an actually existing thing. This means, writes Gilson, "the *creabilia* . . . have a being of their own, an *esse* which is their being *qua* possibles."[10]

The meaning of being, or *esse*, here is then apparently very far from Thomas's understanding. First, we see that natures or essences, similar to Suárez's metaphysical schema, enjoy a sort of being before actual existence, and therefore again essence precedes existence. For Scotus, writes Gilson, "being (*esse*) is nothing other than the intrinsic reality of essence itself," or put another way, "existence is the definite mode of being which is that of an essence when it has received the complete series of determinations." So again *esse* is itself nothing, but not in the way Ulrich understands this to be so. For Scotus, *esse* is a mode of essence because for Scotus "essence always is."[11]

Thus we see that Scotus also reduces *esse* to essence, but rather than in the horizon of reality, as Suárez does, Scotus does this in the horizon of

9. BSP, 85.
10. BSP, 85.
11. BSP, 86.

ideality: here, the essence more or less exists by itself in the divine mind. *Esse* does not enact essence, is not its principle of actuality, but is rather a mode of an essence which already enjoys some sort of being, but a being apart from the actually existing thing. Indeed, for Scotus, "being is always determined by the actual condition of its essence. . . . Essence is a nature itself whereas existence is a mode which happens to created nature."[12]

Gilson points out that though it seems as if Scotus could simply do away with the distinction between *esse* and essence altogether, he does not. Scotus maintains the distinction, describing it as "accidental in a way, though it be not truly accidental,"[13] which, Gilson says means that "existence is so one with essence that it cannot be said to be accidental."[14] Still, though Scotus acknowledges some distinction between *esse* and essence, it is only formal, and it has no real bearing on Scotus's metaphysical schema. Indeed, writes Gilson, "The notion of *esse* so completely absorbs both essence and existence in [Scotus's] doctrine that it correctly applies to both in some sense."[15] This means that Scotus's conception of being is utterly essential, or as Gilson puts it, "we are here in a metaphysical world in which essence is identical with being."[16] While Suárez subsumes being into essence, making being itself a function of essence, and thus can only see the *res*, Scotus subsumes essence into *esse*, meaning that essence becomes a function of being, not really an-other, so to speak, and thus Scotus in a way can only see *esse*, albeit an *esse* than is indistinguishable from essence.

Ulrich on Suárez

Ulrich writes that Suárez's understanding of being "seems simple, but hides within itself a plethora of entirely new consequences."[17] Although Suárez uses familiar terms such as essence, *res*, and *esse*, each of these has a different meaning in his metaphysics of creation than in Thomas's precisely because "Suárez does not recognize the causative act of being."[18] *Esse* is not the first of

---

12. *BSP*, 86.
13. *Op. Ox.* lib. II, dis. 3, q. 3, n. 2: quae est aliquo modo accidentalis, licet non sit vere accidentalis (quoted in *BSP*, 88).
14. *BSP*, 88.
15. *BSP*, 89.
16. *BSP*, 91.
17. "Die Antwort, die Saurez gibt, scheint sehr einfach, birgt jedoch eine Fülle von ganz neuen Konsequenzen in sich" ("Inwiefern," 5).
18. "Suárez kennt den begründenden Seinsakt nicht" ("Inwiefern," 5).

all created effects for Suárez, nor is it the act of actualities, which means the *essentia realis* is not enacted by *esse*. Essence does not here emerge from *esse*, and there is no presupposition of essence by *esse*. Ulrich writes that for Suárez, essence "means an always already perduring thing in being.... [I]t means that the essence exists because existence determines itself immediately on the basis of the positing of reality. It is always already actual, if it actually is essence."[19] In a Suarezian metaphysics, essence itself is the perfection of created being, which includes act and potency, and of which existence is simply a mode. With no real distinction between *esse* and essence, there can be no difference between *res*—the substance with respect to essence—and *ens*—the substance with respect to *esse*. "Ens and res are for Suárez equivalents terms,"[20] writes Ulrich.

This leads to, among other things, a reduction of being in two different ways. (1) Being becomes only beings, rather than that which has been given and created to be the image of the divine goodness. This also means that there can be no movement of mediation or generosity within being itself. If being is only beings, there is no room, so to speak, for a *Subsistenzbewegung* or a transnihilation, in which being hands itself over such that what is truly other can emerge. (2) The ontological status of both form and matter is placed into question. Neither form nor matter are in themselves an essence, at least in a Thomist metaphysics, and so Suárez will have to deal with the status of these constituents.

According to Ulrich, and as we saw above, Suárez's concept of being is a mode or condition of the *essentia realis*, not as fullness of actuality. For Suárez, "the word *existens* can only be used for the actual being. It cannot be predicated of a thing which does not exist." On the other hand, Ulrich continues, *ens* "can be used as a noun, whereby it indicates de formali the essence of a thing, which being has or can have. This means it indicates ipsum esse ... in potentia.... Therefore the word ens can at one point mean the actually existing thing, and at another only potency."[21] Remember that according to Ulrich, the *ens* is in a way the best representation of the moment of bonicity because

---

19. Essenz "bedeutet einen immer schon währenden Seinszustand ... daß die Essenz existiert, denn die Existenz ermittelt sich und unmittelbar aus der Realitätsetzung. Sie ist immer schon wirklich, wenn sie aktuale Essenz ist" ("Inwiefern," 31).

20. "Ens und res sind für Suárez aequivalent Termini" ("Inwiefern," 6).

21. "Das Wort existens kann nur für das Aktual-sein gebraucht werden. Es kann nicht von einem Ding ausgesagt werden, das nicht existiert." And "Das Wort ens dagegen kann auch als ‚Namen' gebracht werden, wobei es de formali die Essenz des Dinges bezeichnet, das das Sein hat oder haben kann, das heißt: es bezeichnet: ipsum esse ... in potentia ... . So kann das Wort ens einmal eine wirkliche existierende Sache meinen, zum anderen aber auch nur die Potenz" ("Inwiefern," 4).

in the *ens* (the creature with respect to *esse*), we see both the individual creature and *esse* as act of existence.[22] The *ens* is and represents their unity, but importantly, in their unity we also see the difference between *ens* and *esse*. *Esse* is the act of being, that is, a perfect and supra-determinate source of what is. By reducing *esse* to essence, Suárez makes *esse* a condition of *ens*, a state that is achieved by *ens*, rather than the overly full and gratuitous ground of reality.

This has many and varied consequences, but if we look at this assertion from the point of view of the *Subsistenzbewegung*, we can recognize one immediately: actuality itself becomes something that is attained or achieved, rather than that out of which everything else in creation emerges. If this is the case, then something else must be ontologically first: that is, the ground upon which everything else is built. And as we will shortly see, this, for Suárez, seems to be matter. Creation is upside down, as it were.

This has another immediate implication if we look at this from the point of view of the *Subsistenzbewegung*: if *esse*'s perfection is not in itself—that is, if it is only "gained" at the end of the *Subsistenzbewegung*, when *esse* has given itself so that substance might be, then it is also the case that this pouring out of itself—this gift—cannot itself be a perfection. Perfection is only gained in the attaining of subsistence by *esse*, and thus any movement of giving itself away can only be seen in a mercenary light: an attempt only to gain that which it does not have, rather than an emptying out of its very self in order that another may be.

This would also seem to indicate that the *non subsistens* of *esse* could not itself be a quality of the perfection of being—rather, it is a privation which must be overcome by the movement of *esse* into subsistence. The *Subsistenzbewegung* thus becomes "necessary" in all the wrong senses of that word: a movement of power rather than gift. Additionally, the understanding of matter that Ulrich proposes—that is, as a privileged image of the *non subsistens* of being—is also impossible. If the non-subsistence of being is simply a stage on the way to perfection—or worse, a lack that must be overcome—then there can be nothing intrinsically revelatory about matter itself. Matter too becomes something that must be overcome or overtaken rather than an image of the Good. And that which must be overcome is then simply a stepping-stone and means nothing in itself. So Suárez must show the why of matter by giving it some sort of subsistence, pseudo though it might be.

Thus we reach the fourth implication for Suárez's identification of being simply with the *essentia realis*: act and potency, in order for each to have any ontological status in his system whatsoever, must each have a kind of pseudo-subsistence. In order for matter to be real, both form and matter must have

---

22. See chapter 2, "Bonicity," above.

some kind of essence, and each has a reality that pre-exists their actuality in a substance, which is a unity. And yet, Suárez maintains that substance is constituted by form and matter, which means that there are two pseudo-substances at the heart of every substance. We have here the ontological situation in which form and matter are part and counterpart.[23] Still more serious is then the implication for how part and counterpart (i.e., form and matter) come together: it can only be in competition, with one of the two parts dominating the other, bringing the other under its control. There is in Suárez's metaphysical system, then, violence at the very heart of being.

Because the *esssentia realis* contains, so to speak, both actuality and possibility, the possible is for Suárez always already actual, or perhaps put better, in Suárez's metaphysics, the possible and actual are subsumed into the concept of essence, since Suárez defines the *essentia realis* as that which really exists or is capable of existing.[24] But how can this be the case for Suárez? Again, we emphasize that Suárez has no concept of *esse creatum* and therefore no understanding of anything like *esse* as the perfect image of the divine goodness out of which all creation emerges. *Esse* is not the ground of all creatures; there is no *Subsistenzbewegung*. We should ask: What is creation for Suárez?

Recall that Suárez, when writing his metaphysics, decides not to treat the principles of metaphysics, but *res ipsa*. Here we encounter the resulting shift in his understanding of the act of creation: "Suárez understands the entity as such from the always already posited reality, and not from the necessary sense

---

23. Ulrich mentions this in *HA*, when addressing the unfolding of being in the moments of reality and ideality. If we do not take the transnihilation of being seriously enough—that is to say, if we do not see being's nothingness (*non subsistens*) as itself "given away" so that essence may emerge from being as totally presupposed by being—then essence becomes that which divides being from without. This would mean that essence is a counterpart to being rather than presupposed, i.e., given, by it. "If we attended exclusively to the essence's procession from being and overlooked the positing of the essence," Ulrich writes, "then we would fail to catch sight of being's transnihilation. Instead, being would split up into part and a counterpart" (*HA*, 132). When the givenness of anything is only seen in the light of wealth, or wealth as the negation of poverty, inevitably the result is that the ground of that thing's being is contradiction: part vs. counterpart. When, however, the coincidence of wealth and poverty is kept in mind, we can see the transnihilative character of causation: the cause presupposes the effect and in so doing, allows the effect to emerge from it while at the same time giving it to be really other.

24. "Inwiefern," 9. See n23, in which Ulrich quotes Suárez: "magis autem exacta huius rei intellentia pendet ex pluribus quaestionibus: prima est, qualis sit entitas essentiae realis, quando actu non existit" (*Disp.*, II.4.6).

of the act of being."²⁵ Every created thing is simply "posited,"²⁶ which means that the mediation of a thing in its concrete existence does not interest Suárez. Indeed, Ulrich calls the *essentia realis* the "medium of immediacy."²⁷ There is no emergence of essence from *esse*, and no further emergence of matter therefrom. For Suárez, creation simply means that essence is posited by God. The resulting creature, Ulrich writes, "remains imprisoned in the 'positing.'"²⁸ This means that any created effect must itself already be an essence in order to be posited. It is difficult to overstate the issue here: Suárez, because he lacks (or passes over) any sense of *esse* as the perfection of all perfections, or the act of existence, also lacks any sense of mediation in the creative act whatsoever.

There are many implications here, not least of which we have already mentioned: every "part" of the substance must have an essential character in order to be considered real. With no sense of mediation—and therefore too no participative character of reality—the unity of every substance must in some sense be extrinsic. The source of unity can no longer be the substance's act of existence, which at one and the same time is the source of unity for all of creation and that out of which an individual substance's form and matter flow, thereby making the substance one in itself. Without mediation, *esse*, form, and matter must either be only logical distinctions within a substance or they must each have some sort of entitative character (each itself being "posited") which come together in order to form a single substance. But then the question is what this coming together could look like without mediation. Either one entity must take over the other completely, or each must exist in its entitative character within the substance, such that there is no real unity. That would lead to questions about which entity we are really seeing when we look at a thing, leading us to believe we may not actually be getting at the "really real."²⁹

---

25. "Somit versteht er die Entität als solche von der immer schon gesetzten Realität her und nicht von der Sinn-notwendigkeit der Seinsbegründung" ("Inwiefern," 9).

26. The word is *getsetzt*, which Ulrich uses generally when speaking of reality. Therefore, it makes sense that if Suárez interprets creation only within the horizon of reality, he will see only this aspect, as it were: that creation is posited, but not that it is also presupposed.

27. "daß [Essenz] bei Suárez so etwas gibt wie ein ‚Medium der Unmittelbarkeit'" ("Inwiefern," 7).

28. "Sie bleibt in der ‚Setzung' gefangen" ("Inwiefern," 9).

29. In this case, reality is not reality, and creation is a cruel trick being pulled by an antagonistic god. We can see this understanding of being if we look at the work of, e.g., Galileo or Descartes. Galileo separates the world into "primary" and "secondary" qualities, with the "secondary" qualities not having any reality outside of man's own mind. Descartes more or less accepts this split, though, wanting to give so-called secondary qualities some sort of reality, he places them into the realm of *res cogitans*. In both cases,

It is also the case that substance, conceived in this fashion, has no dynamism—nor does creation as a whole. We must remember that the *Subsistenzbewegung* is not a motion, insofar as it is not a movement from potency to act, but is a movement in the sense that it is dynamic: an emerging of form and matter from *esse*, or the movement of *esse* into finitude, depending on which way we look at it. In either case, we understand the *Subsistenzbewegung*, and all the creatures resulting therefrom, to be dynamic. The ideal mediation of being, as Ulrich calls it, helps to demonstrate how creation can be dynamic without thereby losing any of its actuality. *Esse* both is mediated to substances by essence with no diminishment of *esse*'s actuality, and it itself mediates existence to essence with no diminishment of actuality there either. Mediation does not require either the mediator or the mediated to be diminished simply because they are part of a mediation. Rather, it is precisely mediation that allows an-other to be and share in the original goodness. And otherness allows dynamism.

Suárez lacks any sense of an ideal mediation or the dynamism of creation. He is, as Ulrich puts it, "completely trapped in posited reality"[30] and his concept of substance is similarly frozen. This puts both God and the world in a precarious position, which should be familiar to us if we recall the temptations of thought outlined in the previous chapter. Being, according to Suárez, is not the image of the divine goodness, but rather what is attained by the *essentia realis* at the end of the positing, rather than what is wholly and completely given as the first act, so to speak, of creation. Ulrich writes that Suárez's conception of the *essentia realis* is the ground upon which Suárez builds up the rest of his metaphysics of creation. But again, we have a redefinition of terms here: "one can no longer say [this essence] receives or limits esse, etc. (Thomas)," nor can one understand essence to be being in the way we will see that Scotus does. Rather, writes Ulrich, "the *essentia realis* is placed and sealed within the 'posited reality' and in turn admits . . . no other concept of reality."[31] The positing of reality is all there is. But this means there is no room for gift in Suárez's metaphysics. Using the language of the last chapter, if the only ontological moment Suárez can see is that of reality, then he only knows that being

---

it seems that the world as presented and perceived must be gotten behind in order to get at what is really real. For more on this point see Burtt, *Metaphysical Foundations of Modern Science*, esp. 72–124; Hanby, *No God, No Science*, esp. 375–405.

30. "Suárez ganz von der Realitätsetzung gefangen ist" ("Inwiefern," 11).

31. "Von dieser Essenz kann man in bezug auf die Substanzkonstitution nicht mehr sagen: sie empfängt das esse, begrenzt es usw. (Thomas)" and "So ist die *essentia realis* ganz in die ‚gesetzt Realität' hineingezogen und hineinversiegelt und läßt wiederum . . . keinen anderen Realitätsbegriff zu" ("Inwiefern," 14).

is *given*. But the gift-nature of reality cannot be seen or understood when we cannot recognize *what* is being given. Instead, we see only that something is there[32]—that is, we are taking being, the gift, for granted. The restricted horizon of reality cannot conceive of a giver, because it takes for granted what is given. But only a metaphysics of being as gift will help us see that there is room, so to speak, for both God and the world. Or, to use Ulrich's language, only a radical metaphysics of being as gift makes it possible that another be presupposed with no threat to or competition with the giver.

Suárez's insistence that the only thing real is essence yields a reality that is entirely constructed rather than mediated. As we saw last chapter, a mediated reality has room, so to speak, for potency which is not in competition with actuality. Indeed, potency reveals certain aspects of reality that it would be otherwise very difficult to see. But a constructed reality—a constructed being—means necessarily that actuality and potency are in, we might say, competition with each other. And if our metaphysics is constructionist, this will necessarily affect our understanding of potency.

Ulrich concludes that Suárez is not ultimately interested in the metaphysical makeup of substance; rather, Suárez takes the world as simply "there," and then must construct his metaphysics from that point. "One places oneself, so to speak, on the 'ground-floor of reality,' and then builds up from there. The essentia realis is the once-laid foundation for all further construction. Thus Suárez identifies the ens ut nomen with the res."[33]

This constructionist metaphysics will profoundly affect our understanding of matter. For Suárez, matter is intrinsically connected to corporeal being, as it should be, but because his understanding of reality is constructed rather than mediated, and because essence is the base-line foundation for substance, in order for it to have any metaphysical status whatever, matter is conceived as *pars essentiae*.[34] Just as being is understood only from the perspective of essence, so too is matter.

What matter is, what service it performs, what it represents—none of this is important for Suárez because, as Ulrich puts it, "There is simply matter!" Again, because Suárez both starts and stops, as it were, at the ontological moment of reality, there is no space in his concept of substance to consider

---

32. Ulrich writes that for Suárez, "Der Zustand ist einfach da" (The condition is simply to be there) ("Inwiefern," 16).

33. "Man stellt sich sozugagen auf den ‚Boden der Realität' und baut von hier auf. Die *essenta realis* ist der einmal gelegte Boden für alle weitere Konstruktion. So setzt Suárez das ens ut nomen gleich mit der res" ("Inwiefern," 16–17).

34. "Denn die Materie geht ganz in die Definition der Essenz des körperlichen Dinges ein, sie ist *pars essentiae*" ("Inwiefern," 22).

the mediative unity of its different constituents. So the question of matter is never really a question for Suárez. This does not mean, however, that matter has no importance for Suárez's metaphysics. He just pays it no real attention in itself. "Matter," says Ulrich, is "moved into the metaphysical distance"[35] because it concerns neither the thing itself nor the perfection of being, which is conceived by abstracting from the thing itself.

Because for Suárez there is only the moment of reality, matter can only be interpreted from within this horizon. But for Suárez, a thing can only exist if it is an *essentia realis*, which means matter must in some sense either be or have an essence. This leads Ulrich to conclude that for Suárez, "matter will also have esse and essentia, even though its esse and essentia is not the integral being and essence of the entire corporeal substance." This is to say that in order for matter to be real at all, for Suárez it must already have some sort of pseudo-*esse* and pseudo-*essentia*; without at least a pseudo-subsistence, whatever it is cannot exist and therefore is absolutely nothing. Therefore for Suárez, "prime matter will have an entitative character in itself, and form will have its own as well."[36] This is because the moment of reality is the only lens through which Suárez can see creation, which implies that both matter and form will have some sort of subsistence before they ever join together for the sake of substance. And it is unclear what matter and form's "coming together" could look like here: if both have an entitative character[37] already—pseudo-subsistence—what could form give matter and vice versa, in order for something new—that

---

35. "Es gibt einfach die Materie!" and "Damit ist die Materie schon in eine metaphysiche Distanz gerückt" ("Inwiefern," 22).

36. "Materie ihr esse und essentia haben wird, wenngleich ihr esse und ihre essentia auch nicht das integrale Sein und Wesen der ganzen körperlichen Substanz ist. Die materia prima wird einen entitativen Charakter an sich haben und die Form auch" ("Inwiefern," 23). From *Disp.*, XIII.4.5: Distingitur ergo materia a forma tamquam res a re. Et confirmatur; nam composito substantiae ex materia et forma est realis et physica et non ex re et modo; ergo ex duabus rebus nemo tamen negare potest quin secundum entitatem essentiae alia sit entitas materiae ab entitate formae, ut rationes factae demonstrant. And again in XIII.4.9: forma autem non componit essentiam materiae, ut per se constat, quia materia essentialiter est entitas simplex, sicut et forma et ex utraque consurgit compositum . . . nam omnis entitas simplex necessario habet per seipsam intrinsece et non per aliam entitatem suam essentiam, quia in hoc consistit ipsamet ratio entitatis seu essentiae simplicis: sed materia est essentia simplex.

37. Ulrich writes, "One wonders at how many times Suárez speaks of matter and form. Indeed, he calls these two different things. Matter as well as form has its own entity. Indeed, because they are 'something' outside of their substance. Therefore each has its own corresponding essence, an entity" ("Man wundert sich oft wie massiv Suárez von der Materie und der Form spricht. Er nennt sie sogar zwei verschiedene res. Sowohl die Materie wie die Form haben eine eigene Entität. Denn essentia entsprechend, eine Entität" "Inwiefern," 31).

is, substance—to come into being? How can there be true unity when there is no real exchange or gift of form giving actuality to matter and matter offering itself, so to speak, as capacity for form? The unity of two pseudo-subsistences can only ever itself be pseudo—that is, (a) unreal because (b) not really united. Such a "unity" is rather a construction: two "things" forced together, with the act of one taking over the other in order to use the other to make itself more real, or to make its pseudo-subsistence into a real subsistence. But real unity generates fruit, it is not a construction. And fruit comes out of two which give over everything of themselves in order that another might be.

Going one step further, it becomes apparent that, for Suárez, the fact that the *essentia realis* happens to be corporeal does not change anything about it, essentially speaking. But reality is essence for Suárez, and the *essentia realis* is already the perfection of being: what does matter contribute to reality for Suárez? Or more simply, what is matter for Suárez? How does he account for it? Suárez conceives of matter as essentially (literally) its own species: it never changes, such that the matter of corporeal things is always the same. Only in the entity of form does matter differentiate, but importantly, this differentiation is a violent process for reasons explained above: form and matter are conceived as part and counterpart, which can never be fruitful of a true unity. It can only be such given Suárez's assigning an entitative status to matter. Matter, Suárez says, is the first of all creation. Again, creation seems to be turned upside down here.

Because matter does not itself contribute anything to the reality of essence, Suárez pushes matter to the outermost edge of his construction of reality; it is "first" but as "inchoate essence."[38] This also helps us make sense of what Suárez could mean when he calls matter *pars essentiae* and the beginning of essence. But essence is reality for Suárez, so matter is in the beginning of reality in a Suarezian metaphysic.[39]

We should notice that in Suárez's constructionist schema, not only matter but *esse* is also pushed to the edge of reality. The two pavers on which Suárez's metaphysics is built are: (1) the *essentia realis* is the perfection of reality (2) essence is the completion of substantial nature with respect to matter. But notice that Suárez leaves no room on either side: (1) if essence is act and perfection in itself, then essence is not intrinsically receptive to that which is more perfect than itself (i.e., *esse*), and (2) if matter is simply inchoate essence

---

38. *Disp.* XIII.3.18: nam essentia materiae est esse quasi fundamentum integrae naturae substantialis et composites et ideo solum est quaedam essenta inchoata . . . per modum potentiae.

39. Ulrich writes that matter is the "Anfang der substantialen Essenz der Konstituti-erten Substanz ist: sit essentia inchoata: angefangene Essenz" ("Inwiefern," 29).

then essence is also potency in some sense. In reality, there is only essence. Here we see that both *esse* and matter are left behind. This points negatively to their being analogically bound. If one is ignored, the other will soon follow its analogical partner into obscurity.

Matter thus also for Suárez has a double character that is impossible to reconcile. On the one hand, matter is truly nothing: it is inchoate essence, with no place in being on its own. On the other, matter has an entitative character. Ulrich writes, "the question of the perspective of 'what-always-already-is' reappears with the question of matter's entity. For whatever is observed of matter can be attributed to essence. It is exactly here that Suárez cannot understand the structure of substance."[40] He cannot see that although a being is truly one, that unity is not threatened if there is more in its oneness than its oneness, so to speak. So matter, in order to be real must be an entity, and in order for a thing to be one, matter cannot really be different from any of the constituents in substance. Matter must therefore be just the beginning of essence: *pars essentiae*, inchoate essence.

In order to reconcile these seemingly irreconcilable facets of matter, Suárez has recourse to God. Because Suárez accepts *creatio ex nihilo*, he asserts that matter is created by God, and exists in composite, even though the nature of the composition necessarily remains unclear. The fact that Suárez's metaphysics is incoherent does not seem to bother Suárez even though—and especially because—God is responsible for it.

Suárez knows that matter must have some existence, because it is created by God, but as we have said, for Suárez, to have existence is synonymous with the statement that "it has real essence."[41] Ulrich calls this absolute identification of existence (being) with the essence "a dead-end."[42] By identifying substance simply with essence, the only way we can know substance is in the horizon of reality. There is literally nowhere to go, metaphysically speaking.

This is what happens when we speculatively halt the *Subsistenzbewegung* at the ontological moment of reality. In this closed horizon of reality, in order for matter to exist, it must have some sort of entity, so Suárez calls it "an *entitas*

---

40. "Und so taucht die Perspektive des ‚Immer-schon-seins' bei der Frage nach der Entität der Materie wieder auf. Denn die Materie läßt sich, was immer beachtet werden muß, auf die Essenz zurückkritisieren. Genau so, wie Suárez bei der Konstruktion der Substanzkonstitution nicht verstehen konnte" ("Inwiefern," 31).

41. "Die Materie muß grundsätzlich fähig sein zu sein. Das ist nach Suárez gleichbedeutend mit der Aussage: habet essentiam realem" ("Inwiefern," 32).

42. "Die essentia realis zeigt sich hier genau so wie bei der Konstruktion der Substanzkonstitution als Sackgasse" ("Inwiefern," 32).

simplex."⁴³ It is *simplex* only because it is the *primum subjectum*, not because of anything of which matter is the analogue or image. Thus, says Ulrich, "matter is essentially an incomplete entity with its own species: essentia inchoata per modum potentia."⁴⁴ But if matter has its own species, then it must have its own proper perfection, which consists in its being able to take on and shed forms without its proper perfection being distorted or changed. Thus matter gains an agency here, rather than being pure potency or pure openness to form. And, ironically this move undermines the very unity of the substance, on which Suárez seems to base his entire metaphysics: substance is not one! It has within it at least two different perfections: form and matter. True unity is lost to Suárez precisely because he cannot see that multiplicity and unity are not opposed.

There is still the fact of matter as *potentia pura* to be reckoned with. For Suárez this is as simple as saying that matter has no form: because matter does not have form as its intrinsic act, it can be pure possibility. "Matter is therefore," according to Ulrich, "only and precisely potentia pura because it has an entitative character and is constituted in its own species."⁴⁵ Thus matter and form are defined over-against each other, each only being itself because the other is excluded. Again the real unity of substance is destroyed. There is no admirable exchange between matter and form—form allowing matter to be and form shining through matter, showing forth in the accidents of substance. Matter for Suárez "is simply always already complete . . . it is as it has always already been."⁴⁶

This seems to present a problem for the overwhelmingly traditional way of understanding matter: as principle of individuation. According to Suárez, matter already has a certain kind of essence and existence, and thus is already individualized: How then could it act as individuating principle when combined with form? Ulrich writes that for Suárez "prime matter is in the thing itself individual and the ground of [the thing's] unity and individuality is its

---

43. Ulrich writes, "Because of the determined horizon, Suárez is obliged to say that prime matter is essentielly an entitas simplex" ("Durch die festgelegten Horizont genötigt muß Suárez sagen, daß die materia prima esentiell eine entitas simplex ist" "Inwiefern," 32.) Ulrich is quoting Suárez, *Disp.* XIII.4.9 when he writes that "prime matter is an entitas simplex." See n36 above.

44. "So ist also die Materie wesenhaft eine inkomplete Entität, mit einer eigenen species: essentia inchoata per modum potentiae" ("Inwiefern," 32).

45. "Die Materie ist also nur deshalb und gerade deshalb potentia pura weil sie einen entitativen Charakter hat und in ihrer Materiespezies konstituiert ist" ("Inwiefern," 36). Emphasis added.

46. "sie ist einfach schon immer fertig . . . sie ist, wie sie immer schon wirklich war" ("Inwiefern," 42).

entity per seipsam, as prime matter, as it is always already reality."[47] Matter then has a pre-existent and individuated reality apart from form. "The individuality of matter is not constituted with reference to [any] specific form; rather it is individuated in itself, it has an indifferent relation to all forms."[48] Matter thus is not presupposed by that which precedes it, and matter does not emerge from form in the *Subsistenzbewegung*, but rather for Suárez, matter seems to pre-exist form and relate, as he says, "indifferently" to it.

This leads us finally to Ulrich's last and most serious charge against Suárez and his metaphysics: that Suárez inverts the order of act and potency, thereby making it impossible for us to see being (*esse*) and ultimately God. Though Suárez considers matter to be, at least nominally, potency, he also considers it to be substantial in some way, as we have shown with Ulrich above. Its substantiality consists in the fact that it is not really potency but rather inchoate essence, and thus matter cannot really be accident and cannot really be other than form. It lies within the same order as form, even if it is only form's first stages. Thus, says Ulrich, "Form and matter are immediate to each other. There is at the bottom of matter no potency which can be conveyed between it and the form that the form was not already."[49] Matter is not truly an-other to form, and therefore neither can give anything to the other: there is no relationship of gift at the heart of being. Matter is merely the first stage of essence, and form is more or less a perfecting condition for matter, the nature of which is to take on and shed different forms while remaining the same.

Thus we see that by pushing matter into the metaphysical distance, a Suarezian metaphysics actually ends up in a sense letting itself by ruled by a pseudo-subsistent matter. Ultimately, Suárez does admit that matter is more dependent on form than vice versa,[50] but, "the causality of form can be nothing other than actual unification of form with matter."[51] Form does not mediate the *actus essendi* to matter, rather, form and matter come together in order to construct a substance which then attains existence. At best, matter can be

47. "Die materia prima ist in der Sache selbst individuell und das Fundament dieser ihrer Einheit und Ungeteiltheit ist ihre Entität per seipsam, wie sie eben immer schon Realität ist" ("Inwiefern," 51).

48. "Nicht der Bezug zu dieser specifischen Form macht die Individualität der Materie aus, sondern sie ist per seipsam individuiert, sie hat indifferenten Bezug zu allen Formen" ("Inwiefern," 50).

49. "Form und materie sind unmittelbar zueinander. Es gibt am Grunde keine Potenz, die zwischen ihr und der Form vermitteln würde" ("Inwiefern," 57).

50. *Disp.* XV.8.19: ergo magis per se pendet materia a forma quam forma a materia (quoted in "Inwiefern," 62n131).

51. "Die Kausalität der Form kann nichts sein außer die aktuale Vereinigung der Form mit der Materie" ("Inwiefern," 58). Ulrich points to *Disp.* XV.6.7 here.

interpreted as equal to form as its counterpart, but then we recall that matter is for Suárez "the beginning of reality," and it seems as though matter is actually ontologically primary. This inversion pervades Suárez's entire metaphysical framework.

We are reminded here of the temptations of thought Ulrich warns against so often in *Homo Abyssus*: giving subsistence to that which does not properly have it, especially for the sake of attempting to elevate it, only leads to an evacuation of that thing's proper nature, an incapacity for real unity, and violence at the very heart of being. We have seen all three of these in Suárez's metaphysics, wherein existence itself is equal to substantiality, leading, ultimately, to matter as substantial in itself. A pseudo-subsistent matter, however, leads us to similar places as a pseudo-subsistent being: there is no *esse creatum*, which grounds and unites all creatures, and which gives itself so completely that another is presupposed within its giving; rather, reality and being are taken for granted, and there is no capacity within this schema for true otherness. In a Suarezian metaphysics, there is no act of being, but this means that *esse* has no room truly to give itself—to mediate—and if *esse* cannot truly give itself, then matter cannot truly be itself.

Ulrich on Scotus

Ulrich next gives his attention to Duns Scotus, who he understands to be Suárez's dialectical opposite. While Suárez cannot see past the ontological moment of reality, Scotus has no framework other than the ontological moment of ideality. Interestingly enough, however, both arrive at the same conclusion about matter: it has an entitative character. And thus a metaphysics entirely encapsulated in the moment of ideality ends up succumbing to the same temptations as one stuck in the dead end of an isolated moment of reality, with similar consequences: a lack of unity, violence at the heart of being, and an inversion of act and potency.

Similar to Suárez, Scotus lacks a sense of *esse* as the first of all created effects and the *actus essendi*, and therefore also lacks any sense of mediation or participation. Unlike Suárez, Scotus's metaphysical schema does not rely on reality being "posited," but rather concentrates on how it comes to be. This coming to be, however, is defined, we might say, in an entirely horizontal fashion: Scotus proposes what Ulrich calls a "vector"[52] for creation: the *possibile*, the *creabile*, the *creatum*: what is possible, what is creatable, what is created. This vector is defined entirely by the horizon of ideality: there is no sense here

---

52. "Inwiefern," 72. The word is *Spanne*.

of the fullness of being, or plenitude poured out into creatures in analogical ways. Again, to use the language of the previous chapter, if Suárez can only see that being is *given*, and therefore blind to what it means that reality is a gift or has a gift-nature, Scotus only sees *being*. For Scotus, there is only being, though it be, as we mentioned above with Gilson, a being utterly defined by essence. Scotus's lack of any sense of a vertical outpouring of *esse creatum* to subsistent creatures traps him in the horizon of ideality, which means that he too cannot see that reality has room, as it were, for transcendence in both the horizontal and vertical planes. Unlike Suárez, however, Scotus does not see reality as "simply there." Rather, Scotus ends up understanding creation as horizontal extension of God himself, albeit in an infinitely smaller way, which as we will see, ends, like Suárez, with an entitative conception of matter.

As mentioned earlier, Ulrich characterizes Scotus's metaphysics as "Greek."[53] De la Tour writes that according to Ulrich, "in the horizon of the Platonic approach to metaphysics, the idea is conceived as the truth of beings," therefore "being is 'located' in the essentiell."[54] Being therefore cannot be thought in its superessentiality in this so-called Greek metaphysics. There is some sense of participation or mediation in a Greek metaphysics, but if the idea is the "location" of being, then the question would be how and to what being is mediated. Ulrich understands Greek metaphysics to answer this problem by making matter into a something: it becomes the "what" to which being is mediated. Again, from de la Tour: "The idea is thought in relief against matter and does not have in itself the power to reveal the otherness of matter. The path of mediation of this otherness is thereby paradoxically 'transnihilated': matter is radicalized as pure potentiality—therefore is thought a nonbeing, i.e., not finally an-other to real beings."[55] The idea or essence can then in a way only gain its superessentiality by being participated in by matter, but in such a way that matter must be assumed to be a thing—i.e., not emerging from a superessentiality that is always already given. We will see shortly how this unfolds in Scotus's metaphysics, but for now it is sufficient to note

---

53. This characterization appears in "Inwiefern," 82–86. See also *GA*, 77–83, for an analysis of this claim.

54. "Im Horizont des platonische Ansatzes der Metaphysik wird die Idee als das in Wahrheit Seiende konzipiert" and "Das Sein ist im Essentiellen ‚angesiedelt'" (*GA*, 77).

55. "Die Idee ist in Abgrenzung gegen die Materie gedacht und hat nicht in sich die Mächtigkeit der Aufhebung der Andersheit der Materie. Der Weg zur Vermittlung dieser Andersheit der Materie wird paradoxerweise dadurch ‚durchnichtet', dass sie radikilisiert wird, die Materie als reine Potentialität—also als ein Nichtseiendes, d.h. schließlich kein ‚Anderes' zum wahrhaft Seienden—gedacht wird" (*GA*, 78).

that when Ulrich calls Scotus's metaphysics "Greek," he means that it identifies being with essence almost completely.[56]

One of the major differences, according to Ulrich, between the way Thomas and Scotus approach the question of creation is where each begins his approach. Thomas, writes de la Tour, "begins with existing beings and asks how God knows them; Scotus proceeds from the *intellectus divinus*—from the ideality of God—and asks how the ideas are given to the *intellectus divinus*—initially independent from the reality of the things of which the ideas are." The question of causality then is completely transformed: for Thomas, divine knowledge is always already included within the frame of the question, whereas for Scotus, says de la Tour, "the question of divine knowledge is isolated and initially separated from causality."[57]

The essences, or natures, as Scotus calls them, are that which the divine intellect knows, but it does not know them as creatures, rather as objects of the divine knowledge. This means that, similar to Suárez's *essentia realis*, Scotus's *natura* prescinds from the question of actual being. Rather, the only condition Scotus sets for a nature to be an object of being is that it is *non repugnat esse*,[58] that is, any being which is not contradictory. *Esse* thus means anything which is not self-contradictory, which, importantly, includes possibility. Indeed, for Scotus, "esse possibile and esse intelligible (or esse objectum) are coextensive."[59]

---

56. Again, I must prescind here from the question of whether this analysis is totally sufficient to either a Scotist or Platonic metaphysics, though I do think there may be room, so to speak, in a Platonic metaphysics for a more flexible understanding of being, though of course not the superessential, perfect, and infinite *esse creatum* that Thomas understands. For more on Plato's understanding of being, see Schindler, *Plato's Critique of Impure Reason*, esp. "Coda: Restoring Appearances," 283–336. Scotus, on the other hand, seems to radicalize the idea that being = essence, simply. For a short but very clear article on this point, see Hoffman, "Duns Scotus on the Origin of the Possibles in the Divine Intellect."

57. "Während etwas Thomas von Aquin beim existierende Seienden ansetzt und fragt, wie Gott es erkennt, geht Scotus vom *intellectus divinus*—von der Idealität Gottes—aus und fragt, wie die Ideen für den *intellectus divinus* gegeben sind—zunächst unabhängig von der Realität der Dinge, deren Ideen sind." And "ist die Frage nach dem Erkennen Gottes isoliert und von der Kausalität zunächst getrennt" (*GA*, 84).

58. *Ordinatio* I, dist. 43, q. unica, n. 7.

59. "so dass für Scotus das esse possibile und das esse intelligibile (oder esse objectum) co-extensiv sind" (*GA*, 85). See also Hoffman, "Duns Scotus." In it he writes, "Because God knows every creature is compatible with existence, every possible creature has intelligible being or cognized being in God's intellect, . . . what is intelligible and what is possible is coextensive. The objective being that creatures enjoy as objects of the divine knowledge and the possible being that they enjoy insofar as they have real existence are only formally distinct" (364).

What differentiates possible being from actual being is then only whether the *voluntas divina* selects or decides that a possible nature should really exist and then is "really created by the divine will, therefore placed into existence,"[60] writes de la Tour. Not only does this introduce a radical separation between the divine intellect and the divine will, it also demonstrates that Scotus's understanding of creation is entirely within the ideal horizon: there is no otherness presupposed here, only a distinction between what is posited into existence or not. Everything is entirely defined by God's ideality. Another way to put this, using Ulrich's language: the moment of necessity or need is not, in a sense, given to creation, that is, placed in its own hands. Rather, the necessity of being "is entirely located in the moment of ideality."[61] The "necessary sense of being," as Ulrich puts it, is not an outpouring of what has always already been given, but a placing of a nature, which in itself is indifferent, into existence by God. Being is then indifferent, as it were, to itself, and being is nothing but essence. Scotus's metaphysical world is radically different than Thomas's.

If there is no *Subsistenzbewegung* or anything like it in Scotus's metaphysics, nor any sense that creation participates in its own coming to be through the mediation of *esse non subsistens*, then we might ask, as we did with Suárez, what unity looks like for Scotus, especially with regard to substance. Again, however, we come up against an understanding of unity that does not look like unity. As Gilson points out, though Scotus does not completely deny a distinction between *esse* and essence, he does collapse being and essence to the point of identity, which means substance cannot be the fruit of a union between *esse* and essence (a union that is so perfect that the difference does seem to fall away at some points), because *esse* has nothing to give essence, and vice versa. They are already the same. There is no prior unity of all creation, the differences within which are held together precisely in the mediation of *esse creatum*. Ulrich writes that "for Scotus, the entities which constitute substance have their own being."[62] We then run into the same problem here as we did with the unity of a Suarezian substance: if each metaphysical constituent has its own being, either (a) there is no real substantial unity, as one of the constituents must take over the others, or (b) the constituents must not really be different in the first place—that is, just different gradations of the same thing.

---

60. "durch die göttliche Allmacht real erschaffen, also in die Existenz gesetzt" (*GA*, 86).

61. "ist doch das Moment der Notwendigkeit des Seins ganz in das Moment der Idealität verschoben" (*GA*, 89).

62. "Genau so wie bei Suárez, so haben auch bei Scotus die Entitäten, die die Substanz konstituieren, ihr eigenes Sein" ("Inwiefern," 79a). Note: "Inwiefern" has two page 79s, and this is the first. I will refer to them as 79a and 79b.

Suárez ultimately tries to resolve this problem in the latter way with his definition of matter as *pars essentiae*. We will see that something similar happens in a Scotist metaphysics.

Scotus affirms matter to be real for at least two reasons: the first is his belief in and affirmation of *creatio ex nihilo*. The second is that he needs something to explain generation and corruption. Scotus contends that substance qua substance cannot change, and so he must place the generation and corruption that we encounter into some ground, and that ground certainly cannot be God. But see already the position in which this puts us (and matter): substances do not change, matter does. The two are already conceived apart from each other. Ulrich writes, "as to the questions of whether things are given over to generation and corruption and if we find a positive entity that we can call matter, and that this positive entity is distinguished from form and has its own being—Scotus answers 'yes.'"[63] So we see that Scotus, starting from the enclosed horizon of ideality, ends up in the same place as Suárez: matter is a thing.

The conception of matter's entitative character does however differ from a Suarezian understanding. Remember that for Scotus, in order for anything to exist, it must already be in the divine intellect as *possibile*. This means that matter too must already exist in some sense in the divine intellect. But if matter pre-exists, in any sense, then it is only—as all other things—as *possibilis esse*.

Ulrich understands the entitative character of matter in Scotus's system in terms of the difference between *potentia objectiva* and *potentia subjectiva*. According to Ulrich, for Scotus, a *potentia objectiva* is the *creabile* in his vector of creation. That is to say, a *potentia objectiva* is a potency that is to be created, so it is not just *possibile* in the divine intellect, but *creabile*. However, says Scotus, before something is actually created, it is technically nothing, even if it some sense exists in the divine intellect.

This means, according to Scotus, matter cannot be *potentia objectiva*, because matter cannot be nothing because it must be able to "receive" form in order for substances to come to be. Since what is *potentia objectiva*—the *creabile*—is itself form, it cannot therefore be the subject of form. Thus, matter, according to Scotus, is *potentia subjectiva*, "that is, a subject whose potency is for form,"[64] writes Ulrich.

---

63. "Auf die Frage, ob sich in den Dinge, die der generatio und corruptio anheim gegeben sind, eine positive Entität findet, die wir Materie nennen können und die als positive Entität von der Form unterschieden ist und ein eigenes Seins hat, antwortet Scotus mit ‚ja'" ("Inwiefern," 79b). Ulrich refers to *Op. Ox.* 1.II.d.12, q.1, n1 here.

64. The full quote: "Die Materie kann nicht eine potentia objectiva sein als Subjekt

The issue of reception or receptivity is key here: Scotus understands that matter is receptive to form, but what he cannot see is that matter simply *is* receptivity and that this very receptivity is generated by the radical giving of being in the first place—that is to say, that being is given so radically in the act of creation that it is given the capacity to (pro-)create matter. The gift of being is not just a static (once-and-done) gift, but rather the power, as it were, to presuppose another in one's own dynamism. Matter, for Ulrich, is the apex (or nadir, looked at in a different light) of this presupposed otherness, precisely because all it "is," so to speak, is receptivity. Scotus cannot see receptivity without a subject to be receptive. Thus being must in a certain sense be in itself first, before being receptive. And so too matter, if it is real.

Though Scotus, as Ulrich says, approaches the metaphysics of creation from the horizon of ideality, he does only from this horizon, and thus his view of *esse*—being—is skewed. Existence for Scotus is attained in the moving of a form from *possibile* in the divine intellect to *creatum* by the divine will. *Esse* is not the fullness of being and actuality, to which the Creator gives everything gratuitously, thus allowing creation to participate in its own creation, that is, to become co-principle in its own causality. Matter's role as pure potency gives evidence of precisely this co-causality. Ulrich writes,

> When the existential act of perfection is firmly held in view [an entirely different concept of matter comes to light]. In that case, the terminus of creation, which we are calling the constitution of substance, remains being. However, existence as the specific act of perfection upon which form follows is so directly communicated to the substance (=esse est intimum cuilibet), that it allows Thomas to understand matter as potentia pura.[65]

This is to say that the Creator holds nothing back from creation—not even the capacity for creation, as it were, to receive itself. God does not need to bring into being a matter separate from the rest of creation, separate from substance, in order for substance to be. Rather, the act of creation is so radically a gift that

---

der Form. Sie könnte die Form aufnehmen. Was ein creabile oder in potentia objectiva ist, dass kann nicht Subjekt der Form sein, folglich muß die Materie ein creatum sein. Sie muß eine Sache sein. Sie ist potentia subjectiva, d.h., ein Subjekt, das Potenz ist für die Form" ("Inwiefern," 80). See *Op. Ox.* 1.II.d.12, q.1, n10.

65. "Daß vom thomistischen Konstruktionsansatz her eine ganz andere Möglichket besteht Materie begriff zu erhellen: wenn der existentielle Perfektionsakt ins Auge gefaßt wird. Dann bleibt der Terminus der creatio, sagen wir der Substanzkonstitution, schon das Sein, aber die Existenz als specifizischer Perfektionsakt, der der Form folgt, ist so unmittelbar der Substanz mitgeteilt (=esse est intimum cuilibet), daß Thomas es sich erlauben darf, die Materia als potentia pura zu fassen" ("Inwiefern," 81).

the reception (and further pro-creation) of the gift is given in the creation of *esse creatum*. Things are not just given, rather the capacity to receive (which itself is a capacity of the triune God) is given, and we see precisely this capacity in matter as unfolded from and emerging out of *esse* in its *Subsistenzbewegung*. If matter is an entity—even an entity formed precisely and only to receive—all of this is lost. Creation, rather than participating in its own creation, rather than having the capacity to receive and therefore co-create itself, becomes indifferent to the fact that it is created. To approach creation only through the horizon of ideality leads to an assumption of all of creation into divine ideality: creation is no longer really other.

Scotus has an a priori approach to understanding how substance comes to be. In his metaphysics, what exists in the divine intellect and must be enacted by the divine will is nature and nothing else. However, Scotus knows that substance is a composite and so matter must enter into the equation somehow. It does so by being already created by God, but not as a substance (simply because God has deigned that it will not be a substance by itself). So matter is not a substance for Scotus, but does have some sort of entitative character. Thus, says Ulrich, for Scotus, "matter is one of the causes of being."[66] We encounter here again the inversion of act and potency: matter is a cause of being rather than the other way around. Indeed, matter has its being before it ever emerges from and unites with form.

The unity of substance would seem to suffer here, but for Scotus, writes Ulrich, "that matter and form are different and distinct entities means nothing for the thing itself. Each ens per se is an unum, be it simple or composite."[67] That is to say a substance for Scotus simply is a unity because God has made it so. He does not see the problem with two entities become one because it has come directly from the divine will. Though Scotus gives more attention to the idea that matter and form are truly distinct from each other than Suárez does, Ulrich understands this not to be from the view of a radical understanding of being as gift, but simply in an a priori way. Ulrich writes that "Scotus splits [matter and form] out of a deep-seated concern for their entitative difference. He wants to assign each its own entity, and does in view of his a priori way of relating to quantities."[68] There is no understanding of a mediative or participatory unity of creation here.

---

66. "Für Scotus ist die Materie eine der Ursachen des Seins" ("Inwiefern," 86). See *Op. Ox.* 1.II.d.12, q.1, n11.

67. "Daß Materie und Form unterschiedene und verschiedene Entitäten sind tut nichts zur Sache. Jedes ens per se ist ein unum, sei es nun einfache oder zusammengesetzt" ("Inwiefern," 87). See *Op. Ox.* 1.I.d.12, q.1, n13.

68. "Scotus trennt sie aus den tiefgreifenden Anliegen der entitativen Unterscheidung

Because of his entitative understanding of metaphysical constituents, Scotus needs different entities in order for substance to come to be. "Precisely the radical entitative difference between matter and form is the ground for Scotus, for the immediate possibility of the unity. Scotus needs therefore two entitative forms."[69] For Thomas, says Ulrich, form follows upon and emerges from *esse* in *esse*'s *Subsistenzbewegung*, and the unity of substance is rooted ultimately in the unity of actuality in *esse non subsistens*, while for Scotus, the unity of a substance is attained in the horizontal joining of two incomplete entities. Substance is a product.

Again we see with Scotus, as we did with Suárez, a violence—or least, opposition—at the heart of things. And as with Suárez, we see an inversion of the order of act and potency. Scotus contends that God must have distinct ideas for what is actually distinct. And if matter is formally distinct from form then it must have its own idea. Scotus avers that God can make matter without form because everything God can create by means of a secondary cause, he can also create unmediatedly.[70] But this means the unity of matter and form is somewhat arbitrary. "There is no necessary connection between matter and form," writes Ulrich, "because matter is potency for form in general and not necessarily connected to a particular form. It needs form only generally."[71] Additionally, because matter exists in God as an idea, it must be the case that matter has a higher degree of being than accidents, because accidents do not pre-exist in God; accidents, however, actually subsist in the substance, and so there is an inversion of a Thomist understanding of matter here. Matter is the subject or place of form, and in order to be receptive—again, in Scotus's entirely horizontal view of creation—matter must precede form. Scotus does affirm that matter's degree of being is lower than that of form, but this seems to have nothing intrinsically to do with matter's (or form's) dependency on or relation to *esse*. Ulrich writes that for Scotus,

> Esse is the effectus imperfectissimus. Therefore [matter's] degree of dependency cannot be deduced from [esse]. This sentence is entirely incomprehensible for Thomas because for him esse is the

---

heraus. Er will ihnen je eine eigene Entität zuschreiben. Er kann das aus den apriorische bezogene Entität Ansatz heraus" ("Inwiefern," 88).

69. "Gerade die radikale entitative Unterscheidung von Materie und Form begründet bei Scotus die unmittelbare Möglichkeit ihrer Vereinigung. Scotus braucht dazu zwei entative Größen" ("Inwiefern," 88). See *Op. Ox.* 1.II.d.12, q.1, n16.

70. See *Op. Ox.* 1.II.d.12, q.2, nn3–4.

71. "Es gibt keine notwendige Verbindung zwischen Materie und Form, da die Materie in Potenz ist für Form überhaupt und nicht notwendig mit einer partikulären Form verbunden ist. Sie bedarf der Form nur im allgemeinen" ("Inwiefern," 91).

perfectio perfectionem. This is why Thomas can conceive of matter even in its unconditional dependency on form, because [matter] exists entirely within the field of the necessary sense of being. For Scotus, it is otherwise. He says of matter: non tamen plus est dependens, imo minus.[72]

This is rather remarkable, and inverts act and potency. Matter, for Scotus, is the least dependent creature. Potency effectively becomes actuality: sufficient in itself and prior to act. Notice too the connotation this metaphysics imparts on dependency: namely that it is bad, or at the very least, undesirable. The least number of steps necessary between a creature and the Creator elevates the creature's dignity. Secondary causality, mediation, is therefore in this light not a giving of giving, but rather a seemingly necessary—if not evil, then neutral—step in creation, rather than a revelation of what it means to be a creature. The fullness of perfection is not here given to creation, which therefore allows creation to participate in its own self-actualization as a unified whole. The participatory structure of creation does not reveal the nature of God, only that creation is essentially (*essentielly*) lower than God.

Lastly, Scotus's metaphysics of creation also leads to problems in understanding individuation, as is the case with Suárez, albeit in a different way. Scotus's idealism has no capacity for the difference and connection between singular and universal: it is literally indifferent to these categories. Ulrich writes:

> The vector of the possibile, creabile, creatum is also the vector of the natura communis, which is indifferent to universality and singularity, i.e., to the determined, concrete, existing, individual nature. The vector of the possibile, creabile, creatum therefore also delineates the original movement and mediation of the nature in its individuation. The vector of possibile, creabile, creatum is therefore simultaneously the principle of individuation. The creatum is the individually constituted substance. Individuation is not therefore immediately in the nature.[73]

---

72. "Sie hat einen höheren Seinsgrad als das Accidenz. Dieser ihr Seinsgrad liegt also niedriger als der der Form. Aber das esse ist der effectus imperfectissimus. Daher läßt sich von ihm aus nicht auf den Grad der Abhängigkeit schließen. Ein Satz, dar für Thomas ganz unverständlich ist; ist doch das esse für ihn die perfectio perfectionum. Deshalb kann Thomas aus die Materie in ihrer unbedingten Abhängigkeit von der Form konzipieren, steht sie doch ganz im Kraftfeld der Sinn-Notwendigkeit des Seins. Für Scotus ist das anders. Er sagt von der Materie: Non tamen plus est dependens, imo minus" ("Inwiefern," 91). See *Op. Ox.* 1.II.d.12, q.2, n10.

73. "Die Spanne possibile, creabile, creatum ist auch die Spanne von der natura communis, die indifferent ist zur Universalität und Singularität, d.h. zur determinierten, konkret existierenden indivduellen Natur. Die Spanne possibile, creabile, creatum

The principle of individuation—here, the only principle that allows the being actually to exist—must then lie within the vector of the *possibile, creabile, creatum*. As possibile and creabile however, the nature is indifferent to universality and singularity, which means individuation only comes about in the *creatum*. The principle of individuation then, writes Ulrich, "is simultaneously the principle of the being of the creatum." Thus, the individuation of a thing is not due to matter, but what Scotus calls haecceity.[74] Haecceity, however, just means the essence qua existence. "Haecceity," writes Ulrich, "is not newly added to the form: it is only the ultimate reality of the form: ista nunquam sumitur a forma addita, sed praecise ab ultima realitate formae."[75] In fact, "the individual entity as such is not a new form but the actus ultimus of the form."[76] Individuation, and in turn, existence, is nothing new, as it were; it is simply the result of the divine will deciding to place a possible into existence.

Thus we see with Scotus that by enclosing the moment of ideality in on itself, we end up with almost the exact same problems as Suárez: an entitative matter, violence at the heart of being, an inversion of act and potency, and perhaps most importantly, a complete misunderstanding of the radicality of the act of creation. In order to escape the dialectic of the moments of reality and ideality, Ulrich says that we must see the meaning and necessity of the moment of bonicity. The moment of bonicity, writes Ulrich, "illuminates the

---

umzeichnet also auch die ursprüngliche Bewegung und Vermittlung der Natur in ihre Individuation. Die Spanne possibile, creabile, creatum ist also zugleich Individuationsprinzip. Das creatum ist die individuelle konstituierte Substanz. Die Individuation liegt also nicht unmittelbar in der natura" ("Inwiefern," 93).

74. Gilson writes this of Scotus's understanding of haecceity: "In Scotism, as in Thomism, there is an act of even the form in concrete reality, and, in both doctrines, that act of the form is not itself a form. In the metaphysics of Thomas Aquinas, it is existence; in that of Duns Scotus, it is 'thisness' (*hecceitas*) that is *ultima actualitas formae*. The Scotist 'thisness' is not the cause of existence, but it is the unmistakable sign that the essence under consideration is now fit to exist; then, as a matter of fact, it does exist. Be it in God or in finite things, existence is a modality of being which belongs to a completely individualized essence. Whether they be such by themselves, which is the case of God alone, or they be such by another one, which is the case of all creatures, fully individualizes essences exist in their own right" (*BSP*, 94).

75. "So ist die Haecceitas keine neu hinzugefügte Foram: sie ist nur die ultima realitas formae: ista nunquam sumitur a forma addita, sed praecise ab ultima realitate formae" ("Inwiefern," 94). Ulrich quotes Scotus in n61 here: "Accipitur individuum, substantia et simul totum stricte prout includit existentia et tempus ut hic homo existens et hic lapis existens" (*Questions on the Metaphysics*. I.VIII.q.13, n19).

76. "Die individuelle Entität als solche ist zwar nicht eine neue Form, aber der actus ultimus der Form" ("Inwiefern," 94).

intimate heart of the absolutely necessary sense of being."[77] The moment of bonicity secures both the gift-nature of creation, and its corollary: matter as an image of the Good. To further demonstrate this we will, with Ulrich, turn to Thomas.

Ulrich writes that both Suárez and Scotus "circle around the Thomistic framework without expressly integrating it."[78] In other words, both Suárez and Scotus pick up some of the pieces of Thomas's metaphysics of creation, but neither see the whole radically enough, which leads each of them, in his own way, to come to an essentially entitative understanding of matter, leading to the problems enumerated above. Thomas's *potentia pura* is transformed into an entity for both Suárez and Scotus because of their dismissal or misunderstanding of Thomas's understanding of *esse creatum* as radically given.

Thomas

It is the radicality of *esse*'s givenness that allows us to understand matter in itself: as *potentia pura*. According to Ulrich this radicality is secured in the ontological moment of bonicity, a moment that neither Suárez nor Scotus sees, but which a Thomistic framework reveals. Notice that Ulrich then sees the moment of bonicity and matter as intrinsically connected: without the prior, the latter cannot be seen in itself, as it were. Only the Thomistic understanding of *esse* as *simplex et completum sed non subsistens* reaches far enough, as it were, to comprehend matter in its nothingness. This understanding of *esse* as the first of all created effects, which then gives its "self" away always already such that there is no self outside of the subsisting substances, is the logic of creation: being is gift, not just as a thing passed from one party to another, but to its very depths, being is the giving of the capacity to give. This capacity, in Ulrich's language, is the presupposition of another: a presupposition so radical that it allows another to come to be.

Recall that in chapter 2, we stated that the non-subsistence of created *esse* is precisely what allows *esse* to be the *similitudo divinae bonitatis* (though of course the reverse is true as well). And therefore it is precisely being's nothingness that allows it to give its perfection to beings themselves so that beings may be subsistent, that is to say, being's very nothingness allows it to be pure mediation. Therefore, for Ulrich, the non-subsistence of *esse* is just as

---

77. "der Herzmitte absoluter Sinn-Notwendigkeit des Seins aufleuchten" ("Inwiefern," 95).

78. "Während es sich bei Suárez und Scotus um die Ansätze in der Realität und der Idealität handelt, umgreift der thomistische Entwurf beide, ohne sie ausdrücklich einzubeziehen" ("Inwiefern," 97).

important for the subsistence and existence of individual beings as *esse*'s being complete and simple. Indeed, the perfection of created *esse* is not possible, so to speak, without its being non-subsistent, that is to say, without its being nothing. Being's transnihilation is exactly where this is brought to light.

By introducing the term transnihilation, Ulrich highlights that the very nothingness of being, if we may put it this way, is being transferred through or to individual beings. In the *Subsistenzbewegung*, *esse* gives its actuality to individual beings, yes, but it also gives another property: its very nothingness. Non-subsistence does not just *make possible* the perfection of *esse*, it *is* a perfection of *esse*. Transnihilation is therefore the name of *esse*'s imparting that very perfection to every individual being. This analogous transference of the perfection of non-subsistence reaches its apex, in a certain sense, in matter. Because matter does not—cannot—exist under its own power, so to speak, and can only ever be seen from the point of view of that which has existence—that is, substance—we can identify its non-substantiality more quickly than any other aspect of being—perhaps even *esse* itself. Indeed, matter's status, so to speak, of being "real" and yet not existing in its own right is perhaps a privileged image of the non-substantiality of being. Matter then is a privileged image of the very perfection of created being.

It is precisely matter's (literally) indeterminate status, however, that leads to its being ignored or misinterpreted time and again. It is sometimes, as we saw in chapter 1, relegated only to the realm of individuation, as opposed to being understood as a key to understanding being and its perfection. Or matter is understood to be what is really real in itself, and given a status that ultimately destroys its integrity.[79] Neither of these gets it right.

Matter is central to the whole of Ulrich's metaphysics of creation. The attention paid to transnihilation—indeed, the recognition of being's transnihilation at all—is evidence of this. Ulrich understands that the very non-subsistence of *esse creatum* is itself a perfection of being. This is what Ulrich repeatedly points to when he refers us to the temptations of thought: if we do not understand the non-subsistence of being itself to be at the core of creaturely perfection (and therefore at the core of its perfection qua gift), then we lapse, in many different ways, into the temptation of substantializing *esse non subsistens*. We saw a few of these paths—or rather, dead-ends—in the

---

79. This, it seems to me, is one of the main problems of the modern scientific method: It treats the creature as if it were mere epiphenomenon of what it is "really real"—that is, matter, though matter as treated as if itself were "something" rather than the pure receptivity that it is (so ultimately, not matter at all). The modern scientific method is built upon, we might say, a forgetfulness of the creature in the name of matter, but in forgetting the subsisting creature—that is, what actually allows matter to be revealed—it forgets matter as well, making it to be something it is not: pseudo-substantial.

last chapter. Put perhaps oversimply, any attempt to substantialize *esse non subsistens* results in a pseudo-subsistent creature that can neither receive itself nor give itself. There can be no such thing as a metaphysics of being as gift.

What, then, is matter? We established last chapter that matter indeed comes forth from *esse non subsistens*, as must be the case if God does really create out of nothing. And in the first chapter we demonstrated that matter is potency, which itself contributes to the form of creation—and the substances therein—while simultaneously emerging from *esse*. All of these point more or less to the function of matter in creation, which is important, to be sure. But the question of what matter is must also be a question of why it exists—or, put another way, what matter reveals. We point here to Thomas's assertion that God "produced many and diverse creatures, that what was wanting to one in the representation of the divine goodness might be supplied by another."[80] Our question then, is what representation of the divine goodness matter supplies.

According to Ulrich, matter brings to light the gift of otherness in a way that no other created effect can. Transnihilation, i.e., the *Subsistenzbewegung* with respect to being's non-subsistence, demonstrates that non-subsistence is a perfection of being, a perfection that goes below being itself, so to speak, to matter. The non-subsistence of being is indeed a gift, because without non-subsistence, *esse creatum* would be nothing other than God. Matter demonstrates the gift that non-subsistence is. In transnihilation, the non-subsistence of *esse creatum* then translates into creation—into substances—as potency. Substances are subsistent, whereas *esse* is not, but substances are not infinite like *esse*. They are also comprised of potency, or matter. Were substances both subsistent and infinite, they could be nothing other than the being of God himself. This means that substances would not exist. Potency in substances, just as non-subsistence in *esse*, is therefore the gift of otherness: of being something other than God. Or to put it more simply: the gift of being at all.

It thus becomes a little more clear why we stated that matter must be included within the aim of creation, that is of the *Subsistenzbewegung*, or being's transnihilation. If the act of creation is ultimately that which allows that which is other than God to be, then it would seem that matter is the silent but

---

80. "Hence we must say that the distinction and multitude of things come from the intention of the first agent, who is God. For He brought things into being in order that His goodness might be communicated to creatures, and be represented by them; and because His goodness could not be adequately represented by one creature alone, He produced many and diverse creatures, that what was wanting to one in the representation of the divine goodness might be supplied by another. For goodness, which in God is simple and uniform, in creatures is manifold and divided and hence the whole universe together participates the divine goodness more perfectly, and represents it better than any single creature whatever" (*ST* I.47.1.c).

necessary key to seeing creation as radically as possible. And matter is not then simply a necessary evil, or an indifferent "part" of creation, but rather a privileged image of the non-subsistence of being, and therefore a radical revelation of the nature of God and his goodness and generosity. We might say tentatively that matter's place in creation is the key to opening up fully a metaphysics of being as gift.

Ulrich describes Thomas as more "extreme" in his understanding of the creation of substance than either Suárez or Scotus. This extremity lies in the radicality of what is given to substance, or, put another way, to creation itself. This is nothing less than the fullness of being, the plenitude of actuality: *esse non subsistens*. Both Suárez and Scotus, in their respective errors, collapse *esse* and essence, albeit within the horizons of different ontological moments. Importantly, however, in this reduction of essence to *esse* (or vice versa), real difference in creation is precluded. The emergence of essence from *esse* is, as we saw, the first presupposition of the other for which creation is given the capacity.

Suárez only sees the *given* (and givenness changes to bare positing when one does not see what is given); Scotus only sees *being*. Thomas sees that *being is given*. He can do so because he regards the *ens* as the excessive reaffirmation of the gift of creation itself: the radical giving of the other to itself with nothing at all held back. "The terminus ens directly means the res but always at the same time refers to the act of existence,"[81] writes Ulrich. That is to say that nothing is held back from the *ens*: subsistence is given, as is the *res*'s own act of existence. The *essentia realis* does not possess substance simply of itself, indeed the opposite is true: *esse non subsistens* gives itself to the substance so completely that the substance possesses its own act of existence. And there is no competition between *esse non subsistens* and the *ens*, precisely because *ens* emerges from *esse non subsistens* and each has the capacity to give the other what it in some sense does not possess itself. Ulrich quotes Thomas's *Commentary* on Aristotle's *Metaphysics*: "ens is something having esse, but this is substance which subsists in itself."[82]

Unsurprisingly, Thomas's entire approach to *ens* must begin with *esse* and *esse* "as radical act of perfection."[83] This perfection consists precisely in *esse*'s being *non subsistens*—indeed, for Ulrich, *esse*'s non-subsistence is entirely the key to its perfection, that is, to *esse* being *completum et simplex*. It is only

---

81. "der Terminus ens direkt die res meint, aber immer und zugleich den Akt der Existenz mitbezeichnet" ("Inwiefern," 99).

82. *Commentary on the Meta* XII.1: Ens dicitur quasi esse habens; hoc autem solum est substantia, quae subsistit (quoted in "Inwiefern," 100).

83. "Die Konstruktion muß die Konstitution auf dieses esse als Perfektionsakt radikal zurückkritisieren" ("Inwiefern," 100).

because *esse* is non-subsistent that it can be, so to speak, non-competitive—and non-competitive with both God and the creature. And when we say that *esse* is non-competitive, we mean that its perfection is entirely gratuitous, in both directions as it were: the perfection given to it by God is radically gratuitous because God creates without hesitation—without guarding or protecting his own being.[84] But we also intend this in the other direction: that *esse* itself gratuitously gives its perfection away—again, in an entirely unjealous and unprotective fashion—to the subsistent creature. Thus, the excessive reaffirmation of the gift of creation itself, which occurs in the *ens*, is only possible in light of the gratuitous and non-subsistent nature of *esse*.

This gratuitous reaffirmation of the gift of creation found in *ens* is, we might tentatively say, a glimpse of the ontological moment of bonicity. Ulrich writes that the fundamental meaning of existence for Thomas is "that there is such a thing as reality, which comes to be through the actuality of reality: this is the really real"[85]—that is to say that the reality of the *ens* is its own existence, which it is totally, radically, given and secured in the moment of bonicity. It is here, in the moment of bonicity, where nothing is held back from *ens*—it is given completely to itself, its form, subsistence, and existence. Thomas's metaphysics of creation always begins with "the moment of existential—i.e., substantial—perfection, with this radical concern for the 'subsisting thing' which is beyond both the moments [of reality and ideality] in its own moment . . . in the moment of the radical perfection of being."[86] Thomas himself writes that *bonum dicit rationem perfecti*.[87] Ulrich then concludes that he can "assign Thomas's concern with substantial perfection its own place in the moment of bonicity, where both the other moments of reality and ideality can in turn be unfolded in their fullness."[88]

---

84. "Let us then state for what reason becoming and this universe were framed by him who framed them. He was good; and in the good no jealousy in any matter can ever arise. So, being without jealousy, he desires that all things should come as near as possible to being like himself" (Plato, *Timaeus* 29e).

85. "daß es so etwas gibt wie Wirkliches, durch Wirklichkeit Wirkliches: in Wahrheit Wirkliches" ("Inwiefern," 100).

86. "Und doch liegt in der Konstruktion der Substanzkonstitution bei Thomas das Moment der existentiellen: d.h., substantialen Perfektion, dieses radikal Anliegen das ‚subsistere' über diesen beiden Momenten hinaus in einem eigenen Moment . . . im Moment der Perfektion des Seins" ("Inwiefern," 101). This ellipsis is in the original text.

87. *ST* I.5.1.ad.1.

88. "So sei es uns erlaubt, diesem Anliegen der substantialen Perfektion bei Thomas seinen eigentlichen Ort im Moment der Bonität zuzuweisen: von woher die anderen Momente Realität und Idealität wiederum in ihrer Fülle entfaltet werden kann" ("Inwiefern," 102).

The moment of bonicity thus encompasses and transcends the moments of reality and ideality. If there is no third moment, each—reality and ideality—encloses or gets stuck in itself, allowing no movement of being beyond that particular moment, as we saw with Suárez and Scotus. However, we must ask what it could mean that it is in the moment of bonicity that ideality and reality are unfolded in their fullness—how is this not an imposition on each of these moments, that is to say, a condition to which each must submit? Is bonicity an infringement?

To answer such charges, we must remember that *esse* "is" nothing. *Esse* adds nothing formal to the substance and thus does not impinge on its substantiality in any sense; nor is *esse* a condition. Rather, writes Ulrich,

> Because being as the act of perfection is so radically posited, it is the "intimum cuilibet": it is so interior to every actual thing—more interior to the thing than the thing itself—that it is every thing's act of existence. But it must not be equated with this simply, but only with inquantum ens est. Ens and res are therefore distinct from the act of existence.... Because "esse habere" understood in the radical sense is the same as subsistere, esse, as the intimum, is the actus of the substance, whereby the substance is actually substance. This is what it means to say that esse is the actuality of all acts and therefore the perfection of all perfections.[89]

Thus, the *res* is distinguished from the act of existence even as it is at the same time given being by it. This means that both being (ideality) and the *res* (reality) are in a sense set free to be themselves by *esse*'s being the *intimum cuilibet*, the act of existence. But notice that they are set free precisely in being united in the subsisting thing—that is, the *ens*. It is in their substantial unity that being and essence can really be themselves, so to speak. Bonicity is thus not an imprisoning condition but the origin and fulfillment of the other two moments.

None of this would be possible if *esse* were not *completum et simplex sed non subsistens*. Again we emphasize that for Ulrich, this phrase is the single most important insight in all of Thomas's metaphysics. To be *completum et*

---

89. "Weil das Sein als Perfektionsakt so radikal angesetzt wird, ist es das ‚intimum cuilibet'. So ganz innerlich jedem Wirklichen, innerlicher als dieses sich selber ist, ist es Existenzakt dieses Wirklichen. Aber es darf nicht schlechthin mit diesem gleichgesetzt werden: sondern nur: inquantum ens est. Ens und res werden daher vom Existenzakt her unterschieden.... Da ‚esse habere', im radikalen Sinn verstanden, das gleiche ist wie subsistere, so ist das esse als das intimum der actus der Substanz, wodurch die Substanz wirklich ist. So ist das esse die Aktualität aller Akte und deshalb ‚Vollendung aller Vollendung'" ("Inwiefern," 102). Ulrich points to *ST* I.8.1.c and ad.4 and *DP* 7.2.9.

simplex sed non subsistens means that ultimately "being is either finite or infinite: because it subsists in the finite or infinite mode of subsistence" and only there. *Esse*'s non-subsistence then indicates that "esse lies in a critical central region: 'critical' because it is as it were still radically open to 'subsistere,' i.e. in the finite or infinite way of existence." In other words, Ulrich continues, "esse lies in a between-region, 'between' infinite and finite being: it does not subsist, and therefore can be nothing other than 'ideal mediation,' between the finite and infinite being. Esse therefore will be visible against the background of the Absolute: and it is precisely here that Thomas places it."[90] The non-subsistence of being is then the foundation of a metaphysics of mediation, which is a metaphysics of both true unity and real difference.

Esse non subsistens is therefore, as we have said above, nothing. Or perhaps better put: nothing but the pure mediation of being itself. *Esse* does not subsist except as infinite (God) or finite (creature), but *esse non subsistens* is the guarantor of the true otherness of the creature—that is, that the creature's being is really its own and not just an extension of the creator's. Still, it is also the case, as Thomas often emphasizes, "that nothing is outside of being except nonbeing." This means that every constituent of substance must somehow emerge from—and be originally given in—*esse creatum*.

Esse non subsistens, we repeat, is *completum et simplex* and nothing can be outside of it except nonbeing. This means, writes Ulrich, that "when we follow this esse into its finite subsistence, matter and form emerge in the illumination of the particular phases: they are ultimately completely dependent on this 'movement into subsistence' of esse and comprehensible from the movement into subsistence, which is the movement of perfection."[91] Matter, then, is taken into—included within—the act of perfection itself: that is, *esse*. For matter is not outside of being and in fact emerges from it. Matter's being included in the act of existence from the beginning means that it must conceived in a completely different manner than that of either Suárez or Scotus.

---

90. "das Sein entweder endlich oder unendlich ist: dann subsistiert es auch im Endlichen oder Unendlichen Modus der Subsistenz!" and "Das esse, das hier gemeint ist, liegt sozusagen in einem kritische Mittelbereich: ‚kritisch' deshalb, weil es gleichsam noch radikal zum ‚subsistens' offen ist, d.h., für die endliche oder unendliche Existenzweise." And "das esse liegt in einem Zwischenbereich ‚zwischen' dem unendlichen und endlichen Sein: es subsistiert aber nicht und kann daher nichts anderes sein als ‚ideele Vermittlung' zwischen dem unendlichen und endlichen sein. Dieses esse wird also auf den Hintergrund des Absoluten sichtbar: und genau hier setzt Thomas an" ("Inwiefern," 105).

91. "Wenn wir dieses esse in seine endliche Subsistenz hineinverfolgen, so werden in der Erhellung der einzelnen Phasen auch die Form und die Materie radikal hervortreten: sie sind letzlich ganz und gar von dieser ‚Subsistenzbewegung' des esse abhängig und von der Subsistenzbewegung als Perfektionsakt her verständlich" ("Inwiefern," 106).

The ontological moment of bonicity is both different from and able to encompass—and therefore unify—the ontological moments of ideality and reality. "It is possible," writes Ulrich, "for [Thomas] to embrace these two 'essentiell' moments because he has the Subsistenzbewegung in view: for him it is the moment [in which] . . . hoc autem solum est substantia, quae subsistit. Because he says bonum dicit rationem perfecti, we are allowed to call the moment of the necessity of being: the moment of bonicity."[92]

The moment of bonicity then in some sense surpasses even being, which is how it can generate and encompass both being (ideality) and essence (reality). The Good too then is in some sense beyond being. There is more to creation than either the moments of ideality or reality can hold, separately or together. And this hints at how much, so to speak, is given in *esse*: not just the *res* or its existence, but its gratuitous reaffirmation in the Good as seen in and through the *ens*. *Esse* is the first of all created effects "and everything is related at the root to esse because nothing is outside of esse except non-ens!"[93]

The Good—the dimension of the *Subsistenzbewegung* which bonicity names—reaches beyond reality and ideality and at the same time, nothing is outside of being except nonbeing. Thomas writes:

> Thus goodness as a cause is prior to being, as is the end to the form. Therefore among the names signifying divine causality, goodness precedes being. Again, according to the Platonists, who, through not distinguishing primary matter from privation, said that matter was nonbeing, goodness is more extensively participated than being; for primary matter participates in goodness as tending to it, for all seek their like; but it does not participate in being, since it is presumed to be nonbeing. Therefore Dionysius says that *goodness extends to non-existence*.[94]

How do we resolve this tension? On the one hand, we may not be able to resolve it fully: if perfection is an infinitely non-jealous or even generous superfluousness of self, then it would seem that the Good must always be self-surpassing in order to be generous, and this self-surpassing would seem to extend the Good, so to speak, beyond the bounds of being, while also always including being. It

---

92. "Er vermag diese beiden ‚essentiellen' Momente . . . zu umgreifen, weil er die Subsistenzbewegung in Auge: es geht ihm das Moment . . . hoc autem solum est substantia, quae subsistit. Weil er sagt: Bonum dicit rationem perfect, so sei es uns erlaubt dieses Moment der Notwendigkeit des Seins: Moment der Bonität zu nennen" ("Inwiefern," 109).

93. "und auf dieses hin wird wurzelhaft alles bezogen, denn nichts ist dem esse fremd außer das non ens!" ("Inwiefern," 111).

94. *ST* I.5.2.ad.1. Emphasis added.

is a paradox, the tension of which is fruitful beyond comprehension. On the other hand, we might venture to say that it is true that the Good is outside of being and therefore non-*ens*. But perhaps "outside of being" can be said in many ways: there is that which is outside of being which is simply nothing. There is also matter, which is not exactly being, simply, but also not nothing, simply. Matter too could be said to be outside of being. Lastly, we could, with Thomas and Dionysius, say that the Good is outside of being in such a way that it transcends being—indeed, perhaps circumscribes it while also being generative of it. What we can say with certainty, however, is that existential perfection is found in bonicity, rather than ideality or reality, because the bonum comprehends more than being.

The telos of the *Subsistenzbewegung*—the telos of creation—is not then simply being or substance, it is rather the Good, or in Ulrich's parlance, the ontological moment of bonicity.[95] The Good is beyond being, and thus we might say can comprehend more than being itself, which includes that which may look like simple non-*ens* from the point of view of being. There is being beyond being itself, *hyper-ousia*: the Good.

This is the radicality of Thomistic metaphysics, according to Ulrich: that Thomas can see the aim of creation extends beyond creation itself, and that creation itself is given the power to self-exceed, self-transcend. This is reflected in the *Subsistenzbewegung*, which "circumscribes the phases esse non subsistens must go through into its subsistence," but is ultimately "a movement into the moment of bonicity, i.e., the perfection of being." Ulrich even goes so far as to give the *Subsistenzbewegung* another name: "*Bonitätsbewegung*."[96]

The *Subsistenzbewegung* is not a motion—not a movement from potency to act—but rather a dynamic emergence of the constituents of substance from that which is *completum et simplex sed non subsistens*, or, from the point of view of transnihilation: the other is presupposed so radically by the giver that the receiver appears, so to speak, in the giver before the receiver exists. This is what it means for essence to emerge from *esse*: that *esse creatum* is given the power of this presupposition. This presupposition of the other is then

---

95. This makes sense in two directions: (1) if creation is given the power to participate in its own creation, then it is given the power to self-exceed: to go beyond being to what is, we might say, hyper-determinate (i.e., the Good) and (2) creation's telos is God: of course it aims beyond being itself!

96. "Die Subsistenzbewegung umschreibt die Phasen, die das esse simplex et completum, sed non subsistens durchlaufen muß in seine Subsistenz hinein. Die Subsistenzbewegung ist eine Bewegung in das Moment der Bonität, d.h., der Perfektion des Seins. ‚Bonum dicit rationem perfect': nomine boni intelligitur esse perfectum. Die Essenz geht ganz aus dieser Subsistenzbewegung, d.h., Bonitätsbewegung hervor. Nur von hier in seine Einheit perseipsam zu verstehen" ("Inwiefern," 112). Emphasis added.

analogically communicated to what emerges from *esse*. To repeat: this means that everything is given to creation all at once, that the unity of creation is always already given and does not need to be attained. Essence emerges from *esse non subsistens* in the *Subsistenzbewegung*, and it is in essence that we find the constituents of form and matter. How form and matter are a unity—or that in which their unity consists—is in a way the test case for Ulrich to determine whether a metaphysics is situated radically enough or not. If form and matter are simply part and counterpart, then there is violence or opposition at the heart of things, rather than gratuity. If, however, there is a real unity between the two, we can understand that bonum is situated in the heart of the being.

We might ask, since Thomas understands everything to be given all at once in the gift of *esse creatum*, why Thomas thinks it necessary to identify different metaphysical constituents of reality. For Thomas, writes Ulrich, "distinguishing the components is exclusively for the sake of determining the perfection of substance."[97] Form and matter make up the essence of a substance, and essence both emerges from and receives being itself in order to form a substance. This means that for Thomas, distinguishing the components of substance allows us to understand being better insofar as we understand (1) how being is substantialized by (2) understanding how being is received. This is the key: to better know and understand being itself, we need to understand not how it is attained, but how being *is given and received*. Here the dynamism between form and matter is key.

Ulrich's question with regard to substance is as follows: "how does the substance—the corporeal substance in our case—remain ever-receptive to being; what makes substance capable of being?" Ulrich asserts that this principle must be essential to substance, and it must be part of the essential definition of substance, along with matter. This principle, says Ulrich, is form. Ulrich writes: "form unlocks substance first for being: thereby it will be the proper recipient of what it is to be."[98] Form emerges from *esse non subsistens*, and simultaneous to its emergence, it opens a space for being, so that *esse* may substantialize. Or perhaps better put: the emergence of form from *esse is* the space of the receiving of being. This is why, writes Ulrich, "Thomas can say that being follows form, which opens the space of receiving."[99]

---

97. "Anliegen des Thomas: die Unterscheidung der Kompositionen ausschließlich um der Perfektion der Subsistenz willen vornehmen" ("Inwiefern," 115).

98. "Wodurch wird die Substanz, die körperliche Substanz in unserem Falle, überhaupt empfänglich für das Sein, was macht die Substanz seins-fähig?" and "Die Form also schließt die Substanz erst für das Sein auf, sie öffnet gleichsam die Substanz für das Sein" ("Inwiefern," 115).

99. "So kann Thomas sagen: daß das Sein durch sich der Form folgt, die diesen

We should note two things before moving further: (1) this does not mean that form precedes *esse*. This cannot be the case. Rather, through transnihilation, *esse non subsistens* gives over its very non-substantiality, and in this pouring out, form emerges as a space in which to receive *esse*. This is what it means to presuppose the other: form is given to itself, so to speak, before it "is" at all. *Esse*, infinite actuality, precedes form; form is in potency relative to *esse*. However, this does not mean that form has no causality of its own. In fact, (2) form has its own proper causality that simply is the reception of *esse*. Thus the causality of form is necessary for substance, while it is also entirely the case that form emerges from *esse* in the procession of essence. So though form unlocks substance for being, being is radically the ground of the *Subsistenzbewegung*, such that form is completely understood from being, even though *esse* follows form. Form, to be sure, has a proper actuality, but form's act is *esse* itself. *Esse* does not thus hold onto its own actuality in a miserly fashion, but gives itself to form as form's own proper actuality.

The next step, we might say, in the *Subsistenzbewegung* is matter. We have already indicated, with both Thomas and Ulrich, that matter is not exactly being, and yet it is also not non-*ens* as such. Because of this, matter can only be properly conceived if it is understood in the horizon of bonicity, because the Good in a certain sense is also outside of being. Ulrich writes that "matter as potentia realis in the middle 'between' ens and non-ens, prope nihil . . . is not possibilis esse . . . but real possibility, potentia subjectiva . . . it is only seen from the point of view of the movement of the perfection of being into the moment of its necessary unity with itself."[100] Matter thus has no need for an entitative character, as it does for Suárez and Scotus, because it has a place in the real, so to speak, without entity: as *potentia pura*.

For both Suárez and Scotus matter needs an entitative character in order to be real: neither can conceive matter as anything but—or at least, the beginning of—an entity in order to be real. This is because neither Suárez nor Scotus can conceive of real otherness simultaneously with real unity. This is why Ulrich emphasizes *ens*: it is from this perspective that we see the real distinction between and the real unity of *esse* and essence in the subsisting thing. But this simultaneous distinction and unity is only possible because

---

Empfängnisraum eröffnet" ("Inwiefern," 115). Ulrich points to *ST* I.104.1.ad.1 here: esse per se consequitur formam creaturae, supposito tamen influxu Dei, sicut nomen sequitur diaphanum aeris, supposito influxu solis.

100. "Die materie als potentia realis in der Mitte ‚zwischen' ens et non ens, prope nihil . . . ist nicht possibiles esse . . . aber reale Möglichkeit, potentia subjectiva . . . sie ist nur von der Perfektionsbewegung des Seins in das Moment seiner notwendigen Einheit mit sich selbst geklärt" ("Inwiefern," 112). The ellipses are in the original text.

the moments of ideality (*esse*) and reality (essence) are comprehended by a third moment: bonicity, or the Good. In order to comprehend the other two moments, however, the Good must transcend them, which means that it is in some sense outside of being (*non ens*). This being beyond being is what allows otherness to emerge: *esse creatum* is other than the Good in its being *non subsistens*; essence is other than *esse* in its definition; form is other than *esse* in its communication of subsistence; matter is other than anything else in its being wholly and entirely receptive. The Good is non-*ens* because it is beyond being; matter is non-*ens* because it is not yet being. They meet, as it were, in the unity of the *ens*, both giving of themselves (asymmetrically and analogically) in order that the *ens* might be. This perspective of the "beyond" and the "not yet" is available to neither Suárez nor Scotus in their respective metaphysical schema.

We saw with both Suárez and Scotus that imparting an entitative character to matter leads in one of two directions: (1) matter simply becomes possible essence, or the shadow of essence, and thus not really distinct from it; and/or (2) matter can exist entirely on its own, such that its union with form can only be conceived extrinsically. Thomas avoids both these issues with his radical understanding of *creatio ex nihilo* in which the act of creation, infinite actuality, is given in *esse creatum* and everything else emerges thence. Ulrich highlights this even more with his articulation of the *Subsistenzbewegung*: *esse non subsistens* pours itself out in its need to be subsistent, and essence emerges. The last presupposition of otherness is then the emergence of form and matter in the *Subsistenzbewegung*/transnihilation.

Matter emerging from essence is, we might say, the end of the transnihilation, as the *non subsistens* of *esse* finally comes to rest here, in that which is not itself subsistent but contributes to substance's coming to be. Recall that transnihilation *is* the *Subsistenzbewegung*, seen, however, from the side of *esse*'s non-subsistence rather than its actuality. *Esse* does not just give away its actuality so that beings may be, but its very non-subsistence as well, leading, ultimately to matter's emergence in the *Subsistenzbewegung*: the emergence of that which is not exactly in being, but that which is also not non-*ens* (matter is "between" *ens* and non-*ens*). The perfection which is *esse*'s non-subsistence comes to expression in matter.

We cannot, however, see matter in or by itself; matter can only be seen from the point of view of being, just as the non-subsistence of *esse* cannot be seen by itself, but is only known in and through knowing the nature of actuality itself. Thus, we only see matter in its unity with form. Ulrich notes that form has two "movements": *effundere* and *redire* (pouring out and returning).[101]

---

101. "Inwiefern," 119.

When essence emerges from *esse*, it too is caught up in the movement of being poured out, or better put, emerges precisely from this kenotic movement, and in that movement is presupposed by essence and therefore given to itself completely. But here, precisely because of the whence and why of the *Subsistenzbewegung*, being given to itself does not mean holding onto itself in stasis, but rather, given the capacity to generate what is truly other. This truly other is matter.

Form and matter both emerge from essence, but form is the principle of actuality, and so form is in a certain sense the ground of matter; thus, it behooves us to look more closely at its place in the *Subsistenzbewegung*. Its emergence from *esse* is not a step to be surpassed but in some sense the steady and abiding place for subsistence. Ulrich writes that form does not "expire in the nullity of matter," nor does it simply "empty itself into the effects" of substance: "no, it abides!"[102] Thus form is always constituting substance, and in corporeal substances, this constitution is made up of two moments that demonstrate form's metaphysical status as also, in some way, "between": (1) matter's ordination to form and (2) substance's ordination to existence.[103] Neither of these ordinations is possible without form being both receptive with regard to *esse* and active with regard to matter. The unity of these two ordinations, says Ulrich, is in the *Subsistenzbewegung*.

This might be seen more easily from the point of view of transnihilation, the "underside," as it were, of the *Subsistenzbewegung*. We recall that transnihilation is the giving of the perfection of being that is non-subsistence to that which emerges from *esse* in the *Subsistenzbewegung*. The "through" of the *Durchnichtung* is *esse*'s communication of its own non-subsistence, albeit in an analogous form at each rung on the ladder of being. Form's emergence from *esse* simply is the dynamism of *esse non subsistens* giving up or giving over its very non-subsistence such that something that is really other than *esse*—that is, form—might come to be. Form thus is *esse*'s non-subsistence given to be in real distinction from *esse*. Therefore, because this non-subsistence is always already a part of created *esse*'s intrinsic nature and it is the foundation of form, there is no violent opposition between *esse* and form: *esse* gives over itself such that another might be, and this other, because relative to *esse*, is nothing but

---

102. "Sie verfällt weder der Nichtigkeit der Materie, noch gießt sie sich in ihrer Rückkehr zu sich selbst in den Effekt aus: nein, sie bleibt!" ("Inwiefern," 119).

103. See "Inwiefern," 119. Ulrich writes, "so findet sich also in der, aus Materie und Form zusammengesetzten Substanz eine zweifache Ordnung. Die eine ist die Hinordnung der Materie auf die Form: name magis est materia propter formam quam forma propter materiam: was nur aus der Subsistenzbewegung ist.- Und die zweite ist die Hinordnung der schon zusammengesetzten Substanz auf die Existenz, was wiederum nur vom Moment der Bonität her verständlich ist."

receptivity (i.e., in potency to *esse*). Thus, seen from the point of view of the *Durchnichtung*, form is recipient of *esse*. *Esse* is the actuality of the form that is act. And yet, because of the necessary sense of being and all that follows from it, *esse* and form are really distinct.

The generativity of *esse* does not, however, end at form. Not only does *esse* give form to be (as other than *esse*), *esse* also gives form to be itself generative—that is, of matter. The gift of being is not simply to let another be, but rather to let another be generous as well.[104] Again, we look at matter through the lens of the *Durchnichtung*: in form we see the non-subsistence of *esse* come to light in perfection of the other, and in matter, we see that even this non-subsistence—that which seems to be, or better is: nothing—is given the capacity to be generative of another. Matter, as in some sense the end of transnihilation, is the image of the non-subsistence of being as a perfection of being itself, which itself is the gift of otherness (that is, the gift of being a *self*), is from the Good, which is beyond being.

Because Thomas views the act of creation as radically as possible—that is, as rooted in the *bonitas divina*—says Ulrich, Thomas never experiences matter as a problem that he needs to deal with, dispense, or resolve. In some sense, *esse creatum* simply is the act of creation: it *is* God's creative act. If that is true, then *similitudo bonitas divinae* does not just apply to *esse creatum*, but analogously to all that emerges therefrom. But *esse* is the image of the divine goodness; it is not itself the divine goodness, which is both beyond being and at the same encompasses being.[105] This means that there is no problem for Thomas in seeing creation as rooted in that which is above being itself: it is rooted in the Good, whose nature it is to be generous.[106] This also means that something that is, as it were, below being, is also not an issue in Thomas's metaphysics of creation; however, for something to be below being, there must be something above being as well—and this is why matter is only intelligible, says Ulrich, in the moment of bonicity.

Matter is, according to Thomas, *potentia pura*—pure receptivity to being itself. This pure receptivity is of course mediated by form. Again, Thomas sees no opposition here between these two principles of nature. There is "no need to ascribe an entitative character to matter because it is a receptivum

---

104. We desire to beget in the beautiful. See Plato, *Symposium* 206B–E, wherein Diotima explains to Socrates that the work of those who love "is bringing to birth in beauty in terms of the body and in terms of the soul. . . . For eros is not, Socrates . . . of the beautiful, as you believe. . . . It is of engendering and bringing to birth in the beautiful."

105. This is why Thomas can refer to *esse* as the most proper name of God and also quote Dionysius affirming that the Good is beyond being without contradiction.

106. See n84 above.

for 'form,'"[107] writes Ulrich. Just as form is both really distinct from but also grounded in *esse non subsistens*, so too is matter both generated by and different from form. Matter's purely receptive nature is no problem for Thomas precisely because he understands creation from the horizon of bonicity: if there is something above being, there can be something (analogously) below being as well. And that which is below being—matter—is not privative, but rather, we might say, pure desire for the Good. This desire would lead "it" to desire to be, for to be substantially is to participate in the Good, to be like God. But this pure desire or pure receptivity to act—as mediated by form—is not visible, as it were, except from the point of view of the Good. Viewed from an isolated moment of either ideality or reality, this pure desire either looks like (a) nothing at all or (b) privation. In this case, in order for matter to be a part of creation, it must be entitative.

Ulrich points out that Thomas does not treat matter systematically; this, however, is because Thomas does not see a problem to be resolved when thinking matter. Rather, thinking *creatio ex nihilo* as radically as possible, Thomas sees no issue with matter as pure receptivity. His concept of matter begins with the Good. Thomas understands form and matter to be two principles of nature per se, and matter to be the subject. Not of course, as an already somehow actual container into which form is emptied, but as *potentia pura*. Form is thus matter's most per se *actus substantialis*. This is key: matter's "actuality," form's "actuality," and *esse*'s actuality are not three different pieces that need to be added together to make a substance, which can only ever lead to an extrinsic unity (which is of course no unity at all). Rather, substance truly is a unity-in-difference: all three metaphysical constituents have the same act: *esse* giving itself over so that (a) another might be and (b) *esse* may come to subsistence. Ulrich writes, "Thomas says simply: insofar as something is, it is an unum and the potency and act are somehow one; because what is in potency will then simply really exist: and so it needs no bond."[108]

Matter thus never has an entitative character for Thomas, and he therefore never needs to figure out a way to put it together with form. This also helps us to understand the infinity of prime matter and the question of individuation: that is, how does matter individuate if it is infinite? It is true that prime matter is infinite, but its infinity must be understood differently from

---

107. "Thomas braucht der materia prima keinen entitativen Charakter zuschreiben, damit sie überhaupt ein receptivum der ‚Form' wird" ("Inwiefern," 122).

108. "Thomas sagt einfach: insoweit etwas ist, ist es ein unum und die Potenz und der Akt sind irgendwie eins, denn was in Potenz ist, wird dann eben wirklich existent: und so bedarf es keines vinculum" ("Inwiefern," 123). Ulrich points to *SCG* 11.70 and *ST* I.76.6.ad.7 here.

the infinity of actuality. It is, writes Ulrich, "the primum subjectum and therefore in no other,"[109] which means prime matter is only infinite considered in itself—once in another, it can no longer be infinite. The infinity of actuality, however, somehow abides even when actuality gives itself over to finitude. Matter's infinity is for the sake of being taken up and realized in the finite— that is to say, matter is literally self-effacing. Actuality's infinity, on the other hand, can give itself over and over and take things up into itself, allowing that which is not itself to be. Matter yearns to be; actuality yearns for another to be.

The infinity of matter then images the infinity of actuality, but is not exactly the same. Ulrich writes that matter "is 'infinite' as it were as the outermost border of the infinity of being (ideality), however entirely and only intelligible from the perspective of the moment of the absolute perfection of being (bonicity)."[110] Matter can thus be the principle of individuation without issue, but importantly, it can be principle of individuation because of what it is and what it reveals: that the Good desires another to be. Ulrich writes: "In the Thomistic framework, materia quantitativa signata must be the principle of individuation, even though form, which subsists in itself is individuated. Because matter is for the sake of the individual subsistence of the finite form, it must be the principle that this individuation takes as its beginning."[111] We might put it this way: individuation is looking at this substance from the point of view of its otherness with regard to the rest of creation, rather than its sameness. Substance's otherness is a result of—and best seen through— transnihilation, that is, the communication of non-subsistence to creation in the form of potency. Potency is thus a gift to the creature: so that it can be truly other. But looking at the creature solely through this point of view—that is, isolating its otherness, its potency—makes individuation a puzzle because it lends matter an entitative character (an actuality) where, in reality, it has none. If however, we always understand transnihilation *as* the *Subsistenzbewegung*, then individuation is no issue: matter's infinity is different from actuality's and matter is always for the sake of form.

Indeed, it is always form that gives being to substance, even as it is matter that allows form to be expressed (in corporeal substances). "Form," writes

---

109. "Die Materie ist primum subjectum und daher in keinem anderen" ("Inwiefern," 125). See *ST* I.3.2.ad.3.

110. "Sie ist ‚unendlich' gleichsam als der äußerste Rand der Infinität des Seins (Idealität) aber ganz und gar verständlich aus den Moment der absoluten Perfektion des Seins (Bonität)" ("Inwiefern," 126).

111. "Vom thomistischen Konstruktionsansatz her muß die materia quantitate signata Individuationsprinzip sein, obgleich die in sich selbst subsistierende Form durch sich individuellen Subsistenz der endlichen Form willen da ist, muß sie das Prinzip sein, von dem her diese Individuation ihren Anfang nimmt" ("Inwiefern," 134).

FERDINAND ULRICH'S UNDERSTANDING OF MATTER

Ulrich, "gives the entire being. In giving being, form is somehow poured out over matter, and even though form has being in itself, it returns back to itself."[112] We could put it this way: form is self-transcending, but the only way it could be so is if matter gives it this possibility. Matter is thus for the sake of form returning to itself in substance, just as form is for the sake of *esse* returning to itself as subsistent. Without each of these metaphysical constituents being really distinct from each other, self-transcendence and self-gift would be metaphysically impossible. Substance would not be the fruit of a metaphysical union, but a product of part and counterpart.

Ulrich reiterates: "Matter has neither entitative [character] nor formal act. It has an infinity 'from below.' [The infinity] is its potentia passiva. The infinity will be limited by form, as also the amplitude of form is enclosed by matter."[113] A properly Thomistic approach to the metaphysics of creation therefore always understands creation in light of the Good—which is to say, generosity. Matter's literal insubstantiality is the occasion for its being so often misunderstood: precisely because in some sense totally hidden from view—that is, matter can never be seen by itself—matter is often given a status it does not have in order to "save" it metaphysically. But this is unnecessary, and indeed as we have seen, ultimately harmful, leading to a violent opposition at the heart of substance itself. Matter's insubstantiality, its status as pure potency, is rather an image and sign of what the Good itself is: pure self-giving, albeit in actuality. Matter's pure receptivity allows it to be the case that even finite actuality can self-transcend, can give itself. It is through matter that we see that creation is not just the giving of being, but the giving of the giving of being.

The question of nothing—the question of matter—is one that goes to the heart of being itself, especially being as conceived in the Christian doctrine of creation. Called as we are out of nothing, we must contend with nothing's meaning for creation. Is nothing an oppositional force to being itself, always privative and therefore violent? Or is it the case that nothing can somehow be held by—comprehended in—being and he who creates being? This is the question of matter. Ulrich claims that it is only from the ontological moment

---

112. "Die Form gibt das ganze Sein. Im Sein-geben wird sie irgendwie über die Materie ausgegossen, indem sie jedoch in sich das Sein hat, kehrt sie wieder in zurück" ("Inwiefern," 135).

113. "Die Materie hat weder einen entitativen noch einen formalen Akt. Sie hat eine Unendlichkeit ‚nach unten.' Sie ist ihre potentia passiva. Die Unendlichkeit wird durch die Form begrenzt, wie ja auch die Amplitude der Form durch die Materie eingeschränkt wird" ("Inwiefern," 134).

of bonicity that matter is intelligible because only starting with the Good can we see far enough to comprehend matter as it is (not as we think it should be). "The metaphysics of substance," writes Ulrich, "is therefore a metaphysics of the overcoming and synthesis of a twofold infinity in the moment of the perfection of being."[114] Matter is an "extreme" image of the creator's generosity: to allow that which is not in any way like himself—pure potency—to be. This is the meaning of creation.

Recall that in the introduction, I included several excerpts from Dionysius's works. Reading Dionysius, it becomes clear that his understanding of the reason for material being—and therefore creation—coincides with much of what Ulrich perceives in Thomas's corpus. Indeed, we can say that with a different vocabulary and different accents many of the same themes which Ulrich highlights in Thomas's work, though Ulrich does this through the lens of Thomas's unique insight that *esse* is *completum et simplex sed non subsistens*.[115] Dionysius, Thomas, and Ulrich all share one central insight (each of course receiving and developing it from the previous): that the only way to make any sense, so to speak, of creation, is love, and it is love that leads the higher to care for and allow itself to be revealed and imaged by the lower. Love is what binds, says Dionysius; love "moves the superior to provide for the subordinate, and it stirs the subordinate in return toward the superior."[116] Love must then ultimately be the answer to our original question: there should be material being because of love.

---

114. "Die Konstruktion der Substanzkonstitution . . . ist also Konstruktion der Überwindung und Synthese eine zweifachen Unendlichkeit im Moment der Perfektion des Seins" ("Inwiefern," 126).

115. This is of course not accidental, since Thomas is greatly influenced by Dionysius, but this influence continues to be a rather ignored aspect of Thomas's corpus, especially in English-language Thomism (see chapter 2, n24, above). The notable exception to this is O'Rourke, *Pseudo-Dionysius and the Metaphysics of Aquinas*. On God as nonbeing, see esp. 79–80; on the meaning of nonbeing for Dionysius and its influence on Aquinas, see esp. 85–94.

116. *Celestial Hierarchy*, 709D.

Conclusion

Matter draws its life from the mystery of being as love.[1]

CARO CARDO SALUTIS EST writes Tertullian: "The flesh is the hinge."[2] The second-century apologist writes with respect to the nature of Christ and the nature of the redemption, but this could also be said simply of creation: the fact that man is embodied is the fulcrum on which much of our philosophy is balanced, be it consciously or unconsciously. Our materiality cannot be run away from or gotten behind, so to speak. Matter will be accounted for, one way or another.

In chapter 1, in addition to providing an overview of a Thomistic metaphysics of creation, we offered a short survey of a fairly standard Thomistic account of matter: it is the principle of individuation. Chapters 2 and 3 were meant to show, in and through the work of Ferdinand Ulrich, that matter understood as the principle of individuation is not in any way wrong, but rather that when it comes to matter, stopping at this point is insufficient. When we give matter our full metaphysical attention, so to speak, we see that its being the principle of individuation is in fact only one sign and consequence of what matter is: a privileged image of the Good.

1. "Die Materie lebt aus dem Gehemnis des Seins als Liebe" (*ES*, 490).
2. *De resurrection carnis* 8,8: PL 2 806.

It is of course true that all of creation is an image of the Good, both individually and as a whole. It may sound strange, therefore, to say that matter, the lowest of all created effects, is a *privileged* image of the Good. And yet, it is precisely matter's lowliness that enables this privilege. As I have said already, matter "is" nothing in itself; it is the principle of otherness. But this otherness does not come from outside being; rather we might say that the other comes from the intimate heart of being itself. Being desires that another might be so radically that it presupposes that the other is, so to speak, already there. Matter indeed emerges from being, but not in such a way that it is powerless and empty; instead, it emerges as already enabled and empowered to participate in the imaging of the Good that is creation. Indeed, being presupposes matter (the other) so radically that it allows matter to give it definition, even though matter in itself is nothing. That matter is the principle of individuation reveals the infinite depths of the relationship between matter and the Good.

The radicality of the Good's desire that another might be, then, leads to the Good, we might say, surrendering itself always already to the other: in order for another to be in freedom, the other must be given everything—even, in a certain sense, power over the Good. This power, we must say, can only ever come from the Good itself—the Good is always the source—and yet the Good's desire for the other—its surrender—is so radical that it looks like this power, this fullness, always belonged to the other from the beginning. It is clear in the act of being's pouring itself out that the Good is not miserly of its own fullness and power, but rather gives it unjealously: matter emerges from being's *Subsistenzbewegung*, and in that emergence it is empowered to define being. The giving of the Good is so radical that, looked at from a certain point of view, it seems as if the lowest of all created effects possessed this power of definition—the fullness that it is given in its very emergence from being itself—from the beginning.

It is to this seemingly already-contained fullness we now turn. Toward the end of the third volume of his work, *Erzählter Sinn*,[3] Ulrich uses three words from a fairy tale to describe, roughly, the different principles of substance: being, form, and matter. *Erzählter Sinn* is a book on fairy tales and their interpretation, what these stories mean (and mean for us), anthropologically and philosophically. "Ulrich understands fairy tales as forms of action,"[4] write Bieler and Oster in their foreword to the book. Not only are these stories examples of how one should (or often, should not) act, but they also open up for us a sense of the world in which we live, and help to form our

---

3. Though *ES* was not published until 1999 (its second edition appeared in 2002), the book is based on a series of lectures Ulrich gave in 1970 on narrative meaning.

4. "Ulrich versteht das Märchen als Handlundsgestalt" (*ES*, XV).

understanding of it. In relating these stories, Ulrich delves into each of them in a way that may first be described as imaginative. This is not to say his descriptions have nothing to do with reality, but rather, as with the very fairy tales on which he reflects, the principles of reality are in some sense here writ large and depicted so that we may more clearly see them. Fairy tales, and the imagination necessary in order to read them well, are not flights of fancy, but a plunging into the depths of reality such that its underlying structure may be seen more clearly. Because of this, *Erzählter Sinn* also has the benefit of being somewhat more directly accessible than some of Ulrich's other work. In a certain way, all of the metaphysical groundwork laid in this book up to this point comes to fruition here.

The exploration of being, form, and matter in this way appears in the third and last fairy tale Ulrich interprets in *Erzählter Sinn*, *Die Drei Sprachen*, or *The Three Languages*. In this fairy tale collected by the Brothers Grimm, a count grows frustrated with his son, who seems to be unable to learn anything from his teachers. The count sends him to a celebrated master; after a year his son comes back and tells his father he has learned what dogs say when they bark. His father is disappointed and sends him to another master; this time his son comes back and says that he has learned the language of the birds. Again the count is disappointed and again he sends his son to yet another master; this last time his son returns and says he has learned what frogs say when they croak. The count falls into a rage, disowns his son, and banishes him. While wandering in the forest, the boy comes across a town that is threatened at all times by wild dogs. He learns from the dogs that they are cursed and how to break this curse. He does so, and the town rejoices and rewards him. The son then decides to go to Rome, and on his way he hears from the frogs that the pope has died. In Rome there has been much disagreement about who should be elected as the new pope, and the cardinals decide that doves will be a sign of whomever should be elected. Just as they decide this, the youth enters the same church as the cardinals, and two doves alight on his shoulders; he is elected pope, and the doves counsel him throughout his papacy.

The Three Languages is a somewhat obscure fairy tale, and one that may sound strange to our ears; it feels almost unfinished, and the moral, if there is one, is not entirely clear (though to be fair, the Brothers Grimm are not Aesop). We may glean something about education: what the world thinks is an education misses precisely the wonder and language of creation ("For the wisdom of this world is foolishness with God" [1 Cor 3:19a]). Ulrich identifies each of the languages as a "linguistic event" [*Sprachgeschehen*], that is, the son does not simply learn a language in the sense of rote translation, but he learns how to be with and understand each of the creatures from within its own experience. The youth learns the way of abiding with each of the creatures, and it is from this that he gains his knowledge. Each of these events represents each of the necessary conditions, we might say, for man to understand himself, his Creator, the world, and the relation of all three.

The three linguistic events are the languages of each of the creatures in the story: the bird, the dog, and the frog, which correspond roughly to being, form, and matter. We will concentrate on the meaning of "frog," but to round out our discussion, we will explain the first two briefly. The bird, says Ulrich, represents "the possibility of freedom and imagination."[5] A bird is "a light, wingéd essence," Ulrich continues, and it can fly, which means that it does not have boundaries in the way most other creatures do. "The environment of this living form is not opened merely in earthly horizontality;"[6] rather air, which is seemingly empty, carries it. We know that air is not empty, but is in fact full, but full in the sense that freedom is full: it "releases the concealed possibility of an ever-greater actuality and thereby soars over the seemingly-fixed boundaries of the concrete in which it opens the astonishing future of what is possible."[7] The bird transcends the earth while always being given shelter by the earth: "Its element is the 'breath of emptiness'"[8] writes Ulrich. The bird, precisely in its flight, shows us that air—*esse*—is not in fact empty, but the overly-full enabler of everything else.

The dog and its barking is the second linguistic event, and it corresponds roughly to form. "The 'dog,'" writes Ulrich, "guards the boundary between inside and outside. He perceives the line between day and night, life and death."[9] A dog's entire environment is defined by boundary: he moves on the earth, but he knows things through his sense of smell, by way of the air. Ulrich focuses on boundaries because they are necessary for the enactment of self. In the behavior of dogs, we see that self-knowledge necessarily includes understanding boundaries—not to close one off or in, but precisely to know and understand who one is vis-à-vis everything and everyone else. The dog "marks" his territory; he needs "confrontation," writes Ulrich, which "articulates, in different

---

5. He uses these words in a section heading: "Der 'Vogel': die Sprache der Möglichkeit der Freiheit und der Einbildungskraft" (*ES*, 430).

6. "Das Umfeld dieser Lebensform wird nicht bloß durch die erdhafte Horizontalität eröffnet" (*ES*, 430).

7. "der je größeren Wirklichkeit entbindet und dadurch über die scheinbar fixem Grenzen des Tatsächlichen hinaus abhebt, indem sie die überraschende Zukunft des Seinskönnens eröffnet" (*ES*, 398).

8. "Sein Element ist der ‚Atem der Leere'" (*ES*, 464).

9. "Der 'Hund' wacht an der Grenze von Innen und Außen. Er spürt an der Scheide von Tag und Nacht, Leben und Tod" (*ES*, 463).

forms and qualities, the outline of the boundary, not merely from without, but just as much from within."[10] He continues:

> In its own self-relation, freedom is "another" to itself—and this is disclosed in the measure by which it receives itself as given and assents to the mystery of its own opacity. By receiving, accepting, and appropriating "itself" (as gift), freedom, in the act of individuation in the midst of unity with the giving origin, points to the boundary between giver and gift, giving and receiving, the poverty of reception and the fruitfulness of self-generation, self-comprehension and selflessness, creative self-actualization and quiet, selfless tranquility. These boundaries differentiate enactment and givenness not in an objectivized sense; they rather reveal much more the distinction through and out of which the selfhood of the act of being creatively emerges; they are signs of the act of being's fullness and fruitfulness.[11]

Boundaries allow us to know ourselves as ourselves and therefore are the very thing that allow us to enact our being, though never as separated from our origin. Boundaries, writes Ulrich, "are not only negating or excluding, but flexibly open to the other on the basis of positive self-reception."[12]

This brings us to the third linguistic event, the frog, which Ulrich says represents "the yes to himself as the act of living in the unending metamorphoses that originate in self-generating freedom."[13] The frog, which roughly corresponds to matter, represents originality, generation, and transformation.

---

10. "Auseinandersetzung . . . sie artikuliert in verschiedensten Formen und Qualitäten des Profil der Grenze, nicht bloß nach außen, sondern ebensosehr nach innen" (*ES*, 407).

11. "Denn Freiheit ist in ihrem Selbstverhältnis sich selbst ‚der Andere' an ihr selbst,—und dies geht ihr in dem Maße auf, wie sie sich als gegebene annimmt und ins Geheimnis ihrer Unverfügbarkeit einwilligt. Indem sie ‚sich selbst' (als Gabe) empfängt, übernimmt und aneignet, zeitigt sie durch diesen Akt der Selbstwerdung mitten in der Einung mit dem schenkenden Ursprung: die Grenze zwischen geber und Gabe, Geben und Nehmen, Armut des Empfangens und Fruchtbarkeit der Selbstauszeugung, Sichergreifen und Sich-los-lassen, schöpferischer Selbstverwirklung und stiller, selbstloser Gelassenheit. Diese Grenzen scheiden die Vollzüge und Gegebenheiten jedoch nicht im gegenständlichen Sinne, sie enthüllen sich vielmehr als Differenzen, durch die und aus denen heraus die Selbigkeit der Grundakte schöpferische aufbricht; sie sind Signum ihrer Fülle und Fruchtbarkeit" (*ES*, 407–8).

12. "Die nicht negierend ausschließende, sondern flexibel offene Grenze zum Andernen, aufgrund der positiven Selbstannahme" (*ES*, 398).

13. "Das Ja zu sich selbst als Lebensakt der sich in unabschließbaren Metamorphosen selbst ur-‚sprünglich' auszeugenden Freiheit" (*ES*, 398).

Speaking or thinking about the frog, says Ulrich, could be awkward or embarrassing to us.[14] It lives in the dank, dark, seemingly formless swamp, and its proper form of communication, if we can call it that, is the almost unintelligible "croak." In this croaking, Ulrich writes, "rationality is in a certain sense sunken into the lightless sensuality, the essenceless light of the material."[15] It seems there is nothing on which to think or reflect here; in the bird we have the wide open freedom of flight, in the dog we have the boundaries necessary to knowing "I" and "Thou," but in the frog and its environment, there seems to be nothing at all on to which we can hold, at which we can point, or know in itself.

This is however just the point. The frog exists in the

> "maternal," life-giving *depths* of the earth, out of whose watery, "formless" womb the forms of life arise: first entirely plastic and flexible, in a certain sense "undifferentiated" and so undefined (: "possibility"), though it is also the case that from the very beginning species are already wonderfully formed and fixed in transparent geometry (: "necessity"), at home in the element of water, intrinsically connected to the rhythm of its movement.

The frog, writes Ulrich,

> dwells and grows not in clear running water, but in standing waters, at the protected edge of ponds ... in a dark, opaque, and dull region in which the diverse forms of life are sheltered and "incubated."[16]

Notice the "role reversal," if we may call it that, to which Ulrich is pointing: air (*esse*) looks like nothing, so light and seemingly empty that we could almost ignore it, if we did not need it for absolutely every thing and action in our lives. The swamp (matter) is overly full, even though it seems unnecessary to us and our actions. We cannot see into it, let alone see through it. Again, this is exactly the point: this overly full opaqueness teaches us patience: a

---

14. "Eine gewisse Unbeholfenheit stellt sich ein, und das ist gut so" (*ES*, 462).

15. "die Rationalität gewissermaßen in die lichtlose Sinnlichkeit, die wesenlose Nacht des Materiellen abgesunken ist" (*ES*, 463).

16. "Der Frosch aber ist ein Wesen aus der ‚mütterlichen,' lebenspendenden *Tiefe* der Erde, aus deren wässerigem, ‚formlosen' Schoß die Lebensformen aufsteigen: zuerst ganz plastich-flexibel, in einem gewissen Sinne ‚undifferentziert' und so unbestimmt (: ‚Möglichkeit'), obgleich von den frühesten Formen an schon wunderbar gestaltet und auch in durchsichtiger Geometrie (: ‚Notwendigkeit') verfaßt ... lebt er nicht in fließenden, reißenden Wassern, sondern in sumpfigen, stehenden Gewässern, am schützenden Rand von Teichen ... eine abgedunkelte, undurchsigtige, dumpfe Region, die mannigfaltige Lebensformen beherbergt und ‚ausbrutet'" (*ES*, 464).

CONCLUSION

patience that allows living forms to emerge, a patience that gives them space to be themselves. This opacity "makes space for [living forms] in the depth and distance of their personal 'generation-of-self.'"[17] The richness of the swamp allows forms to grow—to grow into themselves; the opacity of the swamp allows them to grow unperturbed.

This is not to say things become themselves without another. Of course they do, necessarily so. But the origin, the giver, must let the other go so completely—must give so radically—that the other becomes, at first, and in some way, totally opaque to the origin. We can see then that the origin—the giver—really lets the other be, so much so that the giver relinquishes control over the other's development. We know this to be true, for this is exactly what happens in the womb: parents, having given themselves fully to each other, and therefore allowed another (the child) to come about as a fruit of this giving, must wait in patience and relative blindness to see who their child is.

Matter is then, we could say, not only a principle of otherness, but also the element of patience—not first on the side of the receiver (though that too), but rather the patience of the giver. Matter is the element, so to speak, that the giver bestows on the other so that the other may really be himself. Matter is then a sign of a giver so transcendent that he is able to surrender to what he gives.

Ulrich calls the frog's swamp a womb throughout this part of *Erzählter Sinn* and points out what happens when we try to grasp at what is in the womb before it is ready to reveal itself: objectification, which reduces the other to factical availability. A lack of patience with the other—a refusal to surrender to the other's time—indicates a desire to place the other under one's own power, to make whatever it is an extension of one's self. This kind of power, says Ulrich, is achieved in the attempt of de-materializing living forms: we order them according to precise measurements which we use for our own ends, rather than allowing them to reveal themselves in their own time and according to their own living intensity. This reduction of things to factical availability subjects living forms to "the death-power of the faceless and nameless 'that,'" and "petrifies [them] into a dead 'essentiality' of the existing" (but not coming-to-be), and "freezes [them] into a lifeless substance."[18] In this reduction to factical availability, the only unifying force among the diverse forms is the will of the objectivizer, because there is no sense of anything growing or coming together before his intervention. But the swamp of matter is opaque

---

17. "ihr die Tiefe und Ferne des personalen ‚Her-kommens von selbst' einräumt" (*ES*, 466).

18. "Die Faktizität verfügbarer Sprache (und Welt) hingegen besitzt, unter der Todes-Herrschaft des gesichts- und namenlosen ‚Daß', ... erstarrt in einer toten ‚Wesentlich-keit' des Bestehenden, friert im leblosen Substantiellen ein" (*ES*, 470).

and rich and therefore cannot be wholly objectivized: there, the forms seem all mixed together and emerge together out of the swamp. Therefore, he who wishes to control forms must dematerialize them. "Whoever robs living forms . . . of their material," writes Ulrich, "also takes from them the power to grow together, for them to become concrete (con-crescere) in and by themselves."[19]

The frog's swamp is then the place of metamorphosis, of growth and development. Think of the tadpole: it cannot become the frog without the swamp. All of creation is borne out of matter's womb. It is matter's "positive formlessness," writes Ulrich, that makes possible the appearance of two corresponding (though asymmetrical) elements of metamorphosis: "the act of being and the receiving space of matter."[20] The language of the following passage should sound familiar at this point: "in the gift of creation from the absolute origin, material essential forms arise from superessential being in the act of its finitization (through the gift of its emptying, a giving of being that does not hold on to self), which being receives, defines, determines, holds, and pulls together into finite subsistence, through which it holds onto, shares, and brings itself into subsistence."[21] It is the material forms that allow being to come to subsistence even at the same time those same material forms emerge from being itself.

This, once again, is key: that being gives itself so radically that it presupposes another—in this case, essence, which includes form and matter—is already there to receive it and therefore give it standing, as it were, in creation. Ulrich stresses that this does not mean that the receiver becomes a bare function of the giver. The receiver is really different—so different, in fact, that the giver in a certain sense allows the receiver to be opaque to his origin, to be himself and grow into himself in the womb of the earth. The origin allows the other his own time: past, future, present.

---

19. "Wer den Lebensformen . . . Materiellen raubt . . . der nimmt ihnen zugleich die Kraft, durch die sie mit sich zusammenwachsen, konkret (con-crescere) sie selbst werden können" (*ES*, 467).

20. The full quote: "In der positiven Gestaltlosigkeit des Sprachgeschehens ‚Frosch' enthüllen sich *zwei* (zu-einander radikal a-symmetrische) *Tiefen*, die das Profil der Wesensgestalten (die das Wirkliche in seinem So-sein fügen und an*wesens* sein lassen) einerseits übersteigen, aber anderseits gerade dadurch in ihrem je spezifischen Erscheininen bestimmten ermöglichen: der Akt des Seins under Empfängnisraum der Materie" (*ES*, 471).

21. "Dem überwesenhaften Sein als Schöpfungsgabe des absoluten Ursprungs entspringen im Akt seiner Verendlichung (durch die die Gabe ihr entäußertes, nicht an-sich-haltendes Gegebensein vollbringt) die materiellen Wesensgestalten, die das Sein aufnehmen, bestimmen, begrenzen, zur endlichen Subsistenz zusammen-ziehen: fassen, indem es sich dadurch selbst faßt und vermittelt zu-*stande*-bringt" (*ES*, 471–2).

CONCLUSION

The opacity of the swamp of matter is then a sign of the absolute freedom of the origin, who could not allow this opacity if his intent were anything else than allowing the other really to be other. The other, the receiver, is not mere extension of the origin, in which case there could be no real moment of giving and receiving (to whom would the giver give?), but rather the giver gives there to be real difference between himself and the receiver, so that the receiver may actually receive. Importantly: *this is entirely for the sake of the receiver*. The giver needs nothing here, and only desires that another might truly be other. Thus, "the gift arises from the absolute self-sufficiency of the origin, through pure originality, which is not compelled by any external need. It is the image of [the giver's] overflowing love."[22]

The presupposition of the giver is what enables there to be a receiver at all. That is to say, without the giver giving the gift as if the receiver already exists in order to receive, then the giving can only be an extension of the giver himself. The giver does not give in a piecemeal way, but rather gives the whole gift and allows the receiver to develop, transform, and metamorphize in himself. In short, the giver gives everything to the receiver all at once, including the receiver himself, but also the ability to grow and change.

Metamorphosis, change, development (history and future): none of this could be if matter was "bare possibility."[23] Bare possibility cannot receive. In radical giving, the capacity to receive emerges; the giving is so radical that it looks as if this capacity were always already there. This is why we mistake matter as eternal, as the source of all that we see. Matter, writes Ulrich, is the "ab-bounding result of the act of being 'from below to above.'"[24] As the gift is poured out, so to speak, from above, matter—the capacity to receive—emerges from below. This capacity is already "itself," we might say—that is, it is a capacity to develop into a self, not just an extension of the giver. Bare possibility, on the other hand, is either an extension of the giver or a depotentiation of him. "Because bare possibility cannot receive, it only *seemingly* allows the giving and the gift to affect it fully in its emptiness,"[25] writes Ulrich. Bare possibility "lacks the fertile space of independent receiving, in which act

---

22. "Die Gabe entspringt reiner, durch keine äußere Exigenz ernötigter Ursprünglichkeit, der absoluten Selbstmächtigeit des Ursprungs. Sie ist Gleichnis seiner überstromenden Liebe" (*ES*, 473).

23. "bloße Möglichkeit" (*ES*, 475).

24. "Ur-sprünglichen Resultieren des Seinsakts ‚von unten nach oben'" (*ES*, 475). My thanks to D. C. Schindler for suggesting "ab-bounding" as the translation for "Ur-sprünglichen."

25. "Weil die bloße Möglichkeit nicht nehmen kann, läßt sie den Schenkenden und die Gabe nur *scheinbar* völlig in ihrer Leere sich auswirken" (*ES*, 476).

can be received and come to subsistence."²⁶ Bare possibility "throws the giver back onto himself,"²⁷ thereby making his act of giving sterile, meaning the only thing it can be is an extension of himself.

Matter is surely not the only principle that emerges in the giving of being, but because matter is the lowest of all created effects, it is where we see the radicality of the gift most clearly. None of the foregoing should be interpreted as Ulrich imparting an entitative character to matter; rather, the "swamp," the area of metamorphosis, is only possible because the giver allows it to be, and surrenders himself so radically to that which he gives to be that it in some sense looks to us as if matter "is" in itself. But this is not the case: matter is nothing in itself, but is presupposed by the giver such that it can seem as though it has always already been "something." Matter is capacity to receive, and is presupposed by the giver in the giving. This presupposition "is demonstrated in the radical intensification of the *emptiness* of the dimension of *conception* such that it is *not* presupposed as mere poverty, but rather emerges from the having-received, from the wealth of the having-been-present of the timeless act of being which has been given to it."²⁸ Matter therefore is a sign of the radicality of the gift of creation in two directions: that everything has been given to the receiver "for nothing,"²⁹ and that the receiver is enabled—at the very same time as he is given to himself—in the receiving of the gift to grow and develop in himself. That is to say, matter is the sign of both the always already of the gift and *at the very same time* the gift of the receiver's *future*. As

---

26. "Es fehlt der tragende Raum des selbständig Empfangenden, in dem das Wirken aufgenommen wereden und zu-‚stande' kommen kann" (*ES*, 476).

27. "Die Leere wirft den Geber auf sich selbst zurück" (*ES*, 476).

28. "sondern erweist sich durch eine radikale Intensivierung der *Leere* der *Empfängnis* dimension even dadurch, daß sie *nicht* als Nur-Armut voraus-gesetzt ist, sondern aus dem Empfangen-haben, aus dem Reichtum der Gewesendheit des zeitlos in sie hinein vergangen Seinsaktes heraus aufgeht" (*ES*, 477).

29. The word Ulrich uses is *umsonst*, which appears throughout his work, not just in *Erzählter Sinn*, especially with regard to *why* the giver gives, or to put it another way, why God creates. In fact, the perfection of gift is only achieved, so to speak, when the giver gives "for nothing," that is, without expectation on the giver's side of something in return, without any original neediness on the giver's part. A real gift is one that is given without expectations, without an assumption of anything in return. *Umsonst* communicates this in the sense of *gratis*, but it can also mean "in vain." Ulrich's use of *umsonst* reflects this latter sense as well, especially when looking at creation and redemption from the point of view of human sin—in this sense, it looks as if the giver gives in vain, but does so anyway. Still, this latter sense is not the "last word" on the gift, or on the meaning of *umsonst*, but is rather contained within the prior and primary meaning of *gratis*.

Ulrich puts it, pure potency "makes possible both the future and the continual abiding of being as gift in the present."[30]

The womb of matter—the opacity of the swamp—is the medium of transformation and thus a testament to the desire of the giver to let the other really be an-other. Matter images the pouring out of the act of being, albeit "from below," and thus, the truth of this outpouring is refracted through its own distinctive prism. In matter we can glimpse the "asymmetrical 'in one another' of the self-giving of being as gift (from above to below) and the fruitful self-'task' (from below to above) out of the womb of the material world."[31] Matter's seeming self-generation is then a gift and image of the outpouring of being in the act of creation, but crucially, this capacity to self-generate does not lag behind, so to speak, the original gift. Rather, the capacity of the receiver to self-generate, as it were, is *presupposed* by the origin such that this capacity is always already given in the gift itself. Thus, the gift is both always with the receiver (and in a certain sense, simply *is* the receiver), and also gives the receiver the capacity to become himself. The giver does not then tyrannically control the receiver by giving, but precisely in the presupposition of the other in the act of giving allows the other to transform and express itself "from below." It is in matter that we see this aspect of the gift of creation most clearly: that God allows an-other to be, and to be free. At the very same time, we can see that only a transcendent giver has the power to give like this, to give "for nothing." Matter then, as the lowest of created effects (and thus that which can only be "from below to above"), is an image of both the desire of the Creator to allow another to be and—precisely in this desire—the absolute transcendence and freedom of such a Creator. Matter is a privileged image of the Good, which is not only not jealous, but generous.

The question of matter is perennial, and as I hope I have shown in this book, our response to the question of matter will in turn affect the entirety of our metaphysics. According to Ulrich, when we approach the question of matter,

> we are trying to articulate ontologically the meaning of the immaterial, superessential act of being springing out of the depths of the "dark, shady, formless, stagnant region of matter." It does *not*, to say it once more, emerge from bare possibility, from the fermenting

---

30. "Es vermag beide, Zu-kunft und Gewesendheit des Seins als Gabe im Präsens" (*ES*, 478).

31. "a-symmetrischen Ineinander von Sich-aufgeben des Seins als Gabe (von oben nach unten) und fruchtbarer Selbst-‚aufgabe' (von unten nach oben) aus dem Schoß der materiellen Welt" (*ES*, 484).

"matrix omnium formarum" (G. Bruno), but rather out of the receptive dimension of matter, which already been filled, formed and structured by the essential forms through which it has been given.[32]

For Ulrich, the question of material being is contained within the question of being itself, but given a different accent: How does being give itself? And the answer, which matter helps us to see: completely, wholly, overflowingly, superfluously.

Matter then is an image of the Good because it reveals how and what the Good gives, and therefore what the Good is: love. Only love can give itself in this way: so radically that at times it looks as if matter generates itself. Matter, which in itself is nothing, is given the power to define and limit being, and has been given this power, this capacity, because of the Good's desire that an-other may be. It is precisely matter's nothingness that allows it to be given this power at all. Matter's

> non-essentiality reveals itself . . . as the dimension of emptying and abandonment of superessential being, which reveals its fullness in the poverty of its being finitized and thus itself as the given yes to love, as image which does not grasp after itself, but in absolute freedom expresses the radiating, originless origin: it is the epiphany of the self-communication of the giving![33]

Matter is an image of the Good precisely because matter's very existence, so to speak, points to what the Good desires to give: everything.

---

32. "Versuchen wir das Gemeinte ontologisch auszuworten: Der immaterielle, überwesenhafte Seinsakt springt aus der Tiefe des ‚dunklen, nächtigen, formlosen, trägen, dumpfen Bereichs der Materie' auf, aber, um es nochmals zu sagen: Er resultiert *nicht* aus der bloßen Möglichkeit, der gärenden ‚matrix omnium formarum' (G. Bruno), sondern aus der durch die Wesensformen, durch die er verschenkt ist, schon erfüllten, gestalten, strukturierten materiellen Empfängnisdimension" (*ES*, 479).

33. "Ihre Nicht-Wesentlichkeit enthüllt sich . . . als Dimension der Entäusserung und Hingabe der überwesenhaften Seins, das seine Fülle in der Armut des Verendlichtseins offenbart und sich so als geschenktes Ja der Liebe, als Gleichnis des nicht ansichhaltenden, sondern in absoluter Freiheit sich verströmenden, ursprunglosen Ursprungs ausspricht: Epiphanie der Selbst-mit-*teilung* des Schenkenden!" (*ES*, 489).

Bibliography

Aertsen, Jan A. *Medieval Philosophy and the Transcendentals: The Case of Thomas Aquinas.* Leiden: Brill, 1996.
Aldana, Ricardo. "The Experience of the Unity of Time and Christian Faith in the Thought of Ferdinand Ulrich." *Communio: International Catholic Review* 43 (2016) 388–408.
Aquinas, Thomas. *De ente et essentia.* Translated by Joseph Bobik. Notre Dame: Notre Dame University Press, 2007.
———. *De mixtione elementorum.* Translated by Joseph Bobik. Notre Dame: University of Notre Dame Press, 1998.
———. *De potentia.* Translated by Fathers of the English Dominican Province. Westminster, MD: Newman, 1932.
———. *De principiis naturae.* Translated by Joseph Bobik. Notre Dame: University of Notre Dame Press, 1998.
———. *De veritate.* Translated by Robert W. Mulligan. Chicago: Regnery, 1952.
———. *In duodecim libros Metaphysicorum expositio.* Translated by John P. Rowan. Notre Dame: Dumb Ox, 1995.
———. *Summa contra gentiles.* Translated by Anton C. Pegis. Notre Dame: University of Notre Dame Press, 2009.
———. *Summa theologiae.* Translated by Fathers of the English Dominican Province. New York: Cosimo, 2007.
Aristotle. *Categories.* In *The Basic Works of Aristotle*, edited by Richard McKeon, 7–39. New York: Random House, 2001.
———. *Metaphysics.* Translated by Joe Sachs. Santa Fe: Green Lion, 2002.
———. *Physics.* Translated by Joe Sachs. New Brunswick, NJ: Rutgers University Press, 2008.
Balthasar, Hans Urs von. "The Fathers, the Scholastics, and Ourselves." *Communio: International Catholic Review* 24 (1997) 347–96.
———. *Theo-Logic I: Truth of the World.* Translated by Adrian J. Walker. San Francisco: Ignatius, 2000.

BIBLIOGRAPHY

Bieler, Martin. "*Analogia Entis* as an Expression of Love According to Ferdinand Ulrich." In *The Analogy of Being: Invention of the Antichrist or the Wisdom of God?*, edited by Thomas J. White, 314–37. Grand Rapids: Eerdmans, 2011.

———. "Einleitung." In Ferdinand Ulrich, *Homo Abyssus*, xiii–liv. Freiburg: Johannes Verlag, 1998.

———. *Freiheit als Gabe: Ein schöpfungstheologischer Entwurf*. Freiburg: Freiburger theologische Studie, 1991.

Blankenhorn, Bernard-Thomas. "The Good as Self-Diffusive in Thomas Aquinas." *Angelicum* 79 (2002) 803–37.

Bobik, Joseph. *Aquinas on Being and Essence: A Translation and Interpretation*. Notre Dame: Notre Dame University Press, 2007.

———. *Aquinas on Matter and Form and the Elements: A Translation and Interpretation of the* De Principiis Naturae *and the* De Mixtione Elementorum *of St. Thomas Aquinas*. Notre Dame: University of Notre Dame Press, 1998.

———. "Dimensions in the Individuation of Bodily Substances." *Philosophical Studies* 4 (1954) 60–79.

———. "La doctrine de saint Thomas sur l'individuation des substances corporelles." *Revue philosophique de Louvain* 51 (1953) 5–41.

———. "A Note on a Problem About Individuality." *Australasian Journal of Philosophy* 36 (1958) 210–15.

———. "Saint Thomas on the Individuation of Bodily Substances." PhD diss., University of Notre Dame, 1953.

Burtt. E. A. *The Metaphysical Foundations of Modern Science*. New York: Dover, 2003.

Chesterton, G. K. *Saint Thomas Aquinas: The Dumb Ox*. New York: Image, 1956.

Clarke, W. Norris. "The Limitation of Act by Potency: Aristotelianism or Neoplatonism." *New Scholasticism* 26 (1952) 167–94.

———. *The One and the Many*. Notre Dame: University of Notre Dame Press, 2001.

Dionysius the Areopagite. *The Complete Works*. Translated by Colm Luibheid. New York: Paulist, 1987.

Gilson, Etienne. *Being and Some Philosophers*. Toronto: Pontifical Institute of Medieval Studies, 1952.

———. *History of Christian Philosophy in the Middle Ages*. New York: Random House, 1955.

Hanby, Michael. *No God, No Science*. Malden, MA: Wiley-Blackwell, 2013.

Haggerty, Joseph M. "The Principle of Individuation According to St. Thomas Aquinas: An Interpretation in Embryo." PhD diss., Boston College, 2015.

Heidegger, Martin. *Introduction to Metaphysics*. Translated by Gregory Fried and Richard Polt. New Haven: Yale University Press, 2000.

———. *Pathmarks*. Translated and edited by William McNeill. New York: Cambridge University Press, 1998.

Hoffman, Tobias. "Duns Scotus on the Origin of the Possibles in the Divine Intellect." In *Philosophical Debates at Paris in the Early Fourteenth Century*, edited by Stephen F. Brown et al., 359–79. Boston: Brill, 2009.

John, Helen James. *The Thomist Spectrum*. New York: Fordham University Press, 1966.

Kalkavage, Peter. *Plato's* Timaeus. Indianapolis: Focus, 2016.

Kent, Matthew Alexander. "Prime Matter According to St. Thomas Aquinas." PhD diss., Fordham University, 2005.

Kierkegaard, Søren. *Works of Love*. Translated by David F. Swenson and Lillian Marvin Swenson. Princeton: Princeton University Press, 1949.

BIBLIOGRAPHY

MacDonald, Scott. "The Esse/Essentia Argument in Aquinas's *De ente et essentia.*" *Journal of the History of Philosophy* 22 (1984) 157–72.

McMullin, Ernan, ed. *The Concept of Matter in Greek and Medieval Philosophy.* Notre Dame: University of Notre Dame Press, 1965.

Oster, Stefan. *Mit-Mensch-Sein.* Freiburg: Karl Alber, 2004.

———. "Thinking Love at the Heart of Things: The Metaphysics of Being as Love in the Work of Ferdinand Ulrich." Translated by Adrian J. Walker. *Communio* 37 (2010) 660–700.

Owens, Joseph. "Being and Natures in Aquinas." *Modern Schoolman* 61 (1984) 157–68.

———. "Metaphysical Separation in Aquinas." *Mediaeval Studies* 34 (1972) 287–306.

———. "Thomas Aquinas (b. ca. 1225; d. 1274)." In *Individuation in Scholasticism: The Later Middle Ages and the Counter-Reformation, 1150–1650*, edited by J. J. E. Gracia, 173–94. Albany, NY: State University of New York Press, 1994.

O'Rourke, Fran. *Pseudo-Dionysius and the Metaphysics of Aquinas.* Notre Dame: University of Notre Dame Press, 2005.

Plato. *Symposium.* Translated by Seth Benardete. Chicago: University of Chicago Press, 2001.

———. *Timaeus.* Translated by Peter Kalkavage. Indianapolis: Focus, 2016.

Ravaisson, Félix. *Essay sur la métaphysique d'Aristote.* Vol. 1. Paris: L'Imprimerie royale, 1837.

Rosemann Phillip W. "*Aliquid*: Ein vergessenes Transzendentale." In *Miscellanea Mediaevalia 26: Was ist Philosophie im Mittelalter?*, 529–42. New York: de Gruyter, 1998.

———. *Omne ens est aliquid: Introduction a la lecture du 'systeme' philosophique de saint Thomas d'Aquin.* Leuven: Peeters, 1996.

Sachs, Joe. *Aristotle's* Physics: *A Guided Study.* New Brunswick, NJ: Rutgers University Press, 2008.

Schindler, D. C. *Companion to* Homo Abyssus. Washington, DC: Humanum Academic Press, 2019.

———. "The Grace of Being: Ferdinand Ulrich and the Task of a Faithful Metaphysics in the Face of Modernity." In *Christian Wisdom Meets Modernity*, edited by Kenneth Oakes, 149–64. London: Bloomsbury T&T Clark, 2016.

———. *Plato's Critique of Impure Reason.* Washington, DC: Catholic University of America Press, 2008.

Schmitz, Kenneth. *The Gift: Creation.* Milwaukee: Marquette University Press, 2007.

Scotus, John Duns. *Opus Oxoniense / Ordinatio.* 13 vols. Vatican City: Quaracchi, 1950–2013.

Selner, Susan Canty. "The Metaphysics of Creation in Thomas Aquinas' *De Potentia Dei*." PhD diss., Catholic University of America, 1992.

Siewerth, Gustav. *Der Thomismus als Identitätssystem.* Düsseldorf: Patmos, 1979.

Sweeney, Leo. "Existence/Essence in Thomas Aquinas's Early Writings." *Proceedings of the American Catholic Philosophical Association* 37 (1963) 97–131.

Suárez, Francisco. *Disputationes metaphysicae.* Salamanca, 1597.

Tertullian, *De resurrectione carnis.* Patralogia Latina 2. Edited by Jacques-Paul Migne. Paris: Migne, 1844.

de la Tour, Marine. *Gabe im Amfang: Grundzüge des metaphysischen Denkens von Ferdinand Ulrich.* Stuttgart: Kohlhammer, 2016.

Ulrich, Ferdinand. *Anthropologischen Urgrundlehre: Eine Auseinandersetzung mit her anthropologischen Theologie A. Günthers*. Munich: private printing, 1955.
———. *Atheismus und Menschwerdung*. Einsiedeln: Johannes Verlag, 1966.
———. *Erzählter Sinn: Ontologie der Selbstwerdung in der Bilderwelt des Märchens*. Freiburg: Johannes Verlag, 2002.
———. "Evolution—Geschichte—Transzendenz." In *Evoluzione e storia umana. Atti del XXI. Convegno internazionale del Centro di Studi Filosofici, Gallarate 1967*, 253–321. Brescia: Morcelliana, 1968.
———. *Gabe und Vergebung: Ein Beitrag zur biblischen Ontologie*. Freiburg: Johannes Verlag, 2006.
———. *Gebet als geschöpflicher Grundakt*. Einsiedeln: Johannes Verlag, 1973.
———. *Gegenwart der Freiheit*. Einsiedeln: Johannes Verlag, 1974.
———. *Homo Abyssus: The Drama of the Question of Being*. Translated by D. C. Schindler. Washington, DC: Humanum Academic, 2018.
———. *Homo Abyssus: Das Wagnis der Seinsfrage*. Freiburg: Johannes Verlag, 1998.
———. *Leben in der Einheit von Leben und Tod*. Freiburg: Johannes Verlag, 2000.
———. *Logo-Tokos: Der Mensch und das Wort*. Freiburg: Johannes Verlag, 2003.
———. *Der Mensch als Anfang: zur philosophischen Anthropologie der Kindheit*. Einsiedeln: Johannes Verlag, 1970.
———. "Sein und Materie: Inwiefern ist die Konstruktion der Substanzkonstitution maßgebend für die Konstruktion der Materiebegriffes bei Suárez, Duns Scotus und Thomas?" PhD diss., University of Munich, 1955.
———. *Sein und Wesen: Spekulative Entfaltung einer anthropologischen Ontologie*. Munich: private printing, 1954.
Velde, Rudi A. te. *Participation and Substantiality in Thomas Aquinas*. Leiden: Brill, 1995.
Wippel, John F. "Aquinas's Route to the Real Distinction: A Note on *De ente et essentia*." *Thomist* 43 (1979) 279–95.
———. *Metaphysical Themes in Thomas Aquinas*. 2 vols. Washington, DC: Catholic University of America Press, 1984.
———. *The Metaphysical Thought of St. Thomas Aquinas: From Finite Being to Uncreated Being*. Washington, DC: Catholic University of America Press, 2000.
———. "Thomas Aquinas and the Axiom that Unreceived Act Is Unlimited." *Review of Metaphysics* 51 (1998) 533–64.

Author Index

Aldana, Ricardo, 6
Aquinas, Thomas, 4, 5, 9, 11, 14–44, 45, 54, 114–19, 122, 124, 126, 128, 132–33
Aristotle, 18–23, 39, 41, 42, 118

Balthasar, Hans Urs von, 9, 57
Bieler, Martin, 5, 6, 15, 46, 56, 64, 75, 134
Blankenhorn, Bernard-Thomas, 54
Bobik, Joseph, 28, 39, 40, 41
Burtt. E. A., 98

Chesterton, G. K., 15
Clarke, W. Norris, 42, 43, 54

Dionysius the Areopagite, 1–4, 12, 25–26, 69, 122, 123, 132
Duns Scotus. *See* Scotus, John Duns

Gilson, Etienne, 25, 27, 34, 90–93, 106, 108, 114

Haggerty, Joseph M., 41
Hanby, Michael, 98
Heidegger, Martin, 1, 5, 14, 48, 51, 52, 84
Hoffman, Tobias, 107

John, Helen James, 34–36, 41, 46

Kalkavage, Peter, 14
Kent, Matthew Alexander, 41

Kierkegaard, Søren, 10

MacDonald, Scott, 28
McMullin, Ernan, 41

O'Rourke, Fran, 132
Oster, Stefan, 5, 6, 9, 60, 71, 72, 78, 79, 82, 134
Owens, Joseph, 41

Plato, 14, 18, 21, 43, 107, 119, 128

Ravaisson, Félix, 79
Rosemann, Phillip W., 32

Sachs, Joe, 19
Schindler, D. C., 4, 6, 55, 107, 141
Schmitz, Kenneth, 88
Scotus, John Duns, 5, 6, 73, 81, 89–93, 98, 105–15, 118, 120, 121, 125, 126
Selner, Susan Canty, 18–22
Siewerth, Gustav, 5, 55, 56, 82
Suárez, Francisco, 5, 6, 81, 89–109, 111–15, 118, 120, 121, 125, 126
Sweeney, Leo, 28

Tertullian, 133
de la Tour, Marine, 5, 47, 48, 56, 62, 63, 67, 68, 82, 106–8

AUTHOR INDEX

Ulrich, Ferdinand, 4–13, 15, 18, 21–23, 35, 43–144

Velde, Rudi A., 44

Wippel, John F., 15, 23–40, 42, 46, 51, 54, 80, 83

Subject Index

Note: References following "n" refer to notes.

absolute nonbeing, 33–34, 36–37
accidents of individual substance, 85–87
act and potency, Aristotle's notion of, 18, 22, 40, 42–43n108
    acknowledging existence of prime matter, 21–22
    composition in substances, 18–19
    fourfold causality, 19–21
    Scotus's understandings of being, 112, 113
    Ulrich's charge on Suarez, 95–96, 99, 104
actio ipsum esse subsistens, 69
action, 16, 138
active formal principle, 21
act of creation. *See Subsistenzbewegung*
act of existence. *See actus essendi*
actuality, 95
    fullness of, 23
    to individual beings, 116
    infinite, 27, 36, 130
    infinite pure, 23n37
    limitation of, 41
actus essendi, 24, 27, 36, 104, 105
actus non limitatur nisi per potentiam principle, 42n108
aliquid, 31–32n68
aliud quid, 31–32n68
analogia entis, 6
annihilation
    of being itself, 50
    of beings, 50, 53, 64

Aristotle
    categories of act and potency, 18–22
    fourfold causality, 19, 20
    See also act and potency, Aristotle's notion of
Atheismus und Menschwerdung (Ulrich), 8
Aufgabe. See task of being
Augustine of Hippo, 5
Avicennian, 91–92

bare possibility, 141–42
the Beautiful, 1–2, 3
being (*esse*), 22–23, 41, 42n108, 46, 52, 134–35
    appearance as, 57
    Aquinas's definition of, 23, 24, 46n5, 92
    composite, 37, 38
    contradiction of, 53–54
    and creation, 23–24
    creature's participation in, 74
    crisis of, 54–55, 58, 67
    and *essentia realis*, 91
    existence to everything else, 48
    generativity of, 128
    Gilson's understandings of, 93
    hypostasization of, 47n7, 49
    ideality associated with, 77, 79, 81
    as infinite actuality, 27
    limitation by matter, 15
    logical distinctions, 97

SUBJECT INDEX

being (continued)
  necessary sense of. *See* necessary sense of being
  non-subsistence of, 46–47, 58, 127–28
  nothingness of. *See* nothingness of being
  obedience of. *See* obedience of being
  participation of creatures, 24–25, 26
  presupposition of essence, 88
  prime matter and, 39
  principles, 37–38
  Scotus's views of, 110
  substantiality of, 47n6, 51–52n19
  task of, 62–63, 65, 72, 74
  Ulrich's understanding of, 60
being/beings, ontological difference between, 48n9, 48–51, 53–55
  appearance as being, 57
  horizontal dimension of, 57
  Ulrich's understanding of, 61
  vertical dimension of, 57
Being and Some Philosophers (Suárez), 89
being as being, 24, 52n19
being as gift, metaphysics of, 8–9, 11, 88–89, 99, 115
  in *Gabe und Vergebung*, 9–10
  giver and receiver of gift, 9
  presupposes beings, 10n24
  pure mediation, 9, 26, 79, 121
  understanding creation, 43
  understanding importance of matter, 12, 118, 143
  See also Ulrich's metaphysics of creation
being itself (*esse creatum*), 1, 7, 11, 15, 22, 25, 52, 79, 88, 89, 126
  hypostasization of, 47, 48–50, 51
  non-subsistence of, 46–47
  nothingness in, 51, 59, 69, 121, 131
  participation of creation in existence, 23–24, 26–27, 36
  and prayer, 8
  principle of, 46
  as pure mediation, 9, 26, 79, 121
  similitudo bonitas divinae, 128
  subsistence, 42–43

bonicity, ontological moment of, 12, 76–77, 115, 131–32
  accidents of individual substance, 85–87
  associated with *ens*, 77, 81–82
  for individual creature and creation, 83–84
  kenosis of finite substance in accidents, 86n102, 87
  metaphysical constituent of substance, 77
  in Scotus's understanding, 114–15
  self-affirmation, 84
  substantial perfection in, 119
  surpasses even being, 122
  telos of *Subsistenzbewegung*, 82n92, 82–83
  transnihilation in, 83, 85
  wealth and poverty of being, 83, 84
bonitas divina, 128
bonum dicit rationem perfecti, 119, 122
bonum diffusivum sui, 54n24
Brothers Grimm, 13, 135

capax entis, 60
cause/causality
  efficient, 19n21, 19–21, 22
  father-son example of, 21
  final, 19, 20
  of form, 125
  formal, 18, 19, 20
  material, 20
  secondary, 113
childhood, theme of, 8
chôra (receptacle), 14n1, 43
A Companion to Ferdinand Ulrich's Homo Abyssus (Schindler), 6
complete being/creature, 32–33
completum et simplex, 118, 121
completum et simplex sed non subsistens, 12, 120–21, 123
composite beings, 24, 37, 39
corruption, 37, 109
creabilia, 92
creatio ex nihilo, 22, 40, 62, 74, 88, 92
  Scotus's belief in, 109
  Thomistic concept of matter, 128

152

SUBJECT INDEX

Thomistic radical understanding of, 126
creation, 45, 72, 88–89, 131, 133
    Dionysius's definitions of, 2–3
    drama of, 88n1
    esse and, 23–24
    through lens of matter, 11
    multiplicity and, 70
    participation in self-actualization, 113
    revelation of, 23n37
    Scotist approach through horizon of ideality, 110–11
    Suárez's understanding of, 97
    subject of being in, 24
    telos of, 123
    Ulrich's definition of, 77
creatum (created), 105, 114
creatures, 32–33, 74
    esse commune, participation in, 26–27
    esse creatum, participation in, 26
    esse, participation in, 32, 74
    finite, 7, 47, 49, 74, 79, 87
    incomplete, 39
    material, 40
    ontological moment of ideality, 79–80
    potency, 130
crisis of being, 54, 58, 67

death, 7, 75n78
De ente et essentia (Aquinas), 27–29, 29n61
De potentia Dei (Aquinas), 23
De principiis naturae (Aquinas)
    distinguish between matter, 37
    about prime matter, 38, 39
Der Mensch als Anfang: zur philosophischen Anthropologie der Kindheit (Ulrich), 8
Die Drei Sprachen fairy tale (Brothers Grimm), 13, 135
Dionysius the Areopagite, 1
    Celestial Hierarchy, 2–3
    Divine Names, 1–2, 3
    about love, 3
    matter, statements about, 4
    nonbeing, statements about, 4
diversity in beings, 31–32, 34

divine intellect (*intellectus divinus*), 107–8, 110, 111
Divine Names (Dionysius), 1, 25
    creation, explanation for, 3
    nonbeing, definition of, 1–2
divine will (*voluntas divina*), 50, 92, 108, 110–11, 114
divinity, 33, 35
Duns Scotus. *See* Scotist understandings of being; Ulrich's charge on Scotist understandings of being
Durchnichtung. See transnihilation

Entäußerung, 54
entitas simplex, 102–3
Erzählter Sinn (Ulrich), 5, 8, 12–13, 134–35
essence, 27, 41, 65, 88, 90
    Aquinas's discussion of, 28
    emergence from being, 96n23, 118
    emergence from *esse non subsistens*, 124
    Fabro's definition of, 35–36
    in material and separated substances, 28n57
    non ens, 34
    presupposition of, 80–81
    in reality, 78
    really real, 91
    Scotus's understanding of, 91–92
    in Suarezian metaphysics, 94
    Suárez's understanding of, 90–91
    Ulrich's statements about, 65
    Wippel's understanding of, 36
    See also procession of essence
esse non subsistens, 6, 20, 50, 54, 56, 70, 74, 108, 118
    being's character as, 52
    completum et simplex, 121
    emergence of form from, 124
    essence emergence from, 124
    moment of ideality, 80
    non-substantiality, 125
    nothingness of, 87
    pure mediation of being itself, 121
    temptation of substantializing, 83, 116–17

SUBJECT INDEX

esse non subsistens (continued)
  unity of substance, 112
eternal love, 10–11n24
Expositio in Librum Boethii De Hebdomadibus (Aquinas), 23

the Father, 10n24, 55n26
finite creature, 7, 47, 49, 74, 79, 87
finite freedom, 5
finite reality, 49
finite substance, 57, 67, 68, 78, 84, 85
form, 18, 19, 20, 20n23, 37, 39, 124, 134–35
  act of being, 41
  causality of, 104–5, 125
  definition and understanding of being, 38
  emergence from *esse non subsistens*, 124
  emerging from essence, 126, 127
  essence in, 95–96
  esse's non-subsistence, 127–28
  giving being, 131
  logical distinctions, 97
  movements, 126–27
  ontological situation in, 96
  relationship with matter, 37, 39–40, 41n106
  Scotus's idea of, 112
  subsistence in, 96, 100
formal cause of substance, 18, 19, 20
Freiheit als Gabe (Bieler), 5

Gabe im Anfang: Grundzüge des metaphysischen Denkens von Ferdinand Ulrich (de la Tour), 5
Gabe und Vergebung: Ein Beitrag zur biblischen Ontologie (Ulrich), 9
  being is gift, idea of, 9–10
  presupposition of other, 10
Gebet als geschöpflicher Grundakt (Ulrich), 8
Gegenwart der Freiheit (Ulrich), 7
generation, 37, 109
gift of being, 42, 43n109, 63, 110, 128
  question about limitation, 42–43
  radicality of, 23, 42, 44, 59

  See also being as gift, metaphysics of
God, 2, 3, 9, 18, 24, 25, 69
  creation through *esse creatum*, 42–43
  Dionysius's statement, 25–26
  discussion of existence and nature of, 29
  as fullness of actuality, 23
  ipsum esse subsistens, 47n7
  presupposition of creation, 88
  presupposition of other, 88
  rejection of, 47
  Aquinas's understanding of, 15–16
  See also creation
Good above being. *See* love
the Good, 1–2, 3, 43, 144
  being beyond being, 122, 123, 126
  outside of being, 122, 123, 125
  privileged image, 134
  pure desire, 129
  radicality of desire, 134
  self-surpassing, 122–23
Greek metaphysics, 106–7

haecceity, 114
Holy Trinity, mystery of, 10n24
Homo Abyssus: Das Wagnis der Seinsfrage (Ulrich), 5–7, 9, 13, 45
  Balthasar's writing about, 9
  connection between metaphysics and anthropology, 7
  ontological difference between being and beings in, 48n9, 48–51, 53–55
  temptations of thought, 105
  Ulrich's concept of love, 72
hyper-ousia, 123
hypostasization, 47, 48–50, 51, 98

ideality, ontological moment of, 12, 56n29, 76–77
  closely associated with *esse*, 77, 79, 81
  essence in, 80–81
  metaphysical constituent of substance, 77
  Scotist approach of creation through, 110–11
  in Scotus's understanding, 114–15
  in *Subsistenzbewegung*, 79–80, 82n92

154

SUBJECT INDEX

temptation in, 81
unfolding in fullness, 120
ideal mediation, 98, 121
ideal vacillation (*ideale Schwebe*), 55n27, 64
Immaculate conception, 11n24
inchoate essence, 101–2, 104
incomplete being/creature, 32–33, 39
individuation, principle of, 41, 114, 133
indwelling, kind of, 35–36
infinite actuality, 27, 36, 41, 62, 125, 126
"Inwiefern" (Ulrich), 11–13
ipsum esse, 59–60
ipsum esse non subsistens, 61, 64, 66, 82
ipsum esse subsistens, 47n7, 69

Leben in der Einheit von Leben und Tod (Ulrich), 5
linguistic events, 135–37
  "the bird" story, 136, 138
  "the dog" story, 136–37
  "the frog" story, 136, 137–40
Logo-Tokos (Ulrich), 8
love, 3, 132, 144
  Kierkegaard's about, 10n23
  "presupposing" the other, 66
  and presupposition, 10nn23–24
  Subsistenzbewegung in, 74
  Ulrich's concept of, 72–73

man's freedom, theme of, 7
material being, 1, 3, 4, 11, 14, 77
  Dionysius's understanding of, 132
  question of, 144
  Aquinas's explanation of, 21
material cause of substance, 20
materiality, 67, 133
material substances, 28n57, 67–68
The Metaphysical Thought of Thomas Aquinas (Wippel), 15
Metaphysics (Aristotle), 20
Mit-Mensch-Sein (Oster), 5
motion, 16, 40
multiplicity
  in beings, 31–32, 34
  of creatures, 69–70
  question of why of, 16, 16n5

necessary sense of being, 12, 59, 76, 80, 108
  etymology, 59
  ontological difference between being and beings, 60–61, 65
  similitudo divinae bonitatis, 58, 62, 69, 82, 85, 87
  Subsistenzbewegung, 59–60, 61
  task of being connected with, 62–63, 65
  temptation of hypostasizing being, 62
  See also nothingness of being; obedience of being
Neoplatonic principles, 42–43n108
nihilism
  avoidance of, 52–53
  modern, 51n11
nonbeing (*non ens*), 1–2, 14–15, 32, 34, 39, 65, 123, 126
  absolute, 33–34, 36–37
  above being. *See* God
  Dionysius's statements about, 4
  question of, 41
  relative, 33, 34–36, 80
  status of, 2
  types, 2
  Ulrich's attention to, 46
non-subsistence of being, 46–47, 58, 66, 95, 115–16, 117, 121
non subsistens of esse. *See* non-subsistence of being
no-thing (*non subsistens*), 50, 58
nothingness of being, 33, 35–36, 36n88, 42, 49–51, 69, 131
  avoidance of nihilism, 52–53
  being's meaning, 57–58
  esse as *completum et simplex*, 52
  esse non subsistens, 52
  of *esse non subsistens*, 87
  about *esse*'s perfection, 39
  after matter, 36, 120
  metaphysical issue of, 51
  ontological difference between being and beings, 53–55, 57
  pseudo-subsistent *ipsum esse*, 53
  radicality of gift of being, 59
  real distinction between *esse* and essence, 66–67

SUBJECT INDEX

nothingness of being (continued)
    self-diffusion of being, 58
    Subsistenzbewegung, 55–57
    substantializing of, 52n19
    wealth and poverty of being, 58
    See also necessary sense of being;
        obedience of being
notwendige Seinsinn. See necessary sense
    of being

obedience of being, 65, 66
    nature of God's love, 72–73
    radicalized essence metaphysics, 73
    Subsistenzbewegung in love, 74
    superessential power of being, 73
    task of being, 72, 74
    transnihilation of being, 73
    true interplay between *esse* and
        essence, 74
    See also necessary sense of being;
        nothingness of being
otherness, 28, 52n19, 72, 125
    of creature, 121
    gift of, 117, 128
    of matter, 106
    presupposition of, 71, 110, 126
    principle of, 134, 139
    of substance, 130

pantheism, 24n39, 33
pars essentiae, 99, 101, 102, 109
passive material principle, 21
positive formlessness, 140
positive reality, 74, 78–79
possibile (possible), 92, 105, 109, 114
potency, 130
    generation, 67, 68
    of matter, 67–68
    revealing reality, 99
    in substances, 117
    See also act and potency, Aristotle's
        notion of
potentia objectiva, 109
potentia pura, 103, 115, 125, 128–29
potentia subjectiva, 109
prayer, 8
presupposition
    of another, 115, 140
    of giver, 141
    of other(ness), 10–11, 10–11n24, 66,
        71–72, 88–89, 123–24
prime matter, 33, 38
    Aquinas's personal view, of 40
    and *esse*, 39
    infinity of actuality, 130
    phenomenon of change, 39–40
    principle of being, 40
    Ulrich's charge on Suarez, 100, 103–4
primum subjectum, 103, 130
privation, 37
    matter and, 37–39
    non-subsistence of being, 95
procession of essence, 66
    and multiplicity of creatures, 69–70
    nothingness of being, 66–67
    potency generation, 67, 68
    presupposition of otherness, 71–72
    real distinction between *esse* and
        essence, 74–75
    relative primacy of substance, 75–76
    self-emptying, 72
    Subsistenzbewegung, 68, 69
    substantial independence, 74
    superessentiality of beginning, 68–69
    Verendlichungsbewegung, 65, 67–68
pseudo-hypostasization of being, 47,
    47n7, 55n27
pseudo-subsistence, 49, 100–101
    ipsum esse, 53
    matter, 104–5
pure mediation, 9, 79, 115
    esse commune, 25–27, 34
    esse creatum. See being itself (*esse
        creatum*)
    esse non subsistens. See *esse non
        subsistens*
    ipsum esse non subsistens, 61, 64,
        66, 82
    ipsum esse subsistens, 47n7, 69
    virtue of, 80
pure self-giving, 131
radicality
    of desire, 134
    of *esse*'s givenness, 115

SUBJECT INDEX

of gift of being, 23, 42, 44, 59
real distinction between *esse* and essence, 27, 61, 66, 74–75
   Aquinas's arguments, 28–30, 29n61, 33–34
   complete and incomplete being/creatures, discussion of, 32–33
   diversity and multiplicity in beings, 31–32, 34
   intellectus essentiae argument, 27–28
   multiplication ways of substances, 28–29
   and relative nonbeing, 33, 34–36
   Wippel's arguments, 29, 30–31, 33
real essence (*essentia realis*), 90–91, 94–96, 118
reality, ontological moment of, 12, 56n29, 76–77, 99
   closely associated with *res*, 77, 78
   constructed, 99
   essence in, 78
   finite, 49
   metaphysical constituent of substance, 77
   metaphysical structure of, 49n10, 50
   in Scotus's understanding, 114–15
   in *Subsistenzbewegung*, 78, 82n92
really real, 97, 98n29, 116, 119
relative nonbeing, 33, 34–36
res, 59–60, 74, 75, 77–78, 120

Schwebe. See suspension
Scotist understanding of being, 90
   Avicennian concept, 91–92
   collapsing *esse* and essence, 118
   creabilia concept, 92
   entitative understanding of matter, 115
   focus on being, 118
   possibilia concept, 92
   reducing *esse* to essence, 92–93
   Ulrich's charge on, 105–15
   See also Ulrich's charge on Scotist understanding of being
Seinsschwebe. *See* vacillation of being
self-gift of being, 63, 65–66, 131
self-surpassing, 122–23

similitudo bonitas divinae, 128
similitudo divinae bonitatis, 58, 62, 69, 82, 85, 87
Sprachgeschehen. *See* linguistic events
Suarezian understanding of being, 90
   collapsing *esse* and essence, 118
   entitative understanding of matter, 115
   essentia realis concept, 90–91
   metaphysical schema, 92
   Ulrich's charge on, 93–105
subsistence, 42–43
subsistent being (*esse subsistens*). *See also* God
   addressing nonbeing, 46
   participation of creatures, 24–25, 26
Subsistenzbewegung, 12, 59–60, 89, 134
   bonicity, 76–77, 81–87, 82n92
   dynamic emergence of constituents of substance, 123–24
   essence emerges from *esse non subsistens* in, 124
   esse's perfection, 95
   ideality, 76–77, 79–81, 82n92
   in love, 74
   multiplicity of creatures, 70
   in necessary sense of being, 59–60, 61
   for nothingness of being, 55–57
   potency generation, 67, 68
   presupposition of otherness, 71–72
   procession of essence, 68
   reality, 76–79, 82n92
   resting place, 68
   task of being, 62–63
   telos of, 123
   transnihilation, 126
   very nothingness of being in, 116
   See also Ulrichian metaphysics of creation
substance, 10n24, 18, 19
   accidents of individual, 85–87
   act and potency composition in, 18–19
   actus essendi, 24
   efficient cause of, 19n21, 19–21, 22
   final cause, 19, 20
   finite, 57, 67, 68, 78, 84, 85

SUBJECT INDEX

substance (continued)
    formal cause, 18, 19, 20
    material, 20, 28n57, 67–68
    metaphysical constituent of, 77
    multiplication ways, 28
    otherness, 130
    participation in being, 24
    relative primacy of, 75–76
    Subsistenzbewegung in love, 74
    unity of, 97
substantializing of being, 51–52n19
substantializing of nothing, 52n19
Summa contra gentiles (Aquinas), 16, 18, 29n61, 33, 70
superessentiality of beginning, 68–69
suspension, 55n27

task of being, 62–63, 65, 72, 74
temptation(s)
    in essence, 81
    of hypostasizing being, 62
    in reality, 78
    of thought, 47, 50, 105
thing itself, 19, 21, 28, 74, 103, 111
Thomistic metaphysics of creation, 11–12, 15, 133
    act of creation, 128
    Aristotelian categories of act and potency, 18–22
    creatio ex nihilo, 15
    distinction between *esse* and essence, 27–34
    and God's creation of matter, 17–18
    goodness and, 122
    judging action, motion, and change, 16–17
    question of why of multiplicity, 16, 16n5
    radical understanding of *creatio ex nihilo*, 126
    understanding of God and world, 15–16
    Wippel's arguments, 23–24
    See also matter; Ulrichian metaphysics of creation
Thomistic understanding of *esse*, 115
    esse non subsistens, 118
    focus on being as given, 118
    gratuitous reaffirmation of gift of creation, 119
    non-subsistence of *esse*, 115–16, 117
    radical act of perfection, 118–19
The Thomist Spectrum (John), 41
Timaeus (Plato), 14n1
transnihilation, 64n49, 116, 117, 127, 128
    of being, 60–61, 73
    in bonicity, 83, 85
    in essence, 80
    esse non subsistens, 125
    giving of perfection of being, 126
Treatise on Separate Substances (Aquinas), 34

Ulrich, Ferdinand, 4, 43, 133
    childhood, theme of, 8
    life and work history, 6–7
    linguistic events, 135–40
    man's freedom, theme of, 7
    philosopher's studies on thoughts, 4–6
    presupposition of other, 10
    radicality of gift of being, 23, 44
    See also being is gift, idea of
Ulrichian metaphysics of creation, 4, 8, 15, 45
    being is gift, 8–9, 11
    about emergence of form, 124
    hypostasization of being itself, 47–48
    "little way," 11
    necessary sense of being, 59–65
    non-subsistence of being, 46–47
    nothingness of being, 51–59
    obedience of being, 65–76
    ontological difference between being and beings, 48n9, 48–51, 53–55
    principles of, 6
    pseudo-hypostasization of being, 47, 47n7
    superessentiality, 46
    taking Aquinas's articulation of *esse* principle, 46
    temptations of thought, 47, 50, 105
    See also Thomistic metaphysics of creation

SUBJECT INDEX

Ulrich's charge on Scotist understanding of being, 105
   on approach to composition of substance, 111–12
   on entitative character of matter, 109
   on Greek metaphysics, 106–7
   on *intellectus divinus*, 107–8, 110, 111
   issue of reception or receptivity, 110
   on lack of sense of *esse creatum*, 106
   on metaphysics of creation from horizon of ideality, 110–11
   on moment's ideality, reality and bonicity, 114–15
   on problems in understanding individuation, 113–14
   on unity of matter and form, 112–13
   on unity of Scotist substance, 108–9
   on "vector" for creation, 105–6, 114
Ulrich's charge on Suarezian understanding of being
   on act and potency, 95–96, 99, 104
   on character of substance, 97, 98
   on constructionist metaphysics, 99–100
   on difference between *ens* and *esse*, 94–95
   on *essentia realis*, 93–94, 97, 98–99, 101
   on ideal mediation of being, 98
   on non-subsistence of being, 95
   on prime matter, 100, 103–4
   on pseudo-subsistence, 100–101
   on pseudo-subsistent matter, 104–5
   on *res ipsa*, 96–97
   on understanding of matter, 102–4
unity (*ens*), 2, 90, 120, 125
   Aquinas's entire approach to, 118–19
   bonicity closely associated with, 77, 81–82
   gratuitous reaffirmation of gift of creation, 119
   of substance, 97
universal fullness, 23, 23n37
unmoved mover, 18, 20

vacillation of being, 55n27
Verendlichungsbewegung, 56n29, 65, 67–68
voluntas divina, 50, 92, 108, 110–11, 114

yearning, 3

www.ingramcontent.com/pod-product-compliance
Lightning Source LLC
Chambersburg PA
CBHW032157160426
43197CB00008B/964